Reading 1759

TRANSITS:
LITERATURE, THOUGHT & CULTURE

Series Editor
Greg Clingham
Bucknell University

Transits is the next horizon. The series of books, essays, and monographs aims to extend recent achievements in eighteenth-century studies and to publish work on any aspects of the literature, thought, and culture of the years 1650–1850. Without ideological or methodological restrictions, *Transits* seeks to provide transformative readings of the literary, cultural, and historical interconnections between Britain, Europe, the Far East, Oceania, and the Americas in the long eighteenth century, and as they extend down to present time. In addition to literature and history, such "global" perspectives might entail considerations of time, space, nature, economics, politics, environment, and material culture, and might necessitate the development of new modes of critical imagination, which we welcome. But the series does not thereby repudiate the local and the national for original new work on particular writers and readers in particular places in time continues to be the bedrock of the discipline.

Titles in the Series

The Family, Marriage, and Radicalism in British Women's Novels of the 1790s: Public Affection and Private Affliction
Jennifer Golightly

Feminism and the Politics of Travel After the Enlightenment
Yaël Schlick

John Galt: Observations and Conjectures on Literature, History, and Society
Regina Hewitt

Performing Authorship in Eighteenth-Century English Periodicals
Manushag N. Powell

Excitable Imaginations: Eroticism and Reading in Britain, 1660–1760
Kathleen Lubey

The French Revolution Debate and the British Novel, 1790–1814: The Struggle for History's Authority
Morgan Rooney

Rococo Fiction in France, 1600–1715: Seditious Frivolity
Allison Stedman

For a complete list of titles in this series, please visit http://www.bucknell .edu/universitypress

TRANSITS

Reading 1759

LITERARY CULTURE IN
MID-EIGHTEENTH-CENTURY
BRITAIN AND FRANCE

EDITED BY SHAUN REGAN

LEWISBURG
BUCKNELL UNIVERSITY PRESS

Published by Bucknell University Press
Copublished by The Rowman & Littlefield Publishing Group, Inc.
4501 Forbes Boulevard, Suite 200, Lanham, Maryland 20706
www.rowman.com

16 Carlisle Street, London W1D 3BT, United Kingdom

British Library Cataloguing in Publication Information Available

Library of Congress Cataloging-in-Publication Data

The hardback edition of this book was previously cataloged by the Library of
Congress as follows:

Reading 1759 : literary culture in mid-eighteenth-century Britain and France /
edited by Shaun Regan.
p. cm. — (Literature, thought & culture) Includes bibliographical references and index.
1. Literature and society—Great Britain—History—18th century. 2. Literature and society—
France—History—18th century. 3. Books and reading—Great Britain—History—18th
century. 4. Books and reading— France—History—18th century. I. Regan, Shaun, 1970-
PR441.R43 2012
820.9'006—dc23
2012031639
ISBN: 978-1-61148-478-6 (cloth)
ISBN: 978-1-61148-593-6 (pbk.)
ISBN: 978-1-61148-479-3 (electronic)

 ™

Part III. Authorship and Aesthetics

Part IV. Enlightenment and its Discontents

Part V. Originality and Appropriation

VI. Conclusion: Reading 1759

T HE EDITOR OF A COLLECTION of essays on a diversity
of texts and topics cannot but accumulate a variety of debts. My thanks, first and
foremost, go to the contributors to the volume, both for their scholarly professionalism and for their patience in bearing with my editorial pedantry; they must
surely feel that something like one thousand seven hundred and fifty-nine years
have passed since work on the volume began. For scholarly hints and tips along
the way, I am grateful to Robert Jones, Tom Keymer, and Ian Campbell Ross. The
peculiar clustering of important publications in 1759 first became apparent to me
in the late 1990s during conversations with Robert in the sociable taverns of Ab-
erystwyth. More recently, it has been a pleasure to work with Bucknell University
Press, and I am particularly grateful to its Director, Greg Clingham, for his interest in the project. The reports of the anonymous readers for the Press were also
extremely useful in making revisions and final adjustments.

At Queen's University Belfast, I am especially grateful to the Centre for
Eighteenth-Century Studies, under the auspices of which I ran an interdisci-
plinary conference on "1759" in April 2009. All of my fellow CECS committee
members played some part in the event, and it is with pleasure that I thank
them here: John Bergin, Fiona Clark, Simon Davies, Moyra Haslett, David
Hayton, Sarah McCleave, Daniel Roberts, Gabriel Sánchez Espinosa, and Julie
Steenson. A particular thank you to Moyra for her pertinent and very helpful
comments on drafts of the volume's introduction and concluding essay. Also
at Queen's, I am grateful to various other colleagues in the School of English
for suggestions and practical help along the journey to (and beyond) "1759":
Brian Caraher, David Dwan, Eamonn Hughes, Ed Larrissy, Adrian Streete,

and Caroline Sumpter. Eamonn takes the prize for being the first to jest that, digitally speaking, 1759 is "nearly six o'clock."

Finally, for her love and support, and for enduring vicariously what Johnson termed the "dull duty of an editor," I should like to thank Julie Harvey.

B Y ANY MEASURE, 1759 was a momentous year in British and global history, culture, and ideas. In the international realm, 1759 marked the turning point in the Seven Years' War: a conflict that has been described as "the very first world war" or—in slightly more qualified terms—as "perhaps the first world war."[1] Across Europe, the Americas, and the North Atlantic, the year witnessed a series of key military and naval engagements in which Britain (and its allies) defeated France (and its allies): at Guadeloupe, Ticonderoga, Niagara, Minden, Lagos, Quebec, and Quiberon Bay. In Britain, the victories made national heroes of William Pitt the Elder, General James Wolfe, Admiral Edward Boscawen, and (to a lesser extent) Admiral Edward Hawke—and a villain of Lord George Sackville, the 'Coward' of Minden. The significance of these global events was not lost on British writers and cultural commentators, and the process of monumentalizing 1759 as a crucially important and unprecedentedly successful year in the nation's history was well under way before the year was out. When news arrived of Wolfe's victory on the Plains of Abraham, Horace Walpole wrote to Horace Mann that "like Alexander, we have no more worlds left to conquer"; a further letter to Mann, following news of Hawke's triumph over the French fleet at Quiberon Bay, was dated by Walpole "Nov. 30 of the Great Year."[2] Towards the end of the year, David Garrick's *Harlequin's Invasion* would refer to 1759 as "this glorious year," in the patriotic song "Hearts of Oak"; while, in a review of French war papers, the *Monthly Review* for November could already reflect on "the ever memorable year 1759."[3] As General Wolfe was made to declaim patriotically in a posthumous *Dialogue* between himself and the Marquis de Montcalm: "Masters of the sea, we are become the arbiters of the fate of nations; and *Europe*, jealous of our successes, is forc'd to admire and to fear us."[4] If this fictional Wolfe was as vaingloriously bullish as the living one had been, even during the year itself it was clear that 1759 represented a watershed moment in Britain's international competition with France; a moment that rendered the nation, in Frank McLynn's words, "the global superpower of the eighteenth century."[5]

While extensive attention was given during the year to events across the Continent and at the colonial peripheries, it is not only the waxing and waning of British and French national and imperial fortunes that marks the importance of 1759. A global (or, cosmic) event this year of great scientific and theological significance in Europe was the reappearance in March of Halley's Comet. In Britain itself, 1759 also saw the opening to the public of the British Museum, the founding of Josiah Wedgwood's pottery company, and John Harrison's completion of chronometer Number 4, the eventual Board of Longitude prize-winner. In Dublin, the year ended with the founding of the St James' brewery by Arthur Guinness. Less auspiciously, 1759 also witnessed the deaths of Handel and William Collins and, in France, the death of the *philosophe*, Maupertuis, and the formal suppression of the *Encyclopédie*. From the printing presses, significant histories appeared in the forms of William Robertson's *History of Scotland* and the second (Tudor) installment of David Hume's *History of England*. In the areas of moral philosophy and aesthetic theory, Adam Smith outlined a rational model of sympathy in *The Theory of Moral Sentiments*, while Edward Young published his *Conjectures on Original Composition*, Alexander Gerard an *Essay on Taste*, and Edmund Burke the second edition of *A Philosophical Enquiry into the Origin of our Ideas of the Sublime and Beautiful*, with its important new introduction on "taste." As Richard Taylor notes, it was in 1759 that Oliver Goldsmith "emerged suddenly as a leading essayist in London newspapers and magazines": besides his other work as a periodical essayist and reviewer, Goldsmith's *Enquiry into the Present State of Polite Learning in Europe* and his own periodical, *The Bee*, were both published this year.[6] In the intersecting genres of imaginative fiction and satire, the year also saw the publication of three canonical 'novels of ideas'—Voltaire's *Candide*, Samuel Johnson's *The Prince of Abissinia* (later known as *Rasselas*), and the first two volumes of Laurence Sterne's *Tristram Shandy*—along with less well-known works such as Richard Hurd's *Moral and Political Dialogues*, Sarah Fielding's *The History of the Countess of Dellwyn*, and the unattributed *The Histories of Some of the Penitents in the Magdalen-House*, a pioneering novel of sensibility and social reform.

The purpose of the new essays collected together in *Reading 1759* is to investigate the literary culture of Britain and France during this remarkable year.

As the roster of publications outlined above might suggest, more than simply a single year, 1759 was a singular year of authorial achievement; a year of the new, the novel, and the modern, which saw writers in various fields engaging with pressing issues of nationhood and empire, citizenship and civilization. In various ways, singularity is itself a key aspect of the works explored in this collection. A number of these works were 'one-off' publications, unparalleled within their authors' oeuvres—as in the cases of Johnson's *Rasselas* and Voltaire's *Candide*. Others were works that struck readers at the time as not just singular but singularly odd— Sterne's *Tristram Shandy* being the pre-eminent example. If Sterne's volumes in effect 'performed' singularity, in relation to the generic expectations of the period, singularity itself was thematized (and positively re-evaluated) by Edward Young. As Young argued in his *Conjectures on Original Composition*, "All Eminence, and Distinction, lies out of the beaten road; Excursion, and Deviation, are necessary to find it."[7] Distinction and deviation are not, of course, synonyms; although, for Owen Ruffhead this year, Hume's "passion for singularity" was a function of his "genius," authorial singularity by no means guaranteed exceptional achievement.[8] Yet, as the roster of the year's works indicates, 1759 saw the publication of some outstanding and enduring writings. The essays in *Reading 1759* offer a detailed exploration of the key canonical texts written and published this year, alongside less celebrated works of literature and other kinds of writing that were linked to, and that help to inform our sense of, the literary culture of the moment—works of philosophy and ethics, knowledge and aesthetics. Texts given extended attention within individual essays include *Rasselas*, *Candide*, *Tristram Shandy*, Christopher Smart's *Jubilate Agno*, Smith's *Theory of Moral Sentiments*, and Sarah Fielding's *The History of the Countess of Dellwyn*—along with a group of prostitution narratives that charted the lives and careers of Kitty Fisher, Fanny Murray, and the 'penitent' inmates of the recently founded Magdalen Hospital. Among the major canonical works, *Rasselas* receives particular attention, being the subject of two essays (on colonialism and causation) and a key focus in a third (on constructions of authorship). This recurring attention to Johnson's Oriental fiction—the work of a writer whom Tobias Smollett this year famously called "that great Cham of Literature"—allows for a significant publication of 1759 to be analyzed from a variety of angles: political, philosophical, and artistic.[9] While most of the volume's essays concentrate on British writings and their contexts, the inclusion of two essays on French literary culture (on *Candide* and the *Encyclopédie*) reflects the importance of French writers and thinkers, and of Anglo-French *cultural* relations, at this time. The ongoing conflict between Britain and France forms a significant backdrop to the collection, but neither the war itself, nor the literature of war *per se*, is the central focus. Rather, the volume takes a close but wide-ranging view of the literary culture of 1759. To this end, detailed readings of canonical and non-canonical works are supplemented by three essays on writings relating to this year that illuminate broader issues within the contemporary culture of print: the rise of professional authorship and the emergence of modern assumptions about original composition; encyclopedism and the systematization of Enlightenment knowledge; the formation of taste and the regulation of reading in the new literary review journals.

While 1759 saw the publication of a number of singular, and singularly important, works, this is not to say that literary culture at this time always appeared to those involved to be in a state of rude health. Even as Edward Young wrote of the "pleasures of the Pen" this year, Tobias Smollett—novelist, historian, translator, and editor of the *Critical Review*—claimed in December that "I would not wish my greatest enemy a greater curse than the occupation of an author"; while, earlier in the year, Horace Walpole gave vent to his own authorial ennui: "I am sick of the character of author; I am sick of the consequences of it; I am weary of seeing my name in the newspapers; I am tired with reading foolish criticisms on me, and as foolish defences of me."[10] Walpole's lament partly related to an undesired defense of his *Catalogue of the Royal and Noble Authors of England* (1758) that was published this year by the prolific writer and botanist John Hill; as Walpole wrote to Thomas Gray in February, "that puppy Dr Hill . . . has chosen to make war with the Magazines thro my Sides."[11] Hill's infiltration of the public sphere offers a salutary reminder of a central feature of literary culture during this period: the role of literary warring, of paper skirmishes between authors and critics and amongst authors themselves. Ironically, if the literati in Britain were united in anything this year, it was in their antagonism towards Hill. The beginning of the year saw David Garrick attempting (with difficulty) to shake off the Doctor, after utilizing him against Robert Dodsley and his play, *Cleone*, in late 1758. Perhaps the only positive outcome of these squalid dealings was Garrick's "Extempore" motto on Hill, one of the choice literary put-downs of the age: "For Physick & Farces, his Equal there scarce is, / His Farces are Physick, his Physick a Farce is." Throughout 1759, the reviewers offered unflattering assessments of the successive issues of Hill's pen: as the *Monthly Review* for April noted with marked understatement, "It has often fallen in our way to express our admiration at the unremitted industry of Dr. Hill, though we have not always been able to extol the fruits of his labour." In November, moreover, Hill would twice be denied entry into the "*fame machine*" in Goldsmith's *Bee* essay, "A Resverie."[12] Hill had previously been satirized in Christopher Smart's *Hilliad* (1753) and would find himself maligned again, as the "Proteus" of dunces, in Charles Churchill's *Rosciad* (1761).[13] As his thorny presence in the lists of mid-eighteenth-century authorship attests, literary culture during these years was by no means always a locus of artistic excellence, or indeed of creative harmony.

At the superior end of the spectrum of achievement, 1759 witnessed the publication of a number of important works from the hands of Scottish writers. As Adam Ferguson wrote to William Cullen in April, "We have scarcely heard of any thing this Winter but Scotch Authors," and Ferguson was especially impatient to see what would become one of the key philosophical texts of the period: Adam Smith's *The Theory of Moral Sentiments*.[14] Among the Scots-authored works published earlier in the year was the central text that Colin Kidd cites in arguing for the 1750s as a Scottish "golden age" during which, "having lost its independent nationhood," Scotland "rediscovered a voice": William Robertson's *History of Scotland*. As Kidd outlines, the significance of Robertson's *History* lay in its Unionist ideology; its presentation of "the new 'enlightened' patriotism of Scotland."[15] An important early advocate of Robertson's work was David Hume, the second installment of whose *History of England* also appeared this year. 1759 provides ample evidence of Hume's pivotal role within that group project, the Scottish Enlightenment. The selflessness of Hume's conduct towards his fellow historian was acknowledged by Robertson in a letter of 20 February: "Instead of feeling any emotion of envy on account of the success of an Author, who had intruded into the province of History, of which he was formerly in possession . . . he runs about praising my work, & enjoys the applause it meets with, as if it were bestowed upon himself."[16] For Hume, the national significance of Robertson's *History* was partly founded in a linguistic concern: James Basker has discussed Hume's "Scoto-phobic anxieties" about Scotticisms, those "traces of linguistic Scots or Scottish dialect—in diction, grammar or accent" that continued to provide focal points for anti-Scottish prejudice at the end of the 1750s.[17] Robertson's writing succeeded where other Scottish works had, from an English perspective, appeared verbally imperfect, and Hume's account of the *History*'s success, in a letter to Robertson in February, reveals this anxiety of native influence, albeit at second hand: "Mallet told me that he was sure there was no Englishman capable of composing such a work. The town will have it that you was educated at Oxford, thinking it impossible for a mere untravelled Scotchman to produce such language."[18] In the months that followed, Smith's *Theory* would also receive praise for its purity of style. Indeed, the success of Scottish-authored works in shifting perceptions this year is indicated by the *Monthly Review* for June, which observed that recent publications had shown that Scots could write (if not necessarily speak) English with "great ease, as well as elegance"—even if, in the *Monthly*'s opinion, Robert Maxwell's *The Practical Husbandman* (the work here under review) had not itself managed to achieve this.[19]

Hume's presence within *Reading 1759* usefully signals the critical approach that the collection takes to the year in literary culture. While the second install-ment of his *History of England* is not a specific focus, Hume's philosophical treatises and essays receive extended attention in discussions of moral sympathy, luxury and national progress, and the concept of causation. By attending to such works and contexts, to relevant developments both before and after 1759, and to the audi-ence for literature at this time, *Reading 1759* is informed by a sense of where the writings of this year were coming from, what they were looking towards, and how they were received by their contemporaries. Methodologically, the volume thus takes a two-fold approach, complementing its synchronic focus on a single year with a diachronic sense of the year's contribution to longer-term changes. At the heart of the project is an attempt to produce a kind of Geertzian "thick descrip-tion" of the literary culture of 1759; an analysis that Geertz also describes—fit-tingly for the eighteenth century—as "microscopic."[20] In order to balance this strictly 'synchronic' approach, the volume also draws upon Raymond Williams's model of emergent, dominant, and residual discourses and cultural practices, so as to produce a fuller sense of the writings and ideas that were variously drawn upon, appropriated, overwritten, rejected, and anticipated by works published in 1759.[21] By adopting this dual focus, the essays in the collection aim to explore processes of both continuity and change at a specific moment in eighteenth-century literary history, and to pinpoint the representative, as well as the exceptional, within the year's work in writing.

For all the essays' attention to the diachronic dimension, the focus on 1759 necessarily ensures a predominantly synchronic emphasis. This single-year focus inevitably raises certain issues regarding the selection of texts for analysis. As a basic criterion for inclusion, *Reading 1759* addresses texts written or published in 1759—but even such a seemingly straightforward rubric highlights works that press against the confines of calendrical study. Among texts published this year, for instance, Richard Hurd's *Dialogues* was largely a work of 1757–58, that was mostly printed in 1758, but that was delayed when the manuscript of the final dialogue was lost—in the words of William Mason—"by the carelessness of a Leicester bookseller."[22] In relation to publication, a more marginal case is presented by Sterne's *Tristram Shandy*, the initial volumes of which were printed and perhaps published (depending on how one defines this) in December 1759, though more securely written (and indeed rewritten) during the course of the year.[23] The potential problems involved in attending only to the year of writing or to the year of publication (or indeed to either) are further foregrounded by two part-works that receive essay-length treatment in the collection: Fragment B of Smart's *Jubilate Agno*, which was written during 1759 and 1760 but not published until the twentieth century, and the '1759' volume (volume VIII) of the French *Encyclopédie*, which was at least partly written in 1758, partly written after 1759, and not published until the late 1760s. By including them within our remit, our aim is not to 'claim' these works for 1759 (nor, conversely, to dispute their relevance). Rather, the essays presented in this volume seek to examine a range of activities, emphases, and contexts within literary culture during this single year—such as, in these instances, religious discourse written away from the public, communal realm of print, and the warring forces of Enlightenment knowledge and state censorship in France. It would be misleading, though, not to admit that some blurring necessarily occurs at the edges of the 'synchronic' project—fuzziness that is highlighted in another way when we attend to what was being read during 1759, which inevitably includes some works both written and published in previous years, while largely excluding works that only appeared at the end of the year. As it explores the literary culture of 1759, the collection can then also be regarded as a testing ground for the practice of single-year studies, which brings into focus the practical and conceptual issues presented by such studies, as well as the particular insights and interpretive possibilities that they enable.

Reading 1759 is the first book for thirty years to address a single year in eighteenth-century literary culture—since the publication of *1789: Reading, Writing, Revolution* in 1982.[24] While the volume is the first to examine, together and in detail, the range of works written and published in 1759, it is not the first to focus either on the year 1759 itself or on literature during the period of the Seven Years' War. The most significant previous study of 1759 is Frank McLynn's *1759: The Year Britain Became Master of the World* (2004). McLynn's popular history presents a lively narrative of the key military and political events of the year (with a particular focus on the Anglo-French conflict), while also offering an overview of important literary and cultural events—albeit one that is confined to brief prefaces to chapters.[25] One of the aims of *Reading 1759* is to explore more extensively the literary culture of this important year, and its engagement with some of the most significant texts, ideas, and cultural trends of the era. Among the small number of studies of the literature of the war that have appeared in recent years, the most notable are M. John Cardwell's *Arts and Arms: Literature, Politics and Patriotism during the Seven Years War* (2004) and Carol Watts's *The Cultural Work of Empire: The Seven Years' War and the Imagining of the Shandean State* (2007). Cardwell's study is principally concerned with developments in the political arena during these years (as conveyed in textual forms such as ballads, satiric poetry, and prints), and the "political literature" that he addresses does not include any of the works that form the focus of the essays in *Reading 1759*.[26] Watts's study approaches the topic from a more clearly literary perspective than do McLynn and Cardwell, and her arguments inform a number of the essays in this collection.[27] Neither Cardwell nor Watts, though, shares the present volume's focus on the single year of 1759—a focus that here encompasses, but is not restricted to, the relationship between the writings produced during the year and the events of the Seven Years' War. While Watts in particular does consider a number of the texts that are examined in *Reading 1759*, therefore, the essays in this volume seek to establish more precisely than have previous studies the connections between texts, ideas, and contexts, in relation to 1759 specifically.[28]

A broader publishing context for *Reading 1759* also exists as, within the last ten to fifteen years, something approaching a fashion has developed for studies focused on particular years. Like McLynn's *1759* (and also his *1066*), most of these studies are primarily historical or historical-cultural in focus: as with Adam Zamoyski's *1812: Napoleon's Fatal March on Moscow* (2004) or, in our own period, Sheila O'Connell's *London 1753* (2003). In relation to literature, James Shapiro's *1599: A Year in the Life of William Shakespeare* (2005) is a notable example of a biographically oriented study focused on a single year. Of greater relevance here is James Chandler's *England in 1819* (1998), a work of literary and cultural analysis that, like *Reading 1759*, ranges across the writings of a single year, making connections within the variety of works examined and exploring the participation of these writings in the broader current of events and ideas. Usefully, if somewhat self-consciously, Chandler also reflects on some of the issues raised by "reading the text(s) of a *dated* culture" and, in particular, by the "annualization" of criticism. Of annualized studies specifically, Chandler asks: "Does one 'read' differently a given text that is set in a secular literary history [within the framework of a literary period or era, for instance] and one framed by a single year? Does the difference in framing necessarily alter the object framed, or may one imagine that one is considering the 'same' critical object . . . first within one scale and then another?"[29] These questions are undoubtedly pertinent to the essays in this volume, and a preliminary answer might be that what the 'annualized' reading practiced here represents is a form of analysis that is able to delve more deeply than is often possible into the historical specificity of the critical objects, while also attending as closely as possible to the broader range of texts that constitute the field of literature, and its cultural horizons, during the selected year. Whether this entirely alters the works at issue is moot, but at the very least, the critical connections facilitated by this single-year focus can move us towards a fuller and more precise sense of the literary-historical object and its intertextual richness. If a singular focus on the literary culture of 1759 does not transform wholesale the texts under scrutiny in this collection, it nonetheless brings them into closer, "microscopic" focus (individually), and into closer proximity within the field of critical vision (collectively).

The critical contours of *Reading 1759* are shaped to a significant degree by the concerns of most importance to authors during the year itself. The opening section addresses the larger issues of colonialism and empire-creation that lay at the heart of the ongoing conflict between Britain and France. To begin, James Watt reads *Rasselas* in the context of the war and the wider world. Locating the work within Johnson's wartime oeuvre, Watt teases out the relationship between contemporary events and Johnson's philosophical tale—a text that might initially appear to bear little precise relation to its moment of production. While *Rasselas* may not have addressed the war directly, as did some of Johnson's essays at this time, its adoption of a broad perspective on humanity enabled Johnson to survey both the wider parameters and the "deep origins" of the conflict, which stretched back to the beginnings of European colonialism. In this way, the work's general enquiry into humanity and the possibility of happiness encompassed the particular historical moment at which Johnson wrote. At the same time, *Rasselas* also reveals the difficulties involved both in comprehending large-scale historical processes and in circumscribing the human desire for dominion, which leads Watt towards a more qualified assessment of Johnson's oft-noted anti-imperialism. This consideration of the contemporary resonances of canonical texts is continued in Simon Davies's examination of Voltaire's *Candide* within the broad contexts of empire, slavery, and global conflict. Drawing on Voltaire's diverse oeuvre and on key works by contemporary French authors (notably the mid-century writings on slavery of Montesquieu, Rousseau, and Helvétius), Davies foregrounds the global reach of the work and both the directness and the breadth of Voltaire's interventions into pressing contemporary issues. As Davies argues, Voltaire viewed *Candide* very much as a public text, which was designed to school its readers in current global developments. In doing so, it presented a vision of inter-national relations that was far from ennobling, in which increases in cross-cultural contact led to increasing examples of human injustice. In line with this vision and with Voltaire's sense of his own cultural position in France, the tale thus focused on the key issue of leadership, partly through detailing multiple examples of failures of leadership. If *Rasselas* examined how to live, *Candide* might well be regarded as addressing how to lead.

As well as elucidating their contemporary purchase, this pairing of essays on *Rasselas* and *Candide* enables a reconsideration of the links between the two works. *Rasselas* and *Candide* have often been considered as twinned texts that offer variations on similar themes, nowhere more famously than in the comparative evaluation offered in James Boswell's *Life of Johnson* (1791):

> Voltaire's *Candide*, written to refute the system of Optimism, which it has accomplished with brilliant success, is wonderfully similar in its plan and conduct to Johnson's *Rasselas*; insomuch, that I have heard Johnson say, that if they had not been published so closely one after the other that there was not time for imitation, it would have been in vain to deny that the scheme of that which came latest was taken from the other. Though the proposition illustrated by both these works was the same, namely, that in our present state there is more evil than good, the intention of the writers was very different. Voltaire, I am afraid, meant only by wanton profaneness to obtain a sportive victory over religion, and to discredit the belief of a superintending Providence: Johnson meant, by shewing [sic] the unsatisfactory nature of things temporal, to direct the hopes of man to things eternal.[30]

Both here and in the reflections of other early readers, a consensus quickly developed in Britain that maligned Voltaire's text as impious and that, on occasion, set Johnson's more orthodox and consoling text against it. Both implicitly and more directly, the opening essays of this collection add to our understanding of (if not actually resolving) the relationship between these two intriguing, philosophically tinged prose works, specifying points of connection and difference that move us beyond the period's own, predominant concern with the works' religious import.

Moving from the global and political to the national and personal, section II explores works concerning ethics, sexuality, and social progress. Nigel Wood returns us to the first edition of *The Theory of Moral Sentiments*, Smith's initial working out of his system of moral sympathy and of the role within this of the "impartial spectator"—a figure that (or whom) Alexander Broadie has called "a hero of the Enlightenment."[31] To the extent that the impartial spectator seeks a "complete sentimental knowledge of a situation," Smith's *Theory* might be read as offering an affective variation on what James Watt in his essay terms Johnson's interest in "properly comprehensive forms of knowledge." As Wood argues, though, while the 1759 version of the *Theory* laid the bedrock for later revisions, it also displayed marked uncertainties, and differences of emphasis, that need to be taken into account in any understanding of Smith's ethical philosophy. With regard to the *Theory*'s central figure, the essay traces how Smith's conceptualization of the "impartial spectator" extended the use of such figures in the writings of Addison, Hume, and others, but also how, in the first edition, the Smithian spectator was still a work in progress. Described in ambivalent metaphors of mirrors and acting, the spectator at this stage not only resolved but also raised difficulties concerning the social and psychological bases of moral conduct. Moral sympathy, and sentimental constructions of women particularly, are also central to Mary Peace's discussion of a group of narratives concerning prostitution that were published this year. Peace examines the 'lives' of the well-known prostitutes, Fanny Murray and Kitty Fisher, in relation to the classical-republican narrative of the decline into luxury of a risen nation that indulges excessively in the fruits of its prosperity. As the paradigmatic, degenerate symbol of such decline, the figure of the prostitute lay at the heart of this narrative. Within this political-theoretical context, and in the immediate context of a military conflict that demanded an assertion of national vigor, the prostitute also became a central figure within British culture. If the symbolic currency of the prostitute was traded on by a number of textual 'memoirs,' though, these works also sought to contain the threat that the prostitute appeared to represent. Alongside the prostitutes' 'lives,' Peace examines *The Histories of Some of the Penitents in the Magdalen-House*, a work of charitable intent that might seem to offer a moral foil to the more sexualized narratives of Murray and Fisher. Yet, as Peace's essay shows, to a greater or lesser extent all three texts evinced faith in the British national virtue, notwithstanding the evidence they also provided of the snares to individual morality within mid-eighteenth-century society.

Section III turns to the work of writing itself, to consider the process of authorial creativity as this was discussed and envisioned in 1759. Adam Rounce examines three key works that tackled and touched upon the 'idea' of authorship this year: Young's *Conjectures on Original Composition*, Goldsmith's *Enquiry into the Present State of Polite Learning*, and Johnson's *Rasselas*. Through close analysis of these works (and of contemporaneous texts such as James Ralph's *The Case of Authors by Profession* [1758]), Rounce situates 1759 as a transitional moment that was caught between emergent and residual understandings of the life of writing. Discussions of authorship were rarely able to maintain the clear distinction that was made by William Mason this year, between writing high-mindedly "for Fame, for Posterity, & all sort of fine things" and acts of publishing that were driven by the "motive of Gain."[32] Moreover, while Young's promotion of 'originality' over 'imitation' marked a break with the past, the valorization of individual creativity that this entailed could be reconciled to earlier distinctions between an elite of literary geniuses and the masses of workaday hacks. Notably, Rounce finds Young's *Conjectures* less decisively celebratory of creative originality than is sometimes assumed. In particular, in the work's evasion of the marketplace, Rounce discerns both a defensive denial and a form of wish-fulfillment. As his essay asks, therefore: was the *Conjectures* the harbinger of a new, modern idea of authorial creativity, or a retreat into a pre-commercial fantasy in which patronage was justly distributed and literary talent transparently visible? In comparison with Young, Goldsmith's *Enquiry* was more clearly conflicted about the contemporary abuse of hard-working (and financially hard-pressed) writers; while Johnson was more aware again of the relationship, and the contradictions, between the idealization and the material realities of writing. For all their differences of intention and emphasis, what we thus witness in these works is contemporary authors grappling with the status, function, and conditions of modern authorship, and wavering in their focus between the cosseted creative artist and the put-upon literary laborer. Away from the cut and thrust of commercial publishing this year, the incarcerated Christopher Smart was writing the second fragment of his own literary masterpiece. Moving to the act, and the beauty, of literary creation itself, Rosalind Powell details Smart's attempt to forge a new kind of language to communicate the divine—and to communicate *with* the divine—in his *Jubilate Agno*. Against Burke's association of the deity with the sublime, which had informed his earlier poems and which placed absolute limits on the capacity of language to convey the divine power, Smart connected both the Creator and his Creation with the 'beautiful.' Seeking to extend the palette of signification through which one might both view and represent the divine, Smart pointed to a barely perceptible language of signs beyond the conventional understanding of language, discerning spiritual significance in individual letters, sounds, and colors. Through this process, as Powell shows, the deity might be understood as becoming comprehensible (as against the incomprehensibility of a sublime deity), and the divine power appreciable as "powerfully beautiful."

Section IV shifts the focus from authorship and aesthetics to Enlightenment. As Roy Porter has argued, "enlightened ideologies" in England were "less concerned to lambast the *status quo* than to vindicate it against adversaries left and right, high and low."[33] In stark contrast to this was the situation of the French *philosophes*, whose works were frequently set in opposition to the interests of both Church and State. Rebecca Ford examines 1759 as a crucial year in the progress, and the progression, of the *Encyclopédie*, the central text of the French Enlightenment. It was during this year that the project was formally suppressed by the state authorities—an act that threatened the entire enterprise and that caused rifts among the Encyclopedists themselves. Focusing on volume VIII—the volume that was due to be published in 1759—Ford traces the impact of these pressures and tensions in the context of the broader aims and publishing history of the venture. As she recognizes, the focus on a single volume of this (initially annual) multi-volume work foregrounds some of the methodological issues raised by a synchronic, single-year approach to literary and cultural history. While aware of the difficulties presented by such an analysis, however, Ford's essay proposes a number of ways in which the articles included in volume VIII might be seen to have been influenced and inflected by the events of 1759. Following this broad view of the *Encyclopédie* and its travails, James Ward turns our attention to a specific philosophical issue that troubled writers and thinkers during the mid-eighteenth century: the problem of causation. As they were popularly understood, the writings of Hume—the leading light of the Scottish Enlightenment—had thrown open the conventional understanding of causal relation, as something that was empirically unprovable. Noting that philosophy and literature were regarded at this time as "part of the same enterprise," Ward takes the contemporary quandary over causation as the basis for a re-examination both of *Rasselas* and of the relationship between Hume and Johnson. As he shows, Johnson's tale queries conventional notions of causation (and the beliefs that underpin them), but in a different manner, and with a different emphasis, than Hume. Johnson's favoring of practical ethics over the heady mazes of metaphysics could not entirely override or pre-empt more abstract problems—not least the pressing contemporary question concerning cause and effect. Significantly, *Rasselas*'s latent enquiry into causation is intimately related to its anxiety over the potentially delusive workings of the imagination, while idleness, another central Johnsonian concern, can itself be understood as a symptom of philosophical doubt: the consequence, and the condition, of uncertainty over the possibility of tracing causes and effects. Following the essays by Watt and Rounce, Ward's analysis of Hume, Johnson, and causation thus offers another way of viewing *Rasselas* as a work steeped in the concerns of its contemporary moment.

Staying with prose fiction, Section V elaborates further some of the central concerns of Young's *Conjectures*; specifically, the relationships between original-ity and imitation and between contemporary writers and their predecessors. Voltaire found *Tristram Shandy* "a very unaccountable book; an original one," and Moyra Haslett examines the intertwining of eccentricity, originality, and the novel in the opening volumes of Sterne's text.[34] She begins by recovering a spatial meaning of 'eccentric,' which would have been apparent to contem-porary readers and which illuminates both the local, Yorkshire setting and the initial publication of the work. This placement of the work as geographically 'eccentric' leads into a discussion of the interweaving of eccentricity and origi-nality in *Tristram*'s initial installment, in terms of individual behavior, literary character, and authorial creativity. During a singular year in literary culture, *Tristram Shandy* both depicted eccentric personalities and embodied Young's suggestion that—as Haslett puts it—"singular characters might be thought to write in original ways." Teasing out what was shared or borrowed, and what was distinctive and unprecedented, in Sterne's own use of these terms and ideas, Haslett's discussion addresses the extent to which Sterne's own 'eccentric' char-acters referred back to earlier fictional originals, or forwards to emerging ideas about eccentric national character. Drawing on a broad body of novels published during the 1750s—most notably Thomas Amory's *The Life of John Buncle, Esq* (1756)—the essay thus reconsiders the paradox of a text that can be read both as entirely unique and as typical of the literary experimentalism of prose fiction during that decade. Another prose fiction of 1759—Sarah Fielding's *The History of the Countess of Dellwyn*—provides the focus for Kate Rumbold's discussion of the role of Shakespeare, and Shakespearean allusion, in the mid-eighteenth-century novel. As Rumbold shows, Shakespeare is extensively interwoven into the fabric of Fielding's text, in a manner that exemplifies (and indeed furthered) the eighteenth-century process that Michael Dobson has dubbed "the making of the national poet."[35] Both substantiating and nuancing the role of Shakespeare and of virtuous, and not-so-virtuous, heroines in Fielding's writing, Rumbold examines *The Countess of Dellwyn* in the context of the author's fictional oeuvre from the 1740s to the early 1760s. To specify the precise import of the term 'propriety' that attaches to Shakespeare in *Dellwyn* itself, she also returns us to the use of this term in another key work of 1759: Smith's *Theory of Moral Senti-ments*. While the responses of Shakespeare's characters to their circumstances are judged to be appropriate (and thus exemplary), *Dellwyn* exposes the disjunction between the emotional behavior of its own characters and the situations in which they find themselves. In this richly intertextual and partly comic work, narratorial recourse to the example of Shakespeare's plays thus functions primarily as a benchmark for the propriety, or fittingness, of characters' behaviors—while, more subtly, beginning to cast a moral judgment upon them.

Rumbold's discussion emphasizes the cue to the reader that the word 'propriety' represents in *The Countess of Dellwyn*, in which Fielding sought to cultivate an impartial, discriminating form of reader response; a detached yet sympathetic judgment of characters' behavior. Moving from inscribed, or fictionally projected, readers to real ones, the final essay develops the issue of audience response by considering the evidence for contemporary habits of reading contained in writers' correspondence and literary review journals. The essay acts as a conclusion to the collection, while also broadening the focus to cover important figures within mid-century literary culture who, for various reasons, aren't covered elsewhere in the volume: figures such as William Shenstone and Thomas Percy, Elizabeth Montagu and Elizabeth Carter, William Warburton and Richard Hurd. Situating the diachronic form of the periodical within the synchronic frame of a single year, the essay considers the standing of literary reviewing a decade after the commencement of the *Monthly Review*. If professional reviewers and dedicated review journals might seem to have become entrenched within the literary culture by this time, they were yet far from universally welcomed or fully respected—as James Grainger demonstrated the previous year when referring to "the cruel fangs of those savage beasts the Critical Reviewers."[36] Along with testaments to the reviewers' influence and challenges to their authority, the essay considers how far readers were influenced by prevailing and emerging notions of correct style, originality, and polite "taste"—the latter defined by Burke this year as "that faculty, or those faculties of the mind which are affected with, or which form a judgement of the works of imagination and the elegant arts."[37] More particularly, the essay assesses the extent to which authors' own critical evaluations might have been guided by the views of their authorial acquaintances within literary circles. By surveying the institutions, practices, and protocols of reading in 1759, the essay thus seeks to illuminate both the broad context, and the specific ways, in which the texts discussed in this collection were read and evaluated by their contemporaries. In the process, the essay rounds off the volume's own reading of an extraordinary year in eighteenth-century literary culture.

Notes

1. Tom Pocock, *Battle for Empire: The Very First World War, 1756–63* (London: Michael O'Mara Books, 1998); M. John Cardwell, *Arts and Arms: Literature, Politics and Patriotism during the Seven Years War* (Manchester: Manchester University Press, 2004), 9.

2. Horace Walpole to Sir Horace Mann, 19 October and 30 November 1759, in *The Letters of Horace Walpole, Fourth Earl of Orford*, ed. Paget Toynbee, vol. 4 (Oxford: Clarendon Press, 1903), 314, 326.

3. Frank McLynn, *1759: The Year Britain Became Master of the World* (London: Jonathan Cape, 2004), 392; *Monthly Review* 21 (November 1759), 451.

4. *A Dialogue Betwixt General Wolfe, and the Marquis Montcalm, in the Elysian Fields* ([Coventry?]: Sold by E. Jopson, Rivington and Fletcher, and others, 1759), 6.

5. McLynn, *1759*, 388.

6. Richard C. Taylor, *Goldsmith as Journalist* (Rutherford, Madison, Teaneck: Fairleigh Dickinson University Press; London: Associated University Presses, 1993), 24.

7. Edward Young, *Conjectures on Original Composition: In a Letter to the Author of "Sir Charles Grandison"* (London: A. Millar and R. and J. Dodsley, 1759), 22–23.

8. *Monthly Review* 20 (April 1759), 345, 364.

9. Tobias Smollett to John Wilkes, 16 March 1759, in *The Letters of Tobias Smollett*, ed. Lewis M. Knapp (Oxford: Clarendon Press, 1970), 75.

10. Young, *Conjectures*, 7; Smollett to John Harvie, 10 December 1759, in *Letters of Tobias Smollett*, 85; Walpole to the Rev. Henry Zouch, 14 May 1759, in *Letters of Horace Walpole*, 4:263.

11. Walpole to Thomas Gray, 15 February 1759, in *Correspondence of Thomas Gray*, ed. Paget Toynbee and Leonard Whibley, 3 vols. (Oxford: Clarendon Press, 1935), 2:616.

12. David Garrick to John Hawkesworth, [ca. January 1759], in *The Letters of David Garrick*, ed. David M. Little and George M. Kahrl, 3 vols. (London: Oxford University Press, 1963), 1:299; *Monthly Review* 20 (April 1759), 369; Oliver Goldsmith, *The Bee* no. 5 (3 November 1759), in *The Collected Works of Oliver Goldsmith*, ed. Arthur Friedman, 5 vols. (Oxford: Clarendon Press, 1966), 1:445–46.

13. Christopher Smart, *The Hilliad: An Epic Poem* (London: J. Newbery and M. Cooper, 1753); Charles Churchill, *The Rosciad*, 3rd ed. (London: W. Flexney, 1761), 4 (line 72).

14. Adam Ferguson to [William Cullen], 17 April 1759, in *The Correspondence of Adam Ferguson*, ed. Vincenzo Merolle, 2 vols. (London: Pickering and Chatto, 1995), 1:32.

15. Colin Kidd, "The Ideological Significance of Robertson's *History of Scotland*," in *William Robertson and the Expansion of Empire*, ed. Stewart J. Brown (Cambridge: Cambridge University Press, 1997), 124–26.

16. William Robertson to Janet Hepburn, 20 February 1759, as cited in Stewart J. Brown, "William Robertson (1721–1793) and the Scottish Enlightenment," in *William Robertson and the Expansion of Empire*, 20.

17. James G. Basker, "Scotticisms and the Problem of Cultural Identity in Eighteenth-Century Britain," *Eighteenth-Century Life* 15 (February and May 1991): 83–85, 81.

18. David Hume to William Robertson, [February 1759], in *The Letters of David Hume*, ed. J. Y. T. Greig, 2 vols. (Oxford: Clarendon Press, 1932), 1:297.

19. *Monthly Review* 20 (June 1759), 582.

20. Clifford Geertz, "Thick Description: Toward an Interpretive Theory of Culture," in *The Interpretation of Cultures* (New York: Basic Books, 1973), 21.

21. See Raymond Williams, *Marxism and Literature* (Oxford: Oxford University Press, 1977).

22. William Mason to Gray, 22 January [1759], in *Correspondence of Thomas Gray*, 2:612.

23. On the distinction between the printing and publishing of *Tristram Shandy*, see James E. Tierney, ed., *The Correspondence of Robert Dodsley, 1733–1764* (Cambridge: Cambridge University Press, 1988), 416–17n5.

24. Francis Barker, Jay Bernstein, Peter Hulme, Margaret Iversen, and Jennifer Stone, eds., *1789: Reading, Writing, Revolution* (Colchester: University of Essex, 1982).

25. These prefaces are marred in places by inaccuracy, as in the statement that "the first two parts" of *Tristram Shandy* were published this year, followed by "a third part a few years later": McLynn, *1759*, 254.

26. Cardwell, *Arts and Arms*, 1, 278.

27. Carol Watts, *The Cultural Work of Empire: The Seven Years' War and the Imagining of the Shandean State* (Toronto: University of Toronto Press, 2007).

28. Also worthy of note here are two articles by John Richardson: "Imagining Military Conflict during the Seven Years' War," *Studies in English Literature* 48 (2008): 585–611, and "Sterne's Patriotic Shandeism," *Essays in Criticism* 58 (2008): 20–42.

29. James Chandler, *England in 1819: The Politics of Literary Culture and the Case of Romantic Historicism* (Chicago: University of Chicago Press, 1998), 67, 77.

30. *Boswell's Life of Johnson*, ed. George Birkbeck Hill, rev. L. F. Powell, 6 vols. (Oxford: Clarendon Press, 1934–1950), 1:342.

31. Alexander Broadie, *The Scottish Enlightenment: The Historical Age of the Historical Nation* (Edinburgh: Birlinn, 2001), 101.

32. Mason to Gray, 25 January 1759, in *Correspondence of Thomas Gray*, 2:613.

33. Roy Porter, *Enlightenment: Britain and the Creation of the Modern World* (Harmondsworth: Penguin, 2000), 31.

34. Voltaire as cited in Watts, *Cultural Work*, 50.

35. Michael Dobson, *The Making of the National Poet: Shakespeare, Adaptation, and Authorship, 1660–1769* (Oxford: Clarendon Press, 1992).

36. James Grainger to Thomas Percy, February 1758, in John Bowyer Nichols, *Illustrations of the Literary History of the Eighteenth Century*, 8 vols. (London: J. B. Nichols and Son, 1848), 7:249.

37. Edmund Burke, *A Philosophical Enquiry into the Origin of our Ideas of the Sublime and Beautiful*, ed. J. T. Boulton (London: Routledge, 1958), 13.

Part I

WRITING EMPIRE

1

"WHAT MANKIND HAS LOST AND GAINED": JOHNSON, *RASSELAS*, AND COLONIALISM

JAMES WATT

RECENT ACCOUNTS OF THE BRITISH metropolitan consciousness of the Seven Years' War have argued that "colonial conquest was described and glorified as a manly occupation, the proving ground for national potency," but also that it was attended, in some circles, by an anxiety that this rapid growth of territorial dominion might trouble the very meaning of home and belonging.[1] In the light of Suvir Kaul's contention that eighteenth-century literary texts provide "an invaluable archive of the desires and fears that accompanied the making . . . of an imperial nation," this essay will explore the topicality of Samuel Johnson's *The History of Rasselas, Prince of Abissinia*, assessing how the work might be regarded as "a parable fitted to the times."[2] Although *Rasselas* is in no straightforward sense an allegory, its treatment of human restlessness, together with its juxtaposition of the security of the Happy Valley and the turbulence of life beyond, would surely have resonated with readers aware of the ongoing conflict in its numerous different theatres. Even as the proper direction of human energies remains Johnson's ostensible concern, the experiences of the prince and his party outside the confines of the Happy Valley generate other, more specific forms of enquiry regarding the interconnectedness of an increasingly globalized world and (implicitly, at least) Britain's position within that network of relations.

In order to explore the nature of *Rasselas*'s engagement with its contemporary moment, I will first of all consider it alongside earlier writings by Johnson that attend to general truths about the human condition, and that consequently appear little interested in their immediate historical circumstances. By reading *Rasselas* in the context of Johnson's non-fictional prose of the mid- to late-1750s, especially his essays on the Seven Years' War, I will then discuss the ways in which the politics of the present impinge upon the prince's quest for personal fulfillment, as his travels acquaint him with "the various conditions of men" and thus prompt him to recognize the uneven global distribution of power and knowledge.[3] Johnson understood the Seven Years' War as a conflict that brought the world-historical significance of the European voyages of discovery and the colonization of America into sharper focus, and in another work that he wrote in 1759, his introduction to *The World Displayed*, he speculates pertinently about "What mankind has lost and gained" since the end of the fifteenth century.[4] *Rasselas* similarly broaches such expansive questions, I will argue here, but at the same time it reflexively signals its awareness of the difficulty of answering them, or even of establishing a sufficiently stable vantage-point from which they could be addressed in the first place. As I will suggest in conclusion, the practical priorities of the prince's sister, Nekayah, may provide a potentially compensatory form of orientation for the reader, even as her final claim that the "choice of eternity" matters more than the "choice of life" (175) makes *Rasselas* available to be read as a quietist and otherworldly work that transcends history altogether.

Many of Johnson's diverse writings prior to *Rasselas* combined a focus on human nature in the abstract with an expansive geographical reach. Johnson began his career as an author with the 1735 publication of *A Voyage to Abyssinia* (a part-translation of the French edition of a travelogue written by the Portuguese Jesuit, Jeronimo Lobo), and one of the reasons why he was drawn to this text, he claimed, was that its "modest and unaffected narration" exemplified an essential truth: that "wherever human nature is to be found, there is a mixture of vice and virtue, a contest of passion and reason."[5] In his best-known poem, "The Vanity of Human Wishes" (1749), Johnson likewise appealed to the idea of a universal human condition, famously surveying "the busy scenes of crowded life" across the earth ("from China to Peru"), along with particular instances of the defeat of "wavering man, betrayed by venturous pride."[6] Johnson's experimentation with literary Orientalism, in the form of brief tales or "apologues" previously popularized by periodicals such as *The Spectator* (1711–14), allowed him to explore similarly generalized thematic concerns. Numbers 204 and 205 of *The Rambler* (published early in 1752), for example, tell the story of Seged, "Lord of Ethiopia"—who, once securely established as "the monarch of forty nations," decides to devote himself to the pursuit of pleasure, imagining what it might be "to fill the whole capacity of my soul with enjoyment, and . . . live without a wish unsatisfied." Beset by a series of calamities that culminate in the death of his daughter, Seged gradually comes to appreciate "the uncertainty of human schemes," before finally offering his narrative as proof to future generations "that no man hereafter may presume to say, 'this day shall be a day of happiness.'"[7]

Like the story of Seged, *Rasselas* appears to sponsor an abstract enquiry into the human condition. While it takes from Lobo both the name of its title character and the premise that the sons of the Emperor of Abyssinia are confined until the time of their accession, it otherwise offers an essentially composite Eastern setting.[8] If *Rasselas* is in some ways an extended version of Johnson's earlier 'Ethiopian' tale, however, it also interrogates the process of enquiry itself, insistently returning to the question of how, if at all, properly comprehensive forms of knowledge might be acquired.[9] Unlike Seged, Prince Rasselas is shown from the outset to be dissatis-fied with a life of pleasure and repose, and what he imagines to be the "singularity of his humour" (12) makes him bemoan his inactivity, firing him with an ardent yearning to do "something, though he knew not yet with distinctness, either end or means" (17). The scale of this ambition occupies the prince in a solipsistic state of "visionary bustle" (18), and renders him susceptible to the fantasy of flight prof-fered by an aviation enthusiast he meets, a figure who promises both a means of escape from the Happy Valley and an aerial survey that would afford an Olympian vision of "the earth, and all its inhabitants" (26). This richly suggestive episode at once invokes and undercuts the idea of "observation with extensive view" on which an earlier work such as "The Vanity of Human Wishes" was founded, for the mechanical artist's attempt to fly succeeds only in plunging him into a lake, from which he has to be rescued, "half dead with terrour and vexation" (28).[10] Rasselas's first experiences of life outside of the valley provide a further ironic perspective on his dual quest for knowledge of the world and a constructive oc-cupation, since while he is shown to be fascinated with "the diversity of manners, stations and employments" that he encounters on the approach to Cairo, for ex-ample, he expects to be able not only to stand apart from the activity he witnesses, but also to maintain his position of royal privilege. Just as his sister, Nekayah, is said to be shocked "because those that came into her presence did not prostrate themselves before her," so we are told that Rasselas, "wherever he came, expected to be obeyed" (62).

The prince initially uses his status to command the poet, Imlac, to attend him in the Happy Valley, subsequently appointing Imlac as his "sole director in the *choice of life*" (56). Imlac, for his part, largely indulges the misconceptions of his charges, "for[bearing] to force upon them unwelcome knowledge, which time itself would too soon impress" (157); after leaving Cairo, therefore, he does not challenge the "pleasing delusion" of the prince about the "universal plenty" that he believes he has seen (65). Johnson's text is emphatic throughout that the condition of retirement forced upon Rasselas by his upbringing is productive of naivety rather than disinterested authority, and affords him no purchase on the complex ways of the world. On being told by Imlac that even the most vigilant sovereign "can never know all the crimes that are committed, and can seldom punish all that he knows," for example, the prince's response is one of incomprehension: "This . . . I do not understand" (32). Yet although the relationship between the two men is presented as akin to that of teacher and pupil, with Imlac bemoaning the prince's ignorance yet admiring his curiosity, it is significant that Imlac as much as Rasselas is made to confront the limits of his knowledge. While they are still in the Happy Valley, Rasselas assumes that since he is able to find new things "within the circuit of these mountains," his tutor must inevitably have "left much unobserved" on his previous travels, prompting Imlac to define "the business of a poet" as the examination of "general and transcendental truths" that relate to the species rather than the individual (43). If, as Imlac explains, a poet "must write . . . as a being superior to time and place," such an elevated position is only available to one who has already had a wide-ranging, albeit necessarily superficial, experience of what he calls "variety in life" (35). Imlac's own experience of the world derives from his early initiation into the workings of commerce, and his visiting of countries and regions at different stages of social development. However much he might stress the extent of this experience, though, he also recognizes that poets have to be omnivorous creatures whose basic foundational knowledge, "many languages and many sciences" (45), is all but limitless. After Rasselas concludes from what he has heard that "no human being can ever be a poet," Imlac summarizes his Johnsonian meditation by conceding that the business of a poet is "indeed very difficult" (46).[11]

On a number of occasions, Imlac rehearses the wariness about the workings of the imagination that is evident in Johnson's other writings of the period—most notably *Rambler* 4 (31 March 1750), which famously stated that the true province of prose fiction is "to bring about natural events by easy means, and to keep up curiosity without the help of wonder."[12] While, on the one hand, Imlac stresses that poets face the all-but-impossible task of attending to both the particular ("variety in life") and the general, on the other he makes a positive virtue—and indeed a point of principle—out of not attempting to describe "what I had not seen" (41). *Rasselas* begins with a narratorial warning to "Ye who listen with credulity to the whispers of fancy" (7), and Imlac later issues his pupil with an inclusive caution against "the power of fiction," which is said to exert its "imperious, and . . . despotick" (152) influence over people, like the prince, whose minds are not sufficiently or properly occupied. In keeping with this suspicion of fiction's power to seduce, *Rasselas* makes almost no concession to any readerly demand for Oriental exoticism. While Nekayah's maid, Pekuah, describes being kidnapped by an Arab chieftain who keeps a harem, for instance, she presents her captor as a sufferer from "intellectual famine" (140), who above all else craves stimulating conversation. The tale's apparent lack of interest in non-intellectual pleasures is thrown into relief by William Beckford's *Vathek* (1786), a rewriting of *Rasselas* which begins with a richly detailed description of the title character's magnificent Palace of the Five Senses. For all that *Rasselas* initially presents the Happy Valley as a site of "blissful captivity," the specific content of its pleasures remains unsubstantiated, and the "schemes of delight" (10) that it refers to serve only as a plot device, or a counter in an argument.

As Anna Laetitia Barbauld observed in *The British Novelists* (1810), Johnson had "not, as many authors would have done, painted a luxurious bower of bliss," nor had he "once throughout the work awakened any ideas which might be at variance with the moral truths which all his writings are meant to inculcate."[13] Some contemporary critics complained that Johnson in effect deceived his readers, arguing that the "garb" or costume of *Rasselas* did not live up to the billing of the work's full title, and that the insight that it provided into the human condition might have been acquired—as Owen Ruffhead put it in the *Monthly Review*— "without going to Ethiopia."[14] In his postcolonial reading of a *Rasselas* for the present day, by contrast, Clement Hawes has suggested that the conspicuous absence of "reifying local colour" in the tale should be read as a sign of Johnson's ethical intent, proclaiming his principled belief in the essential sameness of the peoples of the world.[15] The terms of T. B. Macaulay's mid-nineteenth-century attack on *Rasselas* appear to bear out this point, for Macaulay was affronted by the way in which Johnson made the prince and Imlac into "philosophers as eloquent and enlightened as himself or his friend Burke," when real Abyssinians would have been the "filthy savages" described by the Scottish explorer, James Bruce (whose claims Johnson himself refused to credit).[16] At the same time that it presents modern Abyssinians as rational and intelligent beings, *Rasselas* also identifies ancient Egypt, "where the sciences first dawned . . . and beyond which the arts cannot be traced" (111), as the fount of world civilization. Johnson may have been drawn to this region of East Africa as a setting because it was distant and yet still allowed him to present his main characters as Christian. Nonetheless, his work at times also unsettles a normative Eurocentrism, as in its opening reference to the Nile as "the

Father of 'waters'" (7), or in Imlac's description of the pyramids as "the greatest work of man, except the wall of China" (117).

Johnson's treatment of Egypt is far from straightforward, however, for while Imlac considers the pyramids to be "monuments of industry and power before which all European magnificence is confessed to fade away" (111), he goes on to invoke them as evidence not only of the general vanity of human wishes, but also of the particular "folly" of kingly forms of display, which he presents as a function of the "satiety of dominion" (119). A passage such as this exemplifies the way in which *Rasselas* often combines the abstract ethical focus of the Oriental tale with an attention to specifically historical questions concerning human civilization, global commerce, and the rise and fall of empires. At an earlier stage in the work, Imlac speaks of having encountered the present-day bearers of "all power and all knowledge" in the form of people from "the northern and western nations of Europe"—those nations, he tells the prince, "whose armies are irresistible, and whose fleets command the remotest parts of the globe" (46). In response to Rasselas's naïve question about whether "Asiaticks and Africans" would be able to turn the tables on Europeans and "invade their coasts, plant colonies in their ports, and give laws to their natural princes," Imlac tells him that, in the present, Europeans are "more powerful . . . because they are wiser"—although "why their knowledge is more than ours," he continues, "I know not what reason can be given, but the unsearchable will of the Supreme Being" (46–47). The ambiguous reference to the uneven development of the regions of the world in this episode is interpreted by Hawes as further evidence of Johnson's refusal to countenance any kind of racially determinist explanation of human inequality; whereas, for Nicholas Hudson, Imlac's acknowledgement of European superiority provides a resonantly "providential" account of the incipient process of British imperial expansion, at a time when Britain was about to become the world's pre-eminent power.[17] That Imlac's brief discussion of the global distribution of power has generated two such divergent readings testifies to the work's at once complex and oblique engagement with its immediate historical moment—mid-way through the Seven Years' War, and at the beginning of what came to be known as the 'year of victories.' "[T]o judge rightly of the present we must oppose it to the past" (112), Imlac tells the prince, and in passages such as the one just cited *Rasselas* broaches an ambitious enquiry into the early stages of European colonialism and the deep origins of Britain's latest conflict with France.

This enquiry had been initiated by Johnson in the essays that he wrote for the broadly pro-Pitt *Literary Magazine* in 1756. In his "Introduction to the Political State of Great Britain" and its continuation, "Observations on the Present State of Affairs," Johnson traced what he termed "the present system of English politics" back to the reign of Elizabeth, during which America first became "the great scene of European ambition."[18] These essays consistently emphasize the illegitimacy of the seizure of "distant dominions" that began in the sixteenth century, and they also at times consider how indigenous peoples might themselves see the current territorial quarrel between Britain and France, a struggle between "two robbers for the spoils of a passenger" (as Johnson memorably put it) in which the true interest of "Indians" is that "both should be destroyed."[19] *Rasselas* makes no direct reference to this conflict, in striking contrast to Voltaire's *Candide* (published just a few weeks before Johnson's tale, and often regarded as a kind of companion volume to it), which famously invoked the fate of Admiral Byng—executed "[b]ecause he didn't kill enough people"—as an index of the "madness" of the war.[20] Instead, in his account of the debate between Imlac and the prince about the global distribution of power, Johnson sought to rise still further above the politics of the present than did Voltaire. In doing so, he upheld Imlac's definition of the proper role of the poet— namely, that of "presiding over the thoughts and manners of future generations; as a being superior to time and place" (45)—in order better to apprehend the larger world-historical processes of which the war was a product.

The precise nature of Johnson's engagement with the present in *Rasselas* can be illuminated by situating the work in relation to a number of essays that he produced in the late 1750s. In *Idler* 30 (11 November 1758), Johnson gave a specific justification for not writing more about the progress of the war, styling himself as an impartial seeker after truth rather than a patriotic purveyor of "news" about battles "in which we and our friends, whether conquering or conquered, did all, and our enemies did nothing." "Among the calamities of war may be justly numbered the diminution of the love of truth," Johnson contended, "by the falsehoods which interest dictates and credulity encourages."[21] As Donald Greene has argued, Johnson was intent, here and elsewhere, on "stripping off the splendid ideological clothing with which the [war] was invested by the rhetoric of Pitt."[22] If Johnson was concerned to counter the journalistic manipulation of the public, however, his writings of the late 1750s shift between, on the one hand, emphasizing the morally dubious origins of the conflict and, on the other, demonstrating a more worldly understanding of the geopolitical interests that were at stake. What complicates any account of Johnson as a principled anti-imperialist is that he saw the gradual French settlement of lands to the east of Britain's Atlantic colonies as a provocation which, he claimed, "at length forced" the country into war.[23] (As Hudson argues, a further index of Johnson's attention to "the world of *Realpolitik*" is that his *Literary Magazine* essays of 1756 also present the mistreatment of native peoples by British traders as a strategic error as much as a moral injustice—an error which made it harder to forge the local military alliances from which, at that moment, the French appeared to be gaining at Britain's expense.[24])

In *Idler* 81 (3 November 1759), published in the aftermath of Wolfe's victory at Quebec, Johnson developed his earlier attempt to ventriloquize a 'native' perspective on the war in North America, amplifying his 1756 "Observations" with the statement that, since the British and the French were alike "the sons of rapacity," indigenous peoples should "look unconcerned" upon their mutual slaughter and "remember that the death of every European delivers the country from a tyrant and a robber."[25] Oliver Goldsmith would borrow from *Idler* 81 (as well as from *Candide*) in *The Citizen of the World* (1762), in making his Chinese informant, Lien Chi Altangi, observe that given the nature of the contest between British and French forces in Canada, "no honest man can heartily wish success to either party." Whereas Goldsmith focused on the cost of this struggle for Britain (in being drained of its wealth and virtue) as well as for the "savages of Canada," however, Johnson appears to have been more equivocal in his analysis of the situation.[26] The different grievances articulated by the "petty chief" in *Idler* 81 illuminate the conflicted nature of Johnson's response to European expansionism, for among these grievances is that, in addition to offering treaties "only to deceive" and seeking to trade "only to defraud," Europeans have "studiously concealed" their arts and failed to communicate their "written law."[27] For Hudson, the narrator's profession of interest in the Christian gospel in this essay is informed by a vision of "a better colonial relationship."[28] The chief nonetheless also goes on to state that Europeans do not preach Christianity to Indians as they know that their actions violate its precepts, and he concludes by suggesting that what Indians can most usefully learn from Europeans is how to harness their weaponry and military discipline, so as eventually to free themselves from oppression.

Johnson reflected just as ambivalently on the course of past, present, and future contact between the peoples of Europe and the rest of the world in his introduction to *The World Displayed*, written in the same year. Focusing in particular on the exploration of the West Coast of Africa begun by the Portuguese in the fifteenth century, Johnson declared in seemingly definitive fashion that "The Europeans have scarcely visited any coast, but to gratify avarice, and extend corruption; to arrogate dominion without right, and practise cruelty without incentive."

Yet this statement is preceded by a short tribute to Prince Henry "the Navigator," the Portuguese patron of maritime exploration, which offers a calculatedly non-judgmental assessment of his legacy: "What mankind has lost and gained by the genius and designs of this Prince, it would be long to compare and very difficult to estimate." The same paragraph concludes by expressing "reason to hope" that, whatever the grim evidence of the previous three hundred or so years, "good may sometime be produced" out of evil, and "the light of the gospel . . . at last illuminate the sands of Africa, and the desarts of America."[29]

Both *Idler* 81 and Johnson's introduction to *The World Displayed* thus combined an apparent optimism about the progressive effects of the spreading of Christianity with a far more uncertain assessment of the actual consequences of three centuries of contact between Europe, Africa, and America (Asia is largely beyond Johnson's purview here). Despite being comparatively brief as well as indirect, Imlac's account of the global imbalance of power likewise testifies to Johnson's apprehension of the complex entanglement of the different regions of the world, and, in its invocation of "the unsearchable will of the Supreme Being" (47), further suggests that this state of affairs is now entrenched and irreversible. Yet if Imlac might be seen here to present the superior "power" and "knowledge" (47) of Europeans as a product of providential design (as Hudson argues), he does not raise the question that Johnson posed in some of his other works of the same year about "what mankind has lost and gained" as a result of this ascendancy; indeed, the corollary of Imlac's emphasis on the near-impossibility of acquiring a comprehensive social knowledge is that such a question is simply too large to be answered.[30] It is instructive here to consider *Rasselas* alongside an essay that Johnson wrote for the *Adventurer* in June 1753, in which he noted that what a newcomer to London would experience only as a bewildering multiplicity of sights and sounds, an observer with the leisure to reflect might appreciate as the ultimately orderly "concurrence of endeavours" that characterizes an advanced commercial society. Like *Rasselas*, this essay emphasizes that, even for the most well off, such circumstances of material plenty offer no guarantee of individual happiness, because affluence only increases desire. Where the essay and the tale clearly differ, though, is in that while, for the former, the diverse kinds of activity evident within the ostensibly circumscribed bounds of a single city come together in a "secret concatenation," for the latter, the greatly more complicated and multifarious effects of global interconnection exceed any such attempt to discern an underlying pattern or organization.[31] Accustomed to an apparently enclosed and self-sufficient environment which magically offers "consumption without production," in Anna Neill's phrase, Rasselas imagines that once he is outside the Happy Valley he will be in a position to "review [the world] at leisure" (68).³² Shortly before they escape, however, Imlac cautions the prince that although he expects the outside world to be "smooth and quiet as the lake in the valley," the reality will in fact be "a sea foaming with tempests, and boiling with whirlpools," in which he will be "sometimes overwhelmed by the waves of violence, and sometimes dashed against the rocks of treachery" (56).

When recalling the beginnings of his own curiosity about the wider world, Imlac tells Rasselas that his first stop after leaving his father was the Gujarati port of Surat, which would have been known to some as the location of the East India Company's first trading post, established in 1608. Imlac makes no mention of encountering Europeans in India, although he claims to have "conversed with great numbers" of them in Palestine (46). The specificity of this reference to Surat solicits critical attention, nonetheless, since it suggestively connects Imlac's cosmopolitan past, along with the expedition that he goes on to lead, to a larger commercial and colonial history. Surat was taken by an expedition of Company forces from Bombay shortly before *Rasselas* was written (although the news of this probably did not reach Britain until September), and the capture of such a "great and opulent city," as the *Annual Register* for 1759 reported in the following year, offered further confirmation that Britain was going from "success to success" in this theatre of the war.³³ Just as Johnson's introduction to *The World Displayed* emphasizes that the maritime exploration which extended "the power of Europe" also served to foster the "acquaintance" of "distant nations," so *Rasselas* might be seen here to allude to the material basis of the free-ranging enquiry pursued by Imlac and his party, reliant on the technologies as well as the networks of contact that underpinned the system of global commerce.³⁴

Rasselas invites the reader to recognize what makes the mobility of Imlac and his party possible, then, and it also—more insistently—provides a skeptical commentary on the forms of insight provided by their survey.³⁵ The work's final chapter draws attention to this reflexivity, for it announces itself as a "conclusion, in which nothing is concluded" and ends on an intriguingly ambiguous note as the group resolves to "return to Abissinia" (175–76). Whereas *Candide* finishes with the title character's famous entreaty—"we must cultivate our garden"—*Rasselas* offers no such call to purposive action, leaving the reader to question whether this return might also constitute a kind of retreat, to the familiar surroundings and circumstances of the Happy Valley.³⁶ Imlac's apparent position of authority as a tutor to the prince is again undercut at the very end of the tale, too, since in the penultimate paragraph he and the astronomer that the group have just met are said to be "contented to be driven along the stream of life without directing their course to a particular port" (176). Although Imlac himself escapes the "maladies of the mind" (150) from which the work's other philosopher-figures (including the astronomer) suffer, it is significant that the tale here underlines that his lack of attachment to any specific profession or place is a condition of drift rather than a source of critical purchase. "[T]eachers of morality live like men" (74), Imlac counsels Rasselas when they encounter a lecturer who proves unable to live by the Stoic precepts that he professes, and Imlac himself, though initially set up as the prince's "director," is likewise shown to be unable to transcend the harsh inevitabilities of the human condition.

Johnson's *Rambler* 120 (11 May 1751), one of the many short Oriental fictions that he wrote before *Rasselas*, concludes with a "sage" offering judicious advice about the use of riches to the disenchanted Almamoulin, another figure who finds that sensual gratification cannot bring contentment.[37] The conclusion to *Rasselas*, by contrast, emphasizes Imlac's lack of any decisive influence over his pupil, for the prince in effect restates a desire that he had earlier expressed to rule "a little kingdom, in which he might administer justice in his own person, and see all the parts of government with his own eyes" (175–76). Such a realm would not only represent a denial of the social complexity he had previously witnessed, but would also appear to recreate the political conditions from which he began the work trying to escape; Rasselas's restatement of this plan in fact underscores Imlac's initial point about "the effects of visionary schemes," namely that we "familiarise them by degrees, and in time lose sight of their folly" (153). Importantly, Johnson also provides a reminder of the topicality of the idea of human restlessness here, for after the reader is told about the prince's desire for "a little kingdom" of his own to govern, the narrator adds that Rasselas's unchecked delusions additionally encompass the dream of empire: "he could never fix the limits of his dominion, and was always adding to his subjects" (176).

In an illuminating essay on the "politics of empire" in *Rasselas*, Steven Scherwatzky has argued that "Johnson satirizes the conflicted nature of claims for political virtue that include imperial ambition."[38] "Satire" is perhaps too strong a term to use here, though, both because the tale's direct engagement with questions of empire is so minimal, and because it continually suggests that ambition of this kind is a function of an innate human restlessness with an unstoppable momentum, and is therefore no more irrational than Imlac's wish to be "driven along the stream of life" (176). As Carol Watts has argued, "Johnson's very language for the acquisition of knowledge and experience is shaped by the circulating desires and energies of worldly life, as if, despite its protest, it cannot be imagined distinctly from them."³⁹ Perhaps the best-known example of this rhetorical continuity appears in Johnson's "Plan" for his *Dictionary* (1755), in which he likened his monumental task to that of "the soldiers of Caesar," looking on Britain as a "new world, which it is almost madness to conquer." Johnson expressed the hope here "that though I should not complete the conquest, I shall at least discover the coast, civilize part of the inhabitants, [and] make it easy for some other adventurer to proceed farther"—thus "half-mocking the loss of sense of proportion he has incurred," in the words of John Barrell, yet challenging "the scale, but not wholly the nature of the comparison."⁴⁰

If the "conclusion, in which nothing is concluded" only emphasizes that restlessness in all its manifestations is an inescapable facet of the human condition, however, a rather different conclusion is offered at the end of the preceding chapter, where Nekayah declares that "the choice of eternity" now seems a more important question to her than "the choice of life" (175). The project that Nekayah goes on to announce is not depicted as being any more realizable than her brother's scheme (or indeed her own previous desire to "play the shepherdess" [153]), but her enlightened ambition to found "a college of learned women" (175) nonetheless presents a significant counterpoint to Rasselas's visions of empire. While Nekayah initially assumes that the people she meets outside of the Happy Valley will "prostrate themselves before her" (62), she eventually appears to move beyond expecting to be obeyed, whereas the prince—with his dreams of dominion still intact—does not. Nekayah's ambition to "raise up for the next age models of prudence, and patterns of piety" (175) is especially resonant in the context of this essay's concerns, for in its attention to the domestic sphere it invokes an arena of feminine influence that is also a locus of stability, implicitly defined against the ever-shifting horizons of Rasselas's imagined sovereignty. In an earlier dialogue with her brother, Nekayah asserts that families, like kingdoms, may themselves sometimes be "torn with factions and exposed to revolutions" (95). The tale's concluding account of the agency of women might by contrast be seen to establish the domestic sphere as a "line of defence" that, as Watts suggests, at once offers a refuge from the world and a consolidation of home, community, and patriotic belonging.⁴¹ This remedial perspective has no place in other works by Johnson—his *Literary Magazine* essays, his introduction to *The World Displayed*, and *Idler* 81, for example—that engage more directly with the origins or the conduct of the ongoing war. In conjunction with Nekayah's appeal to "eternity," its presence here perhaps goes some way towards closing off the text's previous reflections on the complexity and tempestuousness of the world outside the Happy Valley.

It might be argued then that one reason why "nothing is concluded" in *Rasselas* is that it offers more than one conclusion. Together with her commitment to the education of women, Nekayah's "choice of eternity" might be seen to provide a form of readerly orientation that potentially offsets both Rasselas's dreams of empire and Imlac's readiness to be "driven along the stream of life." Clearly, though, we can only speculate about the extent to which contemporary audiences found themselves to be thus directed by Johnson's text. As is evident from the numerous different generic classifications that it was given—"moral tale," "novel," "romance," "satire," "eastern story," "fable"—*Rasselas* was a difficult text for many eighteenth-century readers and reviewers to assimilate.[42] Moreover, as Thomas Keymer has argued, later re-workings of *Rasselas* supply "powerful evidence of just how unsettling Johnson's inconclusiveness remained."[43] To take just one example of such revisionism: *Dinarbas* (1790), Ellis Cornelia Knight's sequel to *Rasselas*, begins by assuming that Johnson's characters "return to the happy valley," and then offers a more conventional "romance" plot that culminates in the marriages of Rasselas and Nekayah. To John Ferriar, writing in the *Monthly Review*, *Dinarbas*, "by exhibiting the brighter side of the picture, is calculated to enliven and to invigorate hope," whereas *Rasselas* itself "tends . . . to produce a painful uncertainty, and to excite a cheerless scepticism and indifference."[44]

For Sir Walter Scott in *Lives of the Novelists* (1821–24), by contrast, comparison between *Rasselas* and *Candide*—respectively "a wholesome and a poisonous fruit"—made Johnson's work appear to be a reassuring rather than an unsettling text: he attributed to Johnson "the benevolent view of encouraging men to look to another and a better world for the satisfaction of wishes which, in this, seem only to be awakened in order to be disappointed," while he claimed that Voltaire sought to foster "a distrust of . . . the Great Governor of the Universe, by presuming to arraign him of incapacity before the creatures of his will." Scott traduced Voltaire as "a fiend . . . who scoffs at and derides human miseries," but he also misrepresented Johnson in framing *Rasselas* as a work that straightforwardly sought to elevate its readers above worldly concerns.[45] This reading of Johnson against Voltaire is very significant, though, since in seizing upon Nekayah's "choice of eternity" as a kind of extractable moral imperative it ignores how, in much of the rest of the work, any such consideration of the vanity of human wishes is so inextricably bound up with specific questions concerning both the relative "power and . . . knowledge" (46) of Europeans and their others, and the contemporary predicament of Britain, after the global extension of its interests had forced it into conflict with France and its allies across the world. If *Rasselas* dwells on the difficulty of securing an objective and authoritative position from which to arrive at conclusions, either regarding the meaning of its characters' experiences or the long-term consequences of European expansionism, Scott's reading suggests how it has been possible for many readers to ignore the text's reflections on its own historical and material as well as epistemological conditions of production, and to treat *Rasselas* instead as if it were an abstract moral tale. There is no space here to say any more about the reception history of *Rasselas*, or about the enduring association of Johnson with narrowly conceived notions of 'Englishness'. Readings such as Scott's may nonetheless help us to think about the broader cultural processes by which the importance of 1759 has come to be forgotten, as well as about the much larger amnesia regarding Britain's history of empire more generally.

Notes

1. Kathleen Wilson, *The Sense of the People: Politics, Culture, and Imperialism in England, 1715–1785* (Cambridge: Cambridge University Press, 1995), 203; Carol Watts, *The Cultural Work of Empire: The Seven Years' War and the Imagining of the Shandean State* (Toronto: University of Toronto Press, 2007), 28–64.

2. Suvir Kaul, *Eighteenth-Century British Literature and Postcolonial Studies* (Edinburgh: Edinburgh University Press, 2009), 120; Watts, *Cultural Work*, 43.

3. Samuel Johnson, *The History of Rasselas, Prince of Abyssinia*, in *Rasselas and Other Tales*, ed. Gwin J. Kolb, vol. 16 of *The Yale Edition of the Works of Samuel Johnson* (New Haven: Yale University Press, 1990), 56. Further references will be given parenthetically.

4. Johnson, introduction to *The World Displayed*, 20 vols. (London: J. Newbery, 1759–1961), 1:xvi.

5. Johnson, *A Voyage to Abyssinia*, ed. Joel J. Gold, vol. 15 of *Works* (New Haven: Yale University Press, 1985), 3–4.

6. Johnson, "The Vanity of Human Wishes," in *Poems*, ed. E. L. McAdam, Jr., with George Milne, vol. 6 of *Works* (New Haven: Yale University Press, 1964), 91–92.

7. Johnson, *Rambler* nos. 204 and 205 (29 February and 3 March 1752), in *The Rambler*, ed. W. J. Bate and Albrecht B. Strauss, vols. 3–5 of *Works* (New Haven: Yale University Press, 1969), 5:296, 297, 300, and 305.

8. For a full and informative discussion of Johnson's source materials, see Kolb's introduction to *Rasselas and Other Tales*, xxvi–xxxiii. See also Thomas M. Curley, *Samuel Johnson and the Age of Travel* (Athens, GA: University of Georgia Press, 1976), 147–82.

9. This was one of the preoccupations of Johnson's non-fictional writings during the 1750s: John Barrell, *English Literature in History, 1730–1780: An Equal, Wide Survey* (London: Hutchinson and Co., 1983), 40–45. On epistemological boundaries in *Rasselas*, see also James Ward's essay in this volume.

10. Johnson, "The Vanity of Human Wishes," in *Poems*, 91.

11. On the idea of authorship in *Rasselas*, see also Adam Rounce's essay in this volume.

12. Johnson, *Rambler* no. 4 (31 March 1750), in *The Rambler*, 3:19.

13. Anna Laetitia Barbauld, *The British Novelists: With an Essay and Prefaces, Biographical and Critical*, vol. 26 (London: F. C. and J. Rivington, 1820), viii.

14. *Monthly Review* 20 (May 1759), 429.

15. Clement Hawes, "Johnson and Imperialism," in *The Cambridge Companion to Samuel Johnson*, ed. Greg Clingham (Cambridge: Cambridge University Press, 1997), 116.

16. Thomas Babington Macaulay, "Samuel Johnson," in *Selected Writings*, ed. John Clive (Chicago: University of Chicago Press, 1972), 145. On Johnson and Bruce, see Nigel Leask, *Curiosity and the Aesthetics of Travel-Writing: "From an Antique Land"* (Oxford: Oxford University Press, 2002), 58.

17. Hawes, "Johnson and Imperialism," 115; Nicholas Hudson, *Samuel Johnson and the Making of Modern England* (Cambridge: Cambridge University Press, 2003), 183.

18. Johnson, "An Introduction to the Political State of Great Britain," in *Political Writings*, ed. Donald J. Greene, vol. 10 of *Works* (New Haven: Yale University Press, 1977), 130.

19. Johnson, "Observations on the Present State of Affairs," in *Political Writings*, 188.

20. Voltaire, *Candide and Other Stories*, trans. Roger Pearson (Oxford: Oxford University Press, 1998), 73. On *Candide* and the war, see Simon Davies's essay in this volume.

21. Johnson, *Idler* no. 30 (11 November 1758), in *The Idler and The Adventurer*, ed. W. J. Bate, John M. Bullitt, and L. F. Powell, vol. 2 of *Works* (New Haven: Yale University Press, 1963), 95.

22. Johnson, *Political Writings*, 127.

23. Johnson, *Political Writings*, 149.

24. Hudson, *Samuel Johnson and the Making of Modern England*, 183.

25. Johnson, *Idler* no. 81 (3 November 1759), in *The Idler and The Adventurer*, 254.

26. Oliver Goldsmith, *The Citizen of the World*, in *The Collected Works of Oliver Goldsmith*, ed. Arthur Friedman, 5 vols. (Oxford: Clarendon Press, 1966), 2:74, 73.

27. Johnson, *Idler* no. 81, in *The Idler and The Adventurer*, 253.

28. Hudson, *Samuel Johnson and the Making of Modern England*, 208.

29. Johnson, introduction to *The World Displayed*, 1:xvi.

30. See Anna Neill, *British Discovery Literature and the Rise of Global Commerce* (Basingstoke: Palgrave, 2002), 139–42.

31. Johnson, *Adventurer* no. 67 (26 June 1753), in *The Idler and The Adventurer*, 386.

32. Neill, *British Discovery Literature*, 144.

33. *The Annual Register; or, A View of the History, Politicks, and Literature, of the Year 1759* (London: R. and J. Dodsley, 1760), 54.

34. Johnson, introduction to *The World Displayed*, 1:xvi. As Neill puts it, "in an effort to know the world in all its diversity . . . they must pursue the same kinds of investigation that have brought far-flung places and peoples into commercial contact": *British Discovery Literature*, 143.

35. On this, see for example Fred Parker, "The Skepticism of *Rasselas*," in *Cambridge Companion to Johnson*, 127–42.

36. Voltaire, *Candide*, 99.

37. Johnson, *Rambler* no. 120 (11 May 1751), in *The Rambler*, 4:279.

38. Steven Scherwatzky, "Johnson, *Rasselas*, and the Politics of Empire," *Eighteenth-Century Life* 16 (1992): 110.

39. Watts, *Cultural Work*, 45.

40. Johnson, *The Plan of a Dictionary of the English Language* (London: J. and P. Knapton and others, 1747), 33; Barrell, *English Literature in History*, 148–49.

41. Watts, *Cultural Work*, 49.

42. Kolb, introduction to *Rasselas and Other Tales*, xxxiii.

43. Thomas Keymer, introduction to *The History of Rasselas, Prince of Abissinia*, ed. Keymer (Oxford: Oxford University Press, 2009), xxxii.

44. Johnson and Ellis Cornelia Knight, *"The History of Rasselas, Prince of Abissinia" and "Dinarbas: A Tale,"* ed. Lynne Meloccaro (London: J. M. Dent, 1994), 105; *Monthly Review*, n. s., 8 (May 1792), 106.

45. Sir Walter Scott, *Lives of the Novelists* (London: Oxford University Press, 1934), 161.

2

VOLTAIRE'S *CANDIDE* AS A GLOBAL TEXT:

WAR, SLAVERY, AND LEADERSHIP

SIMON DAVIES

IN 1759, VOLTAIRE WAS in his sixty-fifth year. He had gained an international reputation and, when he came to compose *Candide*, he was writing from the vantage point of a wealth of experience. He had known the ups and downs of life on both a personal level and in the political arena. He had travelled widely in Western Europe, to Holland, Prussia, and to that up and coming country, England. He had even acquired a knowledge of English, a language that was of little interest to foreigners before the eighteenth century. He had also had contact with people in the corridors of power. He had been appointed historiographer royal by Louis XV in 1745, and had endured a problematic relationship with Frederick the Great in the early 1750s.

Above all, Voltaire was a public intellectual and polymath. His reputation was founded upon a wide variety of literary and philosophical works. Theatrical success, particularly in the prestigious realm of tragedy, had brought him notoriety. He was an inveterate versifier, a popularizer of the science of Newton, and a bold polemicist. In the latter capacity, his *Lettres philosophiques* (1734), with its championing of aspects of life in England, had caused a scandal which led to the text being condemned by the authorities and burnt in public. His preoccupation with history, through his extensive reading and innovative writings in the field, played an essential role in his vocation as a social and political commentator. While the writing of short stories did not register highly in his aesthetic hierarchy, by the late 1750s he had already published a number of such tales, including the interplanetary satire, *Micromégas* (1752), and *Zadig* (1747), his exploration of destiny.[1]

In the eyes of posterity, however, *Candide* stands as Voltaire's most famous work. The present essay investigates Voltaire's masterpiece from a number of interrelated perspectives. The first three involve significant contemporary aspects of the tale: the global reach of the work, and its relationship to the ongoing war; the issue of slavery; and the question of leadership. The fourth concerns Voltaire's use of *Candide* as a means of influencing or even creating public opinion. In France, with no parliamentary system, Voltaire sought to direct opinion by exploiting a comic mode of writing. Exercising a capacity to be serious without being solemn, his short, satiric tale cast light onto some of the most important issues of its time. It is to the most significant and (in 1759) current concerns of the tale, then, that this essay directs its attention.

Of central importance to our reading of *Candide* is the fact that it was written during a time of war. Voltaire was only too aware of the violent conflicts of his age, which pitted the Russians against the Turks, the English against the French, even the Jesuits against the Spanish in Paraguay. The repulsive brutality of battle is echoed in his correspondence at this time.[2] The conduct of the contemporary war should be regarded as supplying a necessary backdrop for understanding the interrelationship of many features of the tale. Early on in the work, the naïve Candide is booted out of the earthly paradise of the château de Thunder-ten-tronck in Westphalia on account of the sexual advances of the anti-heroine, Cunégonde. Any possibility of return to this spuriously fairy-tale domain is shattered by the Bulgar soldiers, who massacre its privileged inhabitants. (Ironically, without this intrusion, the resurrected Cunégonde would never have been reunited with her beloved Candide). Soon enough, Candide himself is press-ganged into the Bulgar army, only to witness the "boucherie héroïque" of battle (chapter 3). Here, Voltaire conveys the horror of conflict without allowing the reader to identify with the anonymous victims. From early on in the work, we are thus brought to recognize the manner in which personal destinies may become tied up with the destinies of nations.

Such a personal destiny features in one of the most famous episodes in the work: the execution of Admiral Byng. Voltaire appears to have at least glimpsed Byng during his stay in England. At the time of the Englishman's imprisonment, Voltaire intervened on his behalf at the behest of Thomas Pitt, brother of William Pitt the Elder, in early 1757. With the help of the military leader and his longstanding friend, the duc de Richelieu, Voltaire sought to save the Admiral by sending a testimony of his valor to England, but to no avail (indeed, the support of the enemy in a time of war might have been judged inappropriate). However,

in 1759, the inclusion of this judicial execution in Voltaire's tale served a dual purpose. On the one hand, it highlighted the English enemy's injustice; on the other,
it demonstrated Voltaire's own championing of justice on an international scale. If
the ostensible intention of the ironic assertion, "pour encourager les autres" (chapter 23, 224), is to urge English forces to pursue their activities with greater zeal,
the deeper aim is to prompt the work's readers to fight against manifest injustices
in the future, irrespective of location or nation. The fictional Pangloss could be
condemned to death and resurrected; the hapless Byng could not.[3]

In the tale as in reality, war is not confined to Europe. We learn later on in
the work about its prosecution in North and South America, and also in North
Africa, where a series of civil wars has been ravaging Morocco. These conflicts have
provoked considerable slaughter—between blacks and blacks, blacks and brown,
brown and brown, mulattoes and mulattoes (chapter 11). The global dimensions
of war are confirmed in the celebrated passage about the icy wastes of North
America, where the doughty pessimist, Martin, asserts that England and France
are at war "pour quelques arpents de neige vers le Canada, et qu'elles dépensent
pour cette belle guerre beaucoup plus que tout le Canada ne vaut" (223: "for some
acres of land towards Canada and that they spend on this fine war more than the
whole of Canada is worth").[4] It is not without justification that the Seven Years'
War has been labeled a "global conflict."[5]

In tracing the international contours of this conflict, Voltaire's story can
itself be regarded as a global text. Notably, *Candide* was composed just after
Voltaire's major work on world history, the *Essai sur les moeurs* (1756). In the
later text, Voltaire is keen to stress the universal implications of his tale and, accordingly, he provides it with an international cast list. The clutch of German
Westphalians apart, there are Dutch, Spaniards, Portuguese, Italians, Turks, South
American Indians, Poles, English, a Scot, Bulgars, Abars, Moroccans, Tunisians,
Algerians, Russians, and the French. The vast majority of these characters are
seasoned travelers, including episodic characters such as the brutal sailor who was
born in Batavia (now Djakarta) and who had been to Japan on four occasions
(chapter 5). The static, shut-off world of the Westphalian country estate is thus
succeeded by the dynamism of a series of unforeseen, and unforeseeable, journeys.
These journeys should be read not merely as textual representations of physical
movement but, rather, as illustrations of how encounters with other cultures
necessarily open minds to different ideas and practices. Voltaire understood fully
the interconnectedness of the world, not just in terms of similar human preoccupations being manifested globally, but also through the necessity and extent of

international contact. Highlighting the intercontinental market for commodities, for instance, the text covers the vogue for chocolate (chapters 4, 11, and 25), cochineal (chapter 4), and the craving for that luxury commodity, sugar (chapter 19). A very different allusion to the effect of international relations is broached in chapter 4, where the origin of venereal disease is located in the Americas. On this prickly subject, Voltaire was reflecting much current thinking.

During the course of the narrative, the reader follows Candide on his journeys through Europe, to South America, and back to Europe. In Holland, with the exception of the non-conformist Jacques the anabaptist, Candide is treated with a complete lack of Christian compassion (chapter 3). In Portugal, he is arrested by the Inquisition. The reluctant traveler is on a quest not for discovery or self-discovery, but for his very survival. Can he find a place for himself in a world that he does not comprehend, following the woeful education that he has received at the hands of his tutor, Pangloss?[6] Throughout the narrative, the eponymous protagonist is an outsider figure. He is also a challenge to traditional societies, by dint of his marginal status as a bastard. Candide is therefore unlike Rasselas with his position of royal privilege. In the opening chapter, the spotlight is very much on Candide, the low-status character, rather than on the baron and his family. His illegitimacy can be viewed as an opportunity for Voltaire (who wondered whether he himself was illegitimate) to query the validity and effectiveness of those in recognized positions of authority. Candide escapes from Europe in an ambiguous situation. On the one hand, highlighting the mercenary composition of contemporary armies, his military expertise acquired in the Bulgar army has gained him the post of captain in the Spanish army. On the other, he is a fugitive from justice as he is, however unintentionally, a murderer (his training in the Bulgar army has also had that unintended consequence). He thus lands in Buenos Ayres as an undesirable asylum-seeker with the European authorities in hot pursuit. The imminent arrival of the latter forces him to flee again. He is obliged to leave Cunégonde to the multiple attractions of the mustachioed Spanish governor, a national stereotype comically transferred to the New World. Against European expectations, the seemingly savage "Oreillons," having established that he is not a Jesuit, grant Candide and his servant "toutes sortes de civilités, leur offrirent des filles, leur donnèrent des rafraîchissements" (180: "all sorts of courtesies, offered them girls, gave them refreshments").[7] Although Voltaire had received a valuable education at a Jesuit institution, he later turned against the order. In the 1750s, the Jesuits had started to attack him; while, in 1759, the same year as *Candide*, Voltaire published a witty satire on his foes, the *Relation de la maladie, de la confession, de la mort, et de l'apparition du jésuite Berthier.*

If war and murder can be justly labeled forms of human evil, so, in *Candide*, can the frequent practices of religion, particularly those of the Jesuits. Here, Voltaire is in characteristic anticlerical mode, intent on underscoring the havoc that religion can wreak in any part of the world. As depicted in this text, the Jesuit settlement in Paraguay is a noxious export from Europe. The religious order lives out a very comfortable existence and is presented as acting as it pleases:

> C'est une chose admirable que ce gouvernement. Le royaume a déjà plus de trois cents lieues de diamètre; il est divisé en trente provinces. Los Padres y ont tout, et les peuples rien; c'est le chef d'oeuvre de la raison et de la justice. Pour moi je ne vois rien de si divin que Los Padres, qui font ici la guerre au roi d'Espagne et au roi de Portugal, et qui en Europe confessent ces rois; qui tuent ici des Espagnols, et qui à Madrid les envoient au ciel. (chapter 14, 169)

> [This government is a wonderful thing. The kingdom is already three hundred leagues in diameter and is divided into thirty provinces. Los Padres possess everything in them and its peoples nothing; it is a masterpiece of reason and justice. As far as I am concerned, I can see nothing so divine as Los Padres, who here wage war on the king of Spain and the king of Portugal, and in Europe hear the confessions of the very same kings; who here kill Spaniards and in Madrid send them to heaven.]

This immigrant community of Jesuits, supposedly dedicated to spreading Christianity, is thus portrayed by Voltaire as fundamentally (and fraudulently) betraying its proper mission in its lust for power and wealth.

As the above overview suggests, while *Candide* displays a remarkable reach in its depiction of international activity and global movement, Voltaire's approach was entirely distinct from that of modern advocates of 'globalization' (with all its progressive, utopian overtones). Candide's transatlantic excursion comes to an end with a return trip to Europe. Although he has exercised charity through rescuing the fanatical pessimist, Martin, his boon companion is his servant who had accompanied him from Spain: the faithful Cacambo, upon whom Candide has now become dependent for survival. Cacambo patently owes something to the tradition of the resourceful servant of French classical comedy, soon to achieve his sublime incarnation in Beaumarchais's Figaro (or, in fiction, in Diderot's Jacques le fataliste). However, Cacambo embodies more than simply the characteristics of the impertinent, cunning valet of comedy. Voltaire was surely making a point in creating a mixed-race character, someone who might be envisaged as possessing a globalized identity. Cacambo is a quarter Spanish, a quadroon, having a mestizo for a father and thus being of predominantly South-American Indian blood. His multicultural background is complemented by a capacity to adapt flexibly to difficult situations and to negotiate them successfully. In picaresque style, his curriculum vitae contains evidence of impressive multi-tasking: "Il avait été enfant de chœur, sacristain, matelot, moine, facteur, soldat, laquais" (chapter 14, 168: "He had been an altar boy, a sexton, a sailor, a monk, an agent, a soldier, a servant"). His versatility in covering various functions is connected with the church, the military, and commerce. It is Cacambo who pronounces the scathing comments on the Jesuit regime, having already witnessed it at first hand. It is he who will bring his practical survival skills to bear in ensuring that Candide, despite his emotional despair, always has food to eat (food, or the absence of it, being a recurrent theme in *Candide*). His mother tongue, Peruvian, will also prove essential for the odd couple's progress in South America. Indeed, Candide goes so far as to tell his friend that "tu es plus habile que moi" (chapter 19, 197: "you are smarter than me").[8] Cacambo, the servant, is the most constant and trustworthy character in the work. He is the proponent of no extravagant ideas. He is the creation of a miscegenation which cuts across racial divides. In short, he is an admirable citizen of the world.

If Cacambo might thus appear to embody a positive vision of global connectivity, though, relations between races also figure in *Candide* in ways that are less informed by the ideals of comedy, cross-cultural companionship, and enlightened cosmopolitanism. The Jesuits in Voltaire's text, for instance, engage in an activity that is evoked earlier in the tale and that is more explicitly censured later on: slavery. It has been estimated that French ships transported more than a million Africans to the "New World" during the course of the eighteenth century.[9] Slavery had already been roundly denounced by Montesquieu in book 15 of *L'Esprit des lois* (1748). In 1761, moreover, Jean-Jacques Rousseau, in his best-selling novel, *Julie ou la Nouvelle Héloïse*, would have his protagonist, Saint-Preux, in the course of his world journey, express shock at the sight of such inhumanity in Africa:

> J'ai vu ces vastes et malheureuses contrées qui ne semblent destinées qu'à couvrir la terre de troupeaux d'esclaves. A leur vil aspect j'ai détourné les yeux de dédain, d'horreur et de pitié; et, voyant la quatrième partie

de mes semblables changée en bêtes pour le service des autres, j'ai gémi d'être homme.[10]

[I saw those vast and unfortunate countries which seem destined only to cover the earth with herds of slaves. At their vile appearance I turned away my eyes with disdain, horror and pity; and, seeing a quarter of my fellow human beings changed into beasts for the use of others, I groaned at being a man.]

Despite such ringing condemnations, abolitionist campaigns were not to get underway in France until later in the century. Voltaire's attitude to slavery has its own ambiguities, and is certainly a controversial topic.[11] This may be partly explained by the fact that he saw himself not just as a writer but also as a businessman. In a letter of 14 July 1769, he approved of the notion of businessmen as philosophers, "commerçants philosophes."[12] The acquisition of wealth granted Voltaire a degree of independence denied to those who relied on patronage, so that he did not have to write to make a living. In relation to slavery, even if he did not overtly invest in the slave trade, it is possible that Voltaire derived some income from it by placing funds in trading companies. He was pleased in 1768 when a ship was named after him by a member of a family, the Monteaudouin, associated with the slave trade in Nantes. As archival research has shown, the ship itself was used for the transportation not of slaves but of coffee.[13] Nonetheless, slaves would have been involved in the production of that fashionable drink, which was much savored by Voltaire himself.[14]

Slavery is evoked in a number of Voltaire's texts prior to *Candide*. In his celebrated history of Louis XIV, *Le Siècle de Louis XIV*, first published in 1751, Voltaire expressed his disgust at the representation of slaves being crushed. The Sun King had been falsely accused of having his statue in the *place des Victoires* "entourée d'esclaves enchaînés" ("surrounded by chained slaves"). This practice had long been used by sculptors, but Voltaire deemed it unworthy. Far better, in his view, would be the representation of kings surrounded by "des citoyens libres et heureux" ("free and happy citizens").[15] Voltaire had previously evoked slavery in *Zadig* (1747), in which the eponymous hero and his servant are both sold as slaves in an Egyptian marketplace, although "le valet, plus propre à la fatigue, fut vendu plus chèrement que le maître" ("the servant, more accustomed to fatigue, was sold at a greater price than the master").[16] Slavery is more starkly delineated in fictional form in his *Histoire des voyages de Scarmentado* (1756), in which a black pirate captain asserts:

Vous nous achetez aux foires de la côte de Guinée, comme des bêtes de somme, pour nous faire travailler à je ne sais quel emploi aussi pénible que ridicule. Vous nous faites fouiller à coups de nerfs de boeuf dans des montagnes pour en tirer une espèce de terre jaune qui par elle-même n'est bonne à rien.[17]

[You buy us at the markets on the coast of Guinea, like beasts of burden, to make us undertake all sorts of tasks which are as painful as they are ridiculous. You make us dig by whipping us with a bull's pizzle in the mountains to extract a type of yellow earth which by itself is good for nothing.]

Notwithstanding the lack of critical agreement regarding Voltaire's opinion on slavery, it is a phenomenon that also pervades *Candide*. In Paraguay, the Jesuit fathers possess black slaves (as they did in reality at this time); while the admirable Cacambo will himself be forced into slavery later on (chapter 26). Notably, Voltaire also invents an illegitimate daughter for the imaginary Pope, Urban X. He relates that, at the age of fifteen, she had been captured by a corsair sailing from the port of Salé in Morocco. The young girl survives a bloody battle between the various Moorish factions, who slaughter each other while reciting their prayers as Mahomet had commanded, five times a day (a parallel with the *Te Deum* ordered by the Abar and Bulgar kings, in chapter 3). She is treacherously sold into slavery to a dey in Algiers by a Neapolitan castrato. A Tunisian merchant then purchases her. We are subsequently presented with a list of various masters who owned her in Tripoli, Alexandria, Smyrna, and Constantinople (chapter 12). A white slave, she is guarded at one stage by two black eunuchs who are likewise slaves. The latter are eaten at a time of famine, whereas the girl loses merely one buttock. The horrors of this relation are downplayed by their rapid recital. The eunuchs had evidently been castrated for their servile posts, while the girl has clung on steadfastly to life, despite the grotesque treatment of her, and lived on to old age to become known as *la Vieille*. Voltaire, who always complained about his own physical ailments, was evidently keen to convey the brutal reality of life. Moreover, the cutting-off of the buttock prefigures a greater atrocity of particular contemporary relevance.

The most famous and significant depiction of slavery in *Candide* is contained in chapter 19, ironically the only chapter to include the word 'optimism'.[18] In Surinam, Candide encounters a mutilated slave who has suffered the amputation of a right hand and a left leg. This unnamed victim describes the atrocities committed against slaves by using himself as an example:

Quand nous travaillons aux sucreries, et que la meule nous attrappe le doigt, on nous coupe la main: quand nous voulons nous enfuir, on nous coupe la jambe: je me suis trouvé dans les deux cas. C'est à ce prix que vous mangez du sucre en Europe. (195–96)

[When we work in the sugar mills, and the millstone catches one of our fingers, the hand is cut off: when we try to run away, a leg is cut off: both these things have happened to me. It is at that price you eat sugar in Europe.]

Sugar had become the sweetener adopted by civilized, European society. The slave here exposes the process that James Walvin terms the "globalization of taste for slave produce" during this era.[19] Furthermore, the description reflects the actual treatment of slaves, and is in accord with the *Code noir*, the slave code enacted by Louis XIV in 1685 (although Surinam itself was a Dutch possession). This incident did not appear in Voltaire's original draft but was added after he had read a passage in Helvétius's *De l'esprit* in the autumn of 1758:

On conviendra qu'il n'arrive point de barrique de sucre en Europe qui ne soit teinte de sang humain. Or quel homme à la vue des malheurs qu'occasionnent la culture et l'exportation de cette denrée refuserait de s'en priver, et ne renoncerait pas à un plaisir acheté par les larmes et la mort de tant de malheureux? Détournons nos regards d'un spectacle si funeste et qui fait tant de honte et d'horreur à l'humanité.[20]

[No one will deny that no barrel of sugar will reach Europe which is not tainted by human blood. Now what man at the sight of such misfortunes caused by the cultivation and the export of that foodstuff would refuse to give it up, and would not renounce a pleasure bought through the tears and the death of so many unfortunates? Turn our eyes away from such a baleful sight which bestows such shame and horror on mankind.]

The slave's persecutor in *Candide* is again a European—a Dutchman called Vanderdenhur. We are left in no doubt that Europe is supplied with sugar at the cost of such abominations. While the punishments described are appalling, Voltaire ensures that the reader responds intellectually rather than emotionally to this episode, through not individualizing the victim and thus granting him a general status. In so doing, he avoids falling into the problem of much sentimental writing about slavery during this era, in which the encouragement to moral sympathy frequently focused on emotional engagement with individual cases, at the expense of any broader critique of the slavery system as a whole.

What Voltaire also ensures (a point often forgotten by commentators) is that the slave informs Candide that it was his own mother who had sold him into slavery, on the coast of Guinea:

> lorsque ma mère me vendit dix écus patagons sur la côte de Guinée, elle me disait: Mon cher enfant, bénis nos fétiches, adore-les toujours, ils te feront vivre heureux; tu as l'honneur d'être esclave de nos seigneurs les blancs, et tu fais par là la fortune de ton père et ta mère. Hélas! je ne sais pas si j'ai fait leur fortune, mais ils n'ont pas fait la mienne. Les chiens, les singes et les perroquets sont mille fois moins malheureux que nous: les fétiches hollandais qui m'ont converti me disent tous les dimanches que nous sommes tous enfants d'Adam, blancs et noirs. Je ne suis pas généalogiste, mais si ces prêcheurs disent vrai, nous sommes tous cousins issus de germain. Or vous m'avouerez qu'on ne peut pas en user avec ses parents d'une manière plus horrible. (196)

> [when my mother sold me for ten Patagonian crowns on the coast of Guinea, she told me: My dear child, bless our fetishes, worship them always, they will make you happy; you have the honour of being a slave of our lords the white folks, and in that way you are making the fortune of your father and mother. Alas, I do not know whether I made their fortune, but they did not make mine. Dogs, monkeys and parrots are a thousand times less unfortunate than us: the Dutch fetishes who converted me tell me every Sunday that we are all children of Adam, white and black. I am not a genealogist, but if these preachers are telling the truth, we are all first cousins. Now you will admit to me that it is not possible to treat one's relatives in a more horrendous manner.]

The slave clearly recognizes the glaring gap between theory and practice in the sermons of the white priests. In addition, the passage is utilized by Voltaire to assert that black Africans are complicit in the slave trade. Furthermore, he transforms the term 'fetish', itself of Portuguese origin, from its basic meaning of magical object, to apply it to the Dutch priests themselves. He thereby undermines their credibility: their exhortations and doctrine are merely hocus-pocus, and they do not practice what they preach.

In a letter of 24 October 1761 to the comte and comtesse d'Argental, Voltaire would write about an auto da fé which saw the execution of the Jesuit, Gabriel Malagrida, who had acted against the king of Portugal in 1758. This prompts the question "que dira Candide?," which is followed by this diatribe:

> Abominables crétiens, les nègres que vous achetez douze cent francs valent douze fois mieux que vous.[21]

> [Abominable Christians, the negroes that you buy for twelve hundred francs are worth twelve times more than you.]

This brief quotation from the letter reinforces the continuity of Voltaire's thought, and underlines the impact that his own fictional episode had on his imagination. In *Candide* itself, the Surinam slave is, perhaps, implausibly articulate in his protestations, but his message startles the reader. Overall, it is the trade in people which is condemned in the work; a species of exploitation that, as Voltaire indicated, was not confined to white Europeans, but practiced by cultures worldwide.

Given its engagement with the contemporary issues of war, slavery, and global travel, it could be contended that *Candide* is first and foremost a tract for its times. In fulfilling this function, it also deals with the crucial question of leadership. Voltaire viewed himself as the leader of the *philosophes* and, consequently, as their pre-eminent opinion-former. If we look at representations of leadership in the tale, however, we are accorded a very diverse picture. Returning to the opening of the work, for example, it is evident that the hierarchical rule of the Baron de Thunderten-tronck is a form of tyranny, over a domain so ironically depicted as an earthly paradise (chapter 2, 122). The Baron is someone who inspires fear rather than respect, causing everyone to feel obliged to laugh when he tells stories. He employs a tutor, Pangloss, who teaches an absolutist philosophy of values that is totally ineffective in the real world. Whether he is conscious of his role or not, Pangloss brings up his pupils as unquestioning subjects of the status quo, indoctrinating them into the belief that a better regime is impossible. Indeed, Candide is raised not to think for himself: "à ne jamais juger de rien par-lui-même" (234). This supposed paradise is totally swept away by the murderous soldiers of the king of the Bulgars, who maintains his authority through the violence of war. True, the king (who represents Frederick the Great) shows pity in sparing the life of the deserter, Candide; but he is nevertheless a warmonger who permits his soldiers to press-gang unwary recruits into his army (in effect enslaving them), while simultaneously being pre-occupied with public relations. Similarly, in chapter 13, the governor of Buenos Ayres is more interested in womanizing than in governing with equity (as will be the case with the officials in Versailles in Voltaire's *L'Ingénu* [1767]). Meanwhile, the kingdom of the Jesuits in Patagonia is (as we have seen) characterized by shameless injustice, rather than by Christian compassion or humility.

We are granted a picture of the perils of leadership in chapter 26, with its depiction of the tribulations of six dethroned rulers dining together in Venice. The assembled rulers were all real people, although their collective fictional appearance owes nothing to chronological reality. Achmet III overthrew his brother in 1703 to become the sultan of the Ottoman Empire, before being deposed himself in 1730 (he died in 1736). Ivan VI was proclaimed tsar of Russia in 1740, only to be displaced the following year (a prisoner at the time of the composition of *Candide*, he was assassinated in 1764). Charles Edward (Bonnie Prince Charlie) is portrayed as on his way to visit his exiled father in Rome. Augustus III, Elector of Saxony and king of Poland, had been forced to quit his realm by the army of Frederick the Great in 1756. Ludicrously, Stanislaw Leszynski, the father-in-law of Louis XV, had been forced to relinquish the throne of Poland in favor of the very same Augustus III. The final ruler, Theodor de Neuhoff, was a German adventurer who briefly occupied the throne of Corsica and died in debt in 1756. In sum, this multinational assortment of the living and the dead testifies to the precarious nature of the attainment of power. The frequent violence of its acquisition, Voltaire intimates, is often counterbalanced by the rapidity of its loss.[22]

If the Venetian carnival-goers had lost their power, other rulers lose their lives or are enslaved. It is rarely noted that Pangloss supplies a list of such unfortunates in the penultimate paragraph of the final chapter. This list perhaps serves as a skeptical prelude to Candide's concluding remarks, in the modest proposal to cultivate their garden. The one really positive cameo of a king occurs much earlier in the text, in chapter 18. There, it is underlined that the king of Eldorado is readily accessible, receiving even uninvited visitors with courtesy and generosity.[23] Despite its utopian aspects, Eldorado is still a monarchy—a hierarchy in which the king commands his servants. When Candide decides to leave, though, the reaction of the king is telling. His Majesty states that Candide and Cacambo are foolish to depart but, more significantly, he explains the basis of his conduct:

> Je n'ai pas assurément le droit de retenir des étrangers; c'est une tyrannie qui n'est ni dans nos moeurs ni dans nos lois: tous les hommes sont libres. (192)

[I certainly do not have the right to detain strangers; that is a tyranny which is not found in our customs or laws: all men are free.]

Here is an example of enlightened kingship, informed by the country's regulations and manners, in which the ruler's behavior is not dictated by personal whim or anger. This could well be a veiled attack on Frederick the Great, who had tried to prevent Voltaire from leaving Prussia in 1753—an event that had been widely reported.

Finally disabused on all fronts, Candide resolves to take charge of his own life and the lives of his companions. He sets up a small farming community at the end of the tale. He is decisive in his enlightened leadership, a role that is accepted by the other characters. By this point, Candide has lost his comic naivety and his last illusion in relation to the now ugly Cunégonde. He does the decent thing by marrying her all the same. (Here, Voltaire is mocking the convention of employing marriage as a symbol of individual and social harmony at the ends of tales.) Importantly, Candide's leadership is derived from money, rather than from birth. The necessity of money is a recurrent theme throughout the tale. In spite of the disdain for gold displayed by the inhabitants of Eldorado, Candide (like his creator) knows that wealth is an essential possession to survive in the real world. Having aided some companions financially, he has ransomed others: Pangloss, the baron's son, Cacambo, the old woman, and Cunégonde. In his role as leader, he is prepared to listen to advice, but he makes up his own mind. Here, there is no unquestioning endorsement of the views of what might be termed surrogate courtiers. Practical organization, tolerance (even for the incurable Pangloss and Martin), mutual help, useful employment—such are the social guidelines of the now-enlightened Candide. The one important survivor who does not join the community is the baron's son. The latter adheres fanatically to his feudal conceptions in opposing the marriage of his sister to Candide, and is thus returned to the galleys and probably thereafter to Rome. By contrast, Candide, the illegitimate young man with no social pedigree, has learnt through experience to organize his multinational group of companions into a mini-state that works (in both senses of the word). The community appears to have no allegiance to a particular country but recognizes itself as a viable entity, as everyone makes a contribution. By presenting a new beginning in a settled place, the conclusion of the tale marks a stark contrast to the opening in Westphalia; the travelers' journeying is now over. The ending of *Candide* contrasts, accordingly, with that of *Rasselas*, which sees a return to Abyssinia, if not necessarily to the Happy Valley in which the story began.[24]

Finally here, it is intriguing that Voltaire chose to locate the final episode of his story near Constantinople, given his later support for Catherine the Great in her war against the Turks. The absence of a return to Candide's roots in Westphalia demonstrates that it was not merely a physical location, but also a site of closed minds. Nor does Voltaire return to Western Europe—which was, for Candide, a land of deception and disappointment. In the final chapter, Candide is depicted as being much impressed by the wisdom of the old Turkish Muslim, who lives a life detached from the murderous scheming associated with the court and government. Equally important, however, is the fact that Candide is impressed by the *hospitality* of this stranger, who offered him food and drink and the services of his daughters for perfuming his beard without any thought of reward. By contrast, such disinterested hospitality appears to be sadly lacking in the Europe of *Candide*.[25]

Voltaire's tale can, then, be envisaged as an appeal to the enlightened minds of his own age. As both author and historian, he saw the dangers of looking through too Eurocentric a lens, although his text was composed before the great voyages to the Pacific by Cook and Bougainville. Ineffectual leadership, he discerned, was destroying ethical values and peoples across the globe. Although not really a pacifist, Voltaire nevertheless abhorred the brutality of war. As in the case of Canada, he deplored the continuation of European wars in overseas territories. Such colonial ventures, he intimated, facilitated inhumane conduct.[26] In the *Essai sur les moeurs* (1756), he had been ambivalent in his attitude to the Americas. There, he had stated that "cette conquête de l'Amérique" was "si funeste pour ses habitants et quelquefois pour les conquérants memes" ("the conquest of America [was] so disastrous for its inhabitants and sometimes for the conquerors themselves"). Moreover, he had acknowledged that it is "un grave problème de savoir si l'Europe a gagné en se portant en Amérique" ("a serious problem to know whether Europe gained anything in going to America").[27] Against this, the ending of *Candide* prefigures the productive activity of Voltaire's own colony at Ferney, where he settled permanently in 1760. In a sense, one might venture to say that Candide's micro-community was a blueprint for his own.[28] What one may also assert is that, in *Candide*, Voltaire was employing a philosophical tale, one of the most effective media of his day, to comment on the burning issues of the mid-eighteenth-century world.[29]

The contemporary success of the tale is manifest from the multiple reprintings in French and in translation that quickly appeared. In 1759 itself there were at least seventeen French editions—launched in various European centers such as Paris, Geneva, Amsterdam, London—as well as three editions in English. In his study of the genesis of *Candide*, Frédéric Deloffre notes that Voltaire, for the first time, had included contemporary events in this tale, "met en scène des faits contemporains."[30] In this keywork of 1759, we thus see Voltaire the historian employing historical events in fiction as part of his enlightening campaign, raising the issue of whether fiction was more effective than history in terms of social and political impact. One might also suggest that the eponymous protagonist of Voltaire's masterpiece himself ends up as a literary manifestation of the *grand homme*, the influential figure who guides his fellow human beings along the path of mutual toleration and fruitful activity.[31] The illegitimate Candide shows that legitimacy derives from real-life actions and not from the accident of birth. The tale's true purchase, meanwhile, lies not in the creation of the best of all possible worlds, but rather in the exhortation to create a better one, in a finale that advocates a necessary process, rather than an already-defined end product.

In its depiction of extremist thinking with its baleful consequences, the atrocities of war and the slave trade, indeed a raft of injustices, *Candide* was both a manifesto for action and a harbinger of Voltaire's campaigns of the following decades, such as his campaigning for the freeing of serfs in France (whose condition he assimilated to that of slaves). In the abuse of its power, he would assert, the Church was betraying Christianity: "Jésus-Christ n'a pas ordonné aux apôtres de réduire leurs frères à l'esclavage" ("Jesus Christ has not ordered the apostles to reduce their brothers to slavery").[32] To highlight these aspects of his oeuvre is to situate the tale in its Enlightenment context, without recourse to any potentially anachronistic, postcolonial readings. Unlike Denis Diderot, Voltaire was not writing for posterity. From his vantage point outside Geneva, he was targeting his compatriots.[33] His portrayal of the enlightened, monarchical administration of Eldorado, with its use of the pound sterling (the currency of its military antagonist, England), could only be viewed as provocative and revealing in the midst of ongoing hostilities. As Carol Watts suggests, *Candide* can be envisaged as a "political work" in its implications, although none of the characters seeks consolation in politics or indeed in religion.[34] Unlike the "conclusion, in which nothing is concluded" of *Rasselas*, Voltaire draws effective conclusions.[35] The incitement to "cultivate our garden" (note the collective plural) is one of particular and universal application. Perhaps the final irony is that Voltaire did not find it sufficient to cultivate his own garden at Ferney. He may have been viewing the world's events only from afar, but he felt compelled to use his pen to influence and comment upon those events, nowhere more so than in his celebrated campaigns to redress miscarriages of justice. In such ways, *Candide* was a text both for its own time, and for all time.

Notes

1. For an overview of Voltaire's importance as a historian, see Catherine Volpilhac-Auger, "Voltaire and History," in *The Cambridge Companion to Voltaire*, ed. Nicholas Cronk (Cambridge: Cambridge University Press, 2009), 139–52. Roger Pearson provides an assured introduction to the *philosophe*'s tales in *The Fables of Reason: A Study of Voltaire's "contes philosophiques"* (Oxford: Clarendon Press, 1993).

2. See the numerous letters referenced in footnotes to the introduction to the standard scholarly edition of *Candide*, ed. René Pomeau, vol. 48 of *The Complete Works of Voltaire* (Oxford: Voltaire Foundation, 1980), 25. References to *Candide* will be to this edition, and will be given parenthetically (citing chapter and page numbers as necessary). All English translations are my own.

3. For an account of the naval engagement which led to Byng's disgrace, see Edward Freeman, "Le combat naval de Minorque: l'exécution de l'Amiral Byng et l'intervention de Voltaire," in *La Méditerranée au XVIIIe Siècle*, ed. F. Paknadel (Aix-en-Provence: Université de Provence, 1987), 41–59.

4. It is important to bear in mind here that Voltaire's tale was composed and published some months before the British victory at Quebec in September 1759.

5. Frank McLynn, among others, writes of the "global conflict" involving England and France, as opposed to the limited European operations of Prussia: *1759: The Year Britain Became Master of the World* (London: Jonathan Cape, 2004), 2.

6. The tutor-pupil relationship between Pangloss and Candide can be compared with that between Imlac and Rasselas, albeit in a more overtly satiric context in Voltaire's tale. On Imlac and Rasselas, see James Watt's essay in this volume.

7. The idea of such hospitality in exotic lands is found elsewhere in the writings of the *philosophes*, for example in the reception of the chaplain in Tahiti in Diderot's *Supplément au voyage de Bougainville* (1773).

8. This acknowledged superiority of the servant prefigures the master's recognition, in *Jacques le fataliste*, that his servant's skills and acumen are superior to his own. Unlike some valets in French comedy, both Cacambo and Jacques are friends rather than rivals of their respective masters.

9. Madeleine Dobie, *Colonization and Slavery in Eighteenth-Century French Culture* (Ithaca: Cornell University Press, 2010), 4.

10. Jean-Jacques Rousseau, *Julie ou la Nouvelle Héloïse*, ed. René Pomeau (Paris: Garnier, 1960), 396–97.

11. For instance, Christopher L. Miller attacks Voltaire and some of his contemporaries in *The French Atlantic Triangle: Literature and Culture of the Slave Trade* (Durham: Duke University Press, 2008). While Miller is right to question a too rosy picture of the *philosophes* in their reactions to slavery, he is inclined to overstate his case. A committed defence of the *philosophes* is undertaken by the eminent Enlightenment scholar, Jean Ehrard, in *Lumières et esclavage: l'esclavage colonial et l'opinion publique en France au xviiie siècle* (Brussels: André Versaille, 2008). The lack of clear-cut positions in the mid-century is outlined in David Adams, "Slavery in the *Encyclopédie*," in *The Enterprise of Enlightenment*, ed. Terry Pratt and David McCallum (Oxford: Peter Lang, 2004), 127–40. On France and abolitionism, see Dobie, *Colonization and Slavery*, passim.

12. Voltaire to André Morellet, 14 July 1769, in *Correspondence and Related Documents*, ed. Theodore Besterman, vols. 85–135 of *Complete Works* (Oxford: Voltaire Foundation, 1968–1977), D15747. Following standard practice in references to this edition, the number of individual letters is preceded by "D" (which stands for definitive), but the number of the volume is not cited.

13. See my "Voltaire et *Le Voltaire*," *Revue d'histoire littéraire de la France* 4 (1991): 756–61.

14. Jean-François Lopez, "Les investissements de Voltaire dans le commerce colonial et la traite négrière: clarifications et malentendus," *Cahiers Voltaire* 7 (2008): 124–39. Voltaire had a great daily intake of coffee: Christiane Mervaud, *Voltaire à table* (Paris: Desjonquères, 1998), 9.

15. *Oeuvres complètes de Voltaire*, ed. Louis Moland, vol. 14 (Paris: Garnier, 1878), 494, 495.

16. Voltaire, *Zadig*, in *Contes en Vers et en Prose*, ed. Sylvain Menant, 2 vols. (Paris: Garnier, 1992), 1:139.

17. Voltaire, *Histoire des voyages de Scarmentado*, in *Contes en Vers et en Prose*, 1:210–11.

18. 'Optimisme' was a neologism which had entered the French language only in the 1730s. Here, it does not have its modern connotation (implying a hopeful cast of mind) but is, rather, a technical term relating to a philosophy of final causes.

19. James Walvin, *Making the Black Atlantic: Britain and the African Diaspora* (London: Cassell, 2000), 122.

20. Claude Adrien Helvétius, *De l'esprit* (Paris: Durand, 1758), 25.

21. Voltaire to the comte and comtesse d'Argental, 24 October 1761, in *Correspondence*, D10090.

22. A lively analysis of this Venetian meal is provided by Christiane Mervaud, "Du carnaval au carnavalesque: l'épisode vénitien de *Candide*," in *Le Siècle de Voltaire: Hommage à René Pomeau*, ed. C. Mervaud and S. Menant, 2 vols. (Oxford: Voltaire Foundation, 1986), 2:651–62.

23. This again contrasts the Ingénu's reception at Versailles and Mlle de St Yves's fantasy of throwing herself at the monarch's feet to plead her case.

24. On the endings of *Rasselas* and *Candide*, see also James Watt's essay in this volume.

25. Jacques the anabaptist might be cited as an exception in his charity to strangers, which puts his Christian duties into execution. However, even there, it is possible to infer an element of self-interest, given that he also puts Candide and Pangloss to work in his business. For a recent assessment of the theme of hospitality, see Judith Still, *Enlightenment Hospitality: Cannibals, Harems and Adoption* (Oxford: Voltaire Foundation, 2011).

26. Síofra Pierse comments on Voltaire's attitude to colonization in *Voltaire Historiographer: Narrative Paradigms* (Oxford: Voltaire Foundation, 2008), 107–10. Karen O'Brien also notes that prominent historians of the Enlightenment such as Voltaire, Hume, and Gibbon "were all in their different ways profoundly critical of the bloodshed inherent in empire-building": "Empire, History and Emigration from Enlightenment to Liberalism," in *Race, Nation and Empire: Making Histories, 1750 to the Present*, ed. Catherine Hall and Keith McClelland (Manchester: Manchester University Press, 2010), 16.

27. Voltaire, *Essai sur les moeurs*, ed. René Pomeau, 2 vols. (Paris: Garnier, 1963), 2:330, 362.

28. See my "Reflections on Voltaire and his Idea of Colonies," *SVEC* 332 (1995): 61–69.

29. Whether the standard use of the term *conte philosophique* is appropriate is another matter. For a questioning of this usage, see Nicholas Cronk, "The Voltairean Genre of the *conte philosophique*: Does it Exist?," *Nottingham French Studies* 48, no. 3 (2009): 61–73.

30. Frédéric Deloffre, "Genèse de *Candide*: étude de la création des personnages et de l'élaboration du roman," in *Bestiaires de Voltaire, Genese de Candide, et Autres Etudes sur Voltaire*, ed. Christiane Mervaud and Frédéric Deloffre (Oxford: Voltaire Foundation, 2006), 249. The carnage of the Lisbon earthquake of 1755, cited in *Candide*, was a major news item in Europe as well as calling into question divine Providence. There is also a veiled reference to the assassination attempt on Louis XV by Damiens in 1757 (chapter 22).

31. Some years ago, a revisionist article by Roy Wolper challenged the generally positive interpretation of the conclusion of the tale: "Candide: Gull in the Garden," *Eighteenth-Century Studies* 111 (1969–1970): 265–77. Wolper's article contains some provocative insights but fails to convince in the context of Voltaire's self-proclaimed enlightening mission.

32. Voltaire, *Au Roi en son conseil* (1770), ed. Robert Granderoute, in vol. 72 of *Complete Works* (Oxford: Voltaire Foundation, 2011), 290.

33. See my "Whither/Wither France: Voltaire's View from Ferney," in *Peripheries of the Enlightenment*, ed. Richard Butterwick, Simon Davies, and Gabriel Sánchez Espinosa (Oxford: Voltaire Foundation, 2008), 17–27.

34. Carol Watts, *The Cultural Work of Empire: The Seven Years' War and the Imagining of the Shandean State* (Toronto: University of Toronto Press, 2007), 35.

35. Samuel Johnson, *The History of Rasselas, Prince of Abyssinia*, in *Rasselas and Other Tales*, ed. Gwin J. Kolb, vol. 16 of *The Yale Edition of the Works of Samuel Johnson* (New Haven: Yale University Press, 1990), 175.

Part II

3

ADAM SMITH'S *THE THEORY OF MORAL
SENTIMENTS* IN 1759: SPECTATORSHIP,
DUTY, AND SOCIAL IMPROVEMENT

NIGEL WOOD

IN 1759, ADAM SMITH had been Chair of Moral Philosophy at Glasgow University for seven years, after a year-long tenure as the Chair of Logic. Smith's progress to 1759 was a complex affair. Studying Moral Philosophy at Glasgow under Francis Hutcheson from 1737 to 1740, he obtained the Snell exhibition to enable a short stay at Oxford—where, it seems, he first encountered David Hume's *A Treatise of Human Nature.*[1] Following an invitation from Lord Kames, Smith's public lectures at Edinburgh from 1748 focused on rhetoric and *belles-lettres.* These lectures brought him to the notice of Hume and, from 1750 onwards, the two philosophers maintained a lively correspondence. It is significant that Smith's immediate preparation for the *Theory of Moral Sentiments* should have combined a concern for rhetoric with ethics. While he would go on to pen *The Wealth of Nations* (1776), Smith would not have been associated with economic theory in the year 1759.

Even in discussions of Smith's moral theory, the 1759 edition of the *Theory of Moral Sentiments* has often been regarded as merely a staging-post, rather than a destination. From this view, the work in its earliest form is superseded by the revisions that Smith introduced in subsequent editions: the second (1764), third (1767), fourth (1774), fifth (1781), and the most extensive re-vision of them all, the sixth edition of 1790. Within a few months of its first publication in April 1759, Smith was drafting a second edition, the "papers" of which he sent to Sir Gilbert Elliot on 10 October.[2] As D. D. Raphael and A. L. MacFie show in their record of the variants between the editions, there were three main areas where the first edition required (and received) emendation: in the enhanced realization that the role of what Smith termed the "impartial spectator" had a socially useful purpose; the greater point given to the distinction between "sympathy" and ethical approval; and the greater depth afforded to the approbation of Stoical self-command that is evident in the 1790 edition (III.3), along with the inclusion for the first time of a Part VI.[3] The emphasis on the prudence of political continuity and the acknowledgement of system in this new Part VI have been regarded as an older man's reaction to Revolutionary change.[4] It is not that the 1759 edition did not indicate all of these points to some extent, but rather that the independence of the *Theory* from earlier models of the social utility of "propriety" and "sympathy" took time to deepen and grow.

Yet despite this gradual maturation of his ideas and the changes that Smith made to the work during his lifetime, the first edition of 1759—the focus of this essay—remains an important document in its own right. As I shall argue, the first edition of the *Theory* was, in fact, a significant intervention in a persistent debate, during the 1750s, about one's social obligations, and about whether self-regulation of the baser, asocial passions was either feasible or sufficient as a basis for (moral) social conduct. Moreover, while the prevalence within the work of visual metaphors, frequently of mirrors and spectating, might seem to be of a piece with previous studies of ethical instincts, these metaphors are often used by Smith in ways that were particular to the *Theory* itself.

The most pivotal figure that Smith employs in his theory is the 'impartial spectator'. This figure is not so much an actual body as an internalized and corrective sense of how society would approve or disapprove of any action. Given the precedent of the *Spectator* series (1711–1714), it is unlikely that Smith would have regarded this figure as original. In creating his *persona* for the *Spectator*, Joseph Addison had partly aimed to carve out a perspective that owed little to any specific power group. The result was a figure of learned silence and gravity; one who appears "rather as a Spectator of Mankind, than as one of the Species," and who has never meddled "with any practical Part in Life." Whether Mr Spectator was intended to be exemplary has been much debated, and queried. His imperturbable empiricism meant, for example, that he was distinguished by "a profound Silence" at University; where—except when absolute necessity demanded—he "scarce uttered the Quantity of an hundred Words" during the course of eight years. Although a great frequenter of crowds in the metropolis, he only converses in his "own Club," and he aims to discern the truth of a situation more quickly than those intimately involved, "as Standers-by discover Blots, which are apt to escape those who are in the Game."[5] Such detached and taciturn observation was hardly a template for responsible citizenship and, in his *Theory*, Smith was clear to associate some of Addison's apparent stylistic 'virtues' with this bloodless reclusiveness, contrasting his "often tedious and prosaic languor" to Pope's "nervous precision" (380).

Nevertheless, in *The Spectator*, Addison and his co-editor, Sir Richard Steele, had popularized issues that are at the core of Smith's 1759 *Theory*. Adopting the *persona* in *Spectator* no. 274 (14 January 1712), Steele attempted to apportion genuine blame (or, at least, moral desert) by acting as an "impartial SPECTATOR" who "looks upon [those who are taken simply to be criminals] with all the Circumstances that diminish or enhance the Guilt," rather than taking the view of the "Pedantick Stoick" who "thinks all Crimes alike."[6] For this early-century 'Spectator', the exhaustive analyst could, by garnering all the available evidence, ascertain the degree of guilt, acquiring accurate knowledge by careful accretion. One of the later numbers of the periodical (number 564 for 7 July 1714, written by Eustace Budgell) considers closely the case of a hypothetical "Philosopher" who subdues his passions so as to lay aside his prejudices. Such a "Philosopher," the paper suggests, would act as "an impartial Spectator" and have no eye to how the objects of his analysis might "advance or cross [his] own private Interest."[7] Moving beyond both partisan strife and frenetic involvement, the ideal 'Spectator' of Addison and Steele's journal was thus situated both within society and outside of it.

For Smith, the impartiality of his own "spectator" is available to all truly sociable citizens. Impartiality is not the special quality that the Addisonian figure cultivates, but, as the successive editions make increasingly clear, an abstract goal, the angel on one's shoulder.[8] At the core of Smith's own sense of sociable sympathy is the need for such a pitch of fellow-feeling that identification—either from pity or revulsion—provides a necessary supplement to a code of ethics. This is made clear in the opening discussion of sympathy, where the intensity of fellow-feeling is only produced by the spectacle of some deep emotions: "The furious behaviour of an angry man is more likely to exasperate us against himself than against his enemies" (7). Any distinct ethical judgment is liable to be overridden by the passions. The spectator strives to attain a complete sentimental knowledge of a situation, yet this knowledge is necessarily gained from external appearances: "Grief and joy . . . strongly expressed in the look and gestures of any one, at once affect the spectator with some degree of a like painful or agreeable emotion" (6). Consonance is necessary to any useful spectatorial gaze, as "the man whose sympathy keeps time to my grief, cannot but admit the reasonableness of my sorrow," whereas a lack of such coincidence might lead to disapproval "on account of their dissonance with his own" (23). Smith's "spectator" is not, then, the passive and distanced *savant* that Addison describes. Rather, in the *Theory*, the whole system of ethical justification is produced by the notion of the actively sympathetic observer, who "must adopt the whole case of his companion with all its minutest incidents; and strive to render, as perfect as possible, that imaginary change of situation upon which his sympathy is founded."[9] The hortatory purchase of "must" and "strive" should not be missed here, for Smith finds it incumbent on civilized citizens to feel ethically; and yet this goal of "compleat sympathy," whilst it may be "passionately" desired, is even a painful aspiration, for an "entire concord" of a spectator's affections with those of another is rarely attainable. Consequently, Smith suggests that it might be strategic to lower the pitch of one's passion nearer to that of an imperfect spectator, who fails to provide such desirable congruence (36–37).

In 1759, Smith was engaged with this process of sympathy more as a foundation for social action than as a contribution to an abstract ideal of spectatorial impartiality (which would occupy him more in the 1790 edition of the *Theory*). The 1759 edition comes near to enshrining the "impartial spectator" as an exemplar of a possible model of social improvement, far from the brutishness of the "rude vulgar of mankind" (44). At the same time, instinctive sympathy overrode volition, and this was to be recognized as a social as well as a psychological fact. It led to a duty of "beneficence," the nearest we can come to "a perfect and compleat obligation" (172), and its worldly manifestation would appear to be 'justice'. This was certainly the conclusion of Henry Home, Lord Kames; who, in the second edition of his *Essays on the Principles of Morality and Natural Religion* (1758), attempted to establish a necessary distinction between general justice and more personal ethical choices, such as (in Smith's words) "friendship, charity, or generosity" (174).[10] The passions exacted a level of dutiful observance for Kames, but only insofar as they encouraged the social institution of justice. Smith, though, required more of one's instinctive self. His example of the impulse to assist those in distress (such as a man about to be robbed) is deployed to illustrate how relatively feeble the "institution of civil government" might be in exacting certain forms of impulsive behavior (175). The very necessary abstraction of the juridical principle is of little help in the immediate instance, and Smith is dubious about how such abstracted notions could effect genuine social improvement. Far more radically effective, in his view, is the fear of social disgrace, the anticipated gaze and judgment of the "impartial spectator." Crucially, this fear is also the most direct way by which "self-love" is tempered, a self-censorship that brings aspiration and appetite "down to something which other men can go along with":

They will indulge it so far as to allow him to be more anxious about, and to pursue with more earnest assiduity, his own happiness than that of any other person. Thus far, whenever they place themselves in his situation, they will readily go along with him. . . . But if he should justle, or throw down any of them, the indulgence of the spectators is entirely at an end. (182–83)

It is up to legal redress to supply a remedy to the consequences of anti-social behavior, but the restraints upon unbridled egotism derive less from religious commandment or concern about any external legal measure than from the intensely perceived possibility of social ostracism. Yet if one's empathic experience has not been embedded by memory or reflection, then one might not be able to identify just what any spectator would expect, and thus how one should act as an impartial spectator. Consequently, when Smith focuses on a "system" of moral sentiments, he becomes increasingly preoccupied by the possibilities for failure and transgression.

When Smith assesses how society really functions, he proceeds, reassuringly, from the premise that man can "subsist only in society" and "was fitted by nature to that situation for which he was made." The cement of this system derives from "the agreeable bands of love and affection" that attract all into "one common centre of mutual good offices" (188). This postulate is the positive side of the coin; the negative alternative resides in the potential for denial and willful isolation, where duty is ignored and "habitual reflection" is missing (269). The possession of correct moral sentiments depends on precision, while virtue stems from "habit and resolution of mind" (512)—or else one would merely be tied to a common consensus. On the other hand, this system would require "prudence and a strong sense of propriety" to prevent it from tipping over into an unwelcome curiosity, where the consultation of "relevant" moral sentiments could in effect be a charter for prying eyes (542).

Just over a century earlier, in *Leviathan* (1651), Thomas Hobbes had concluded that "our naturall Passions . . . carry us to Partiality, Pride, Revenge, and the like."[11] The ethical models most available to Smith strove to prove the opposite—anything to avoid both the conclusion that the human passions were not to be trusted and the resort to centralized enforcement that Hobbes favored. Smith reserved his most acerbic comments for Bernard Mandeville and François de la Rochefoucauld—who both, in their own ways, regarded private vices as a contribution to public benefits (482–86). However, he was more exercised by the need to intervene in recent uses of his key terms. It is no hyperbole to claim that Smith's theory would not have been grounded in the nuances of moral choice and justice had he not had Francis Hutcheson and David Hume before him. For both Joseph Butler and Anthony Ashley Cooper, the third Earl of Shaftesbury, the psychology of moral action had appeared to be the result of intense introspection, so that it always carried a tincture of self-interest. For Hutcheson, by contrast, it was the very disinterestedness of the moral sense that explained how so many of our ethical distinctions were consistent and enduring—just as the category of the beautiful had varied so little through the ages. The lynchpin for this consistency, though, was the spectator. Whereas the agents in an action were bound up in the here-and-now, the spectator possessed the capacity to weigh up—and to be pleased or distressed by—the actions of these agents. Within this process, as outlined by Hutcheson, the externals of such a scene were enough to help the moral sense take shape: "Now, when the natural Air of a Face approaches that which any Passion would form it unto, we make a conjecture from this concerning the leading Disposition of the Person's Mind."[12] In Hutcheson, this evaluative exercise stemmed from the "moral sense" of the observer, that inevitably conferred value on the action observed.[13]

For Hume, similarly, this "moral sentiment" is partly a matter of human judgment—but only partly. It is the resort to sentimental assessment that determines morality, where virtue is not merely utilitarian but rather "*whatever mental action or quality gives to a spectator the pleasing sentiment of approbation*; and vice the contrary." For Hume, the specular is not merely figurative, as it wavers between indicating an introspective and an exterior scrutiny. In his *An Enquiry concerning the Principles of Morals* (1751), it is the "love of fame" that produces a regard for a "moral sentiment," where it is one's standing in the world's eye that encourages correct ethical choice. The path to this argument involves a sense of visual scrutiny, whereby one is constantly "in review," and yet this gaze is internalized, and becomes a "constant habit of surveying ourselves, as it were, in reflection."[14] This internalization is instinctive for the most morally advanced members of society, and cannot be a result of calculation. Indeed, in an implicit rebuke to Mandeville and Shaftesbury, "Self-Love" cannot alone account for moral sentiments, as "Usefulness is only a Tendency to a certain End; and 'tis a Contradiction in Terms, that any Thing pleases as a Means to an End" (84). Social pressure is thus useful, yet cannot alone produce ethical agreement. The agenda that Smith gleaned from both Hume and Hutcheson is, then, part psychological and part sociological in inspiration: to be admitted fully into society one needs to respond and recognize the demands of sociability.

In responding to Hume (and also to Kames), Smith's *Theory* contributed to a specifically 1750s debate about how, *contra* Hobbes, society might allow for personal choices, and how self-scrutiny might aid social cohesion.[15] This is not to claim that the *Theory* was derivative; rather, that it can only be fully understood as the next stage in a line of reflection that had predecessors in Addison, Hutcheson, and Hume. Earlier in the century, Hutcheson had relied on a disinterestedness of view that was conditioned by a predisposition to find benevolent actions acceptable and progressive and the egotistical ugly and destructive. For Hume, as John Mullan describes, there existed a kind of mental flux: "a mutuality of sentiments without distinction, a continuous passing from one 'mind' to another."[16] What is indispensable in Smith's appeal to social control is the scrutiny of the impartial spectator.[17] If the role of the spectator here is not entirely original, in Smith's hands the figure becomes beneficially coercive and even corrective. For Smith, as Mullan notes, society is a "'mirror' which is 'placed in the countenance and behaviour of those he lives with.'"[18] The nature and function of this mirror are themselves, though, subject to debate. Does Smith, for instance, intend to encourage a society's scrutineering as an acceptable alternative to strenuous central control (if still a charter for well-motivated spying)? Or should the mirror be regarded as an internalized ideal, where the fear of social disgrace preemptively corrects behavior? In other words, is the mirror the tenor or the vehicle, signified or signifier?

Smith's revisions to the *Theory* exhibit a generally constructive receptiveness to comment, which was sometimes helpful, sometimes simply negative.[19] If we concentrate on the 1759 edition, we discover a theory that is more tentative in significant areas than it would become in subsequent editions. Two examples will suffice: the first extended introduction of the concept of the impartial spectator in section III.ii ("Of Duty"), and the closing comments on how a concept of the deity might bolster purely social control through the legal process (section II.ii.3). The reliance on dutiful control through intense self-reflection is less assured here than it would become in later editions, and the fear of God more diffuse and mediated. The precise treatment of these issues—duty and the deity—in the first edition thus merits closer consideration.

In principle, the idea that one should observe and appreciate what it is to do one's duty was uncontroversial for writers of the moral-sense and sympathy schools. Hutcheson's "moral sense" had explained moral conduct in terms of an innate reflex, Hume by an appreciation of utility that is seen as beautiful but only insofar as it is beneficial.[20] Despite the qualifications that both had introduced, conscience had to be understood either as a benevolent instinct or as a conscious appreciation of social benefit. Smith, though, could not accept either proposition. Any recourse to an innate 'moral sense' by-passed the potential for both humane and inhumane responses, and failed to establish a necessary degree of account-ability for human action. Similarly, Hume's reliance on "utility" required either a necessary extra gloss (to render more exact whose sense of utility was reliable), or a distinction between simple function and the more abstract benefit of moral advancement. This becomes clear in Smith's chapter "Of the beauty which the appearance of utility bestows upon the characters and actions of men; and how far the perception of this beauty may be regarded as one of the original principles of approbation" (III.iv.2). In this chapter, Smith almost pours scorn on Hume's functional apology for duty:

> first of all, it seems impossible that the approbation of virtue should be
> a sentiment of the same kind with that by which we approve of a con-
> venient and well-contrived building; or that we should have no other
> reason for praising a man than that for which we commend a chest of
> drawers. (359)[21]

The question still remains, though: how might social improvement be possible through individual ethical choice? Or, more simply, how can a focus on the in-dividual and local choice lead to a more comprehensive application, where the amelioration of a whole society is concerned?

This problem explains why Smith relies so much upon "propriety," the suit-able reaching out to others that is the hall-mark of "self-command." As he puts it, "When we act in this manner [with due regard for others and their views on our behavior], the sentiments which influence our conduct seem exactly to coincide with those of the spectator" (361). The isolated voice, crying in its own wilderness, may indeed be logical and correct, yet it returns no sound.[22] This "coincidence" in the sentiments of the observer and the observed is no collective error; rather, it is an insurance that one's judgments are not merely self-love in disguise. For Smith, this insurance is provided by the anticipated reflection, and consequent judgment, on our public conduct. As he remarks in a crucial passage that is only to be found in the first edition:

> To judge of ourselves as we judge of others, to approve and condemn
> in ourselves what we approve and condemn in others, is the greatest
> exertion of candour and impartiality. In order to do this, we must look
> at ourselves with the same eyes with which we look at others: we must

imagine ourselves not the actors, but the spectators of our own character and conduct, and consider how these would affect us when viewed from this new station, in which their excellencies and imperfections can alone be discovered. (257)[23]

This is a form of negotiation with public *mores*, in that regulation of individual conduct—and its social force—is under threat if there is no consonance between the public and the private. Such introspection is achieved not by a communion with an inner calling or intuition, but by imagining ourselves in society and under its regulatory gaze. Moral accountability thus involves an anticipated giving of an account of ourselves "to some other, and that consequently must regulate them [our actions] according to the good-liking of this other" (257). Conformity to this abstract yardstick should bring spectator and agent together. Smith then proceeds to liken such self-correction to the checking of one's appearance in a looking-glass before entering into company: "It is evident . . . that we are anxious about our own beauty and deformity, only on account of its effect upon others. If we had no connection with society, we should be altogether indifferent about either" (259). A further passage that did not survive the first edition, though, evinces some doubt about the accuracy of the reflective metaphor:

> Unfortunately, this moral looking-glass is not always a very good one. Common looking-glasses, it is said, are extremely deceitful, and by the glare which they throw over the face, conceal from the partial eyes of the person many deformities which are obvious to every body besides. But there is not in the world such a smoother of wrinkles as is every man's imagination, with regard to the blemishes of his own character (260–61).

As these propositions and qualifications show, in 1759, Smith's theory tussled with the duality of the self. The crucial difficulty here was whether it was possible to imagine oneself, simultaneously, as both actor and spectator—not least as this projected social scrutiny depended on a self that, as Smith recognized, had a tendency to be partial *to* itself.[24]

If the precise mechanism of pre-emptive self-spectatorship remained somewhat cloudy in the 1759 version of the *Theory*, more clear is that, within this process, God became merely a secondary cause of moral reform. Smith's *Theory* does not so much omit a sense of the deity as place it within a more complex account of how, pragmatically, a recognition of divinity might produce certain beneficial results. This is not to say that he ever quite forsook a theistic perspective;

rather, that he resorts to the deity as a kind of social and philosophical safety-net. What Smith does resist in 1759—in terms that are 'clarified', and thus diluted, in each successive edition—is the notion that human judgment might be capable of identifying clear and decisive instances of divine intervention. A passage that was later excised (from the sixth edition) posits that God's providence operates to allow mankind its own initial freedoms, even if the final tribunal of judgment is unshunnable and remote:

> Man, when about to appear before a being of infinite perfection, can feel but little confidence in his own merit, or in the imperfect propriety of his own conduct. . . . To such a being, he can scarce imagine, that his littleness and weakness should ever seem to be the proper object, either of esteem or of reward. (204–5)

The gap between human discernment and divine justice is, then, an unbridgeable chasm. In the draft revisions that Smith collected in 1759 for the second edition of 1764, we are told that, "for the wisest reasons," the "Great Judge" of the world

> thought proper to interpose, between the weak eye of human reason and the throne of his eternal justice, a degree of obscurity and darkness which tho it does entirely cover that great tribunal from the view of mankind, yet renders the impression of it faint and feeble in comparison of what might be expected from the grandeur and importance of so mighty an object. (203–4)

This explanation of God's obscurity has the advantage of confirming divine glory and justice whilst at the same time denying its immediate relevance to regular human affairs. In this manner, Smith confirmed that it was in this world, rather than the next, that "esteem" and "reward" would have to be attempted and experienced—all under the stewardship of the impartial spectator.

There is no single trend in how Smith emended the first edition, but the most urgent decision—suggested by Sir Gilbert Elliot himself (the recipient of Smith's draft of a second edition)—surrounded the possibility that conscience could merely derive from popular opinion.[25] Without a clear sense of providential authority on the one hand or the demands of simple utility on the other, one was left merely with conformity to currents of opinion that were potentially transient. This problem is likely to have led Smith to clarify and recommend his brand of

Stoicism, where self-command was set above a mere need for approval.[26] The *Theory* commences with a tableau of agonistic energy, an example of human torment that alludes to Cicero's illustration of Stoic ethics in his *De Finibus*, in which we are asked to spectate (in Smith's words) "our brother on the rack."[27] Our senses themselves cannot provide an exact correspondence of feelings, Smith suggests, but our imagination can help in this process: "it is by the imagination only that we can form any conception of what are his sensations. . . . By the imagination we place ourselves in his situation, we conceive ourselves enduring all the same torments, we enter as it were into his body, and become in some measure the same person with him, and thence form some idea of his sensations" (2–3). This is not the coolly analyzing spectator of Addison's coinage, nor is it a Lockean process whereby we merely open the eye and the scene enters.[28] As Nicholas Phillipson observes, such "moral encounters" in Smith are, rather, "two-way affairs," whereby "my attempt to make sympathetic sense of your conduct is likely to be reciprocated by your attempt to make sympathetic sense of mine." Such "mutual sympathy" is thus achieved by a process of sensitive adaptation—although we should note the qualification provided by the word "likely" in Phillipson's summary of this process.[29]

Social benefit emerges in the *Theory*, then, not from a weighing of communal norms and a balancing of utilitarian profit and loss but from its opposite, by intuiting our social responsibility and scaling down the drive towards individualistic advancement. Notably, the 1759 version also shows an insistent awareness of the crucial difference between the roles of actor and spectator, an issue that leads to Smith's use of a theatrical context to frame such assessment. A more traditional sense of the theatre of the world (an allusion to the *theatrum mundi* figure) might have laid greater stress on the divine playwright. If all the world's a stage then there must be some *scriptor* whose original will had assigned parts and outcomes. This emphasis would be an item in any early-century explanation of natural religion. John Wilkins, quoting Epictetus in 1722, for example, had advocated the "reasonableness and fitness of Mens resigning themselves up to God's Disposal":

> Did not he appoint the Time, and Place, and Part you are to act upon the Theatre of this World? And this is properly your Business, to apply your Self to the fittest Means of representing the Part allotted to you, not to take upon you to murmur or repine against it.[30]

This awareness could be a cause of consistent characterization—or of the need to pursue it in developing your own part in this world. The gloss supplied by the translator, George Stanhope, to chapter XLII of Epictetus's *Morals*, usefully sums up this Stoical creed:

> The Duties owing to a Man's self, are the next thing to be learn'd; and those he begins to treat of here, advising his Proficient, (for to such a one he writes now) to make it his first Care to determine with himself, what Figure he intends to make, and what Part to play upon this Theatre of the World: and when that once is done, the next must be so to model all his Actions, as that they may conspire together to the maintaining of that Character.[31]

Smith noted Epictetus's invitation to acquiescence to the divine script in the sixth edition of the *Theory of Moral Sentiments* and did not wish to accept the invitation, despite his overall reinforcement of Stoical principles.[32] In 1759, though, the theatrical metaphor was less easily dealt with. If Smith uses it generally in an orthodox fashion, there are also passages where the equivalence between the world and the stage is not wholly trusted. Tragedy's decorum in depicting stricken aristocratic heroes, for example, does not survive translation to a common reality, for a situation in which it is only kings and lovers that earn our sympathy—the default setting of the theatre—is an effect of "the prejudices of the imagination," that paint the advantages of such figures as much to be desired (114). The Greek theatre may have breached such decorum by depicting directly the effects of pain on many of its protagonists, yet it was the fortitude of the sufferer, rather than their grimace, that was truly persuasive (59).[33] For Smith in 1759, an audience's imagination might be won by effects that were only rhetorical ploys, or because conventional expectations clouded what might otherwise have been authentic responses.

For Smith, then, theatrical illusion was necessary, yet also to be regarded with a measure of reserve.[34] The 'society' of a theatre audience could be likened to the social world at large, but the first edition and the immediate revisions of the 1759 edition of the *Theory* show some doubt as to the equity or impartiality of theatrical response. By contrast, the metaphor of holding a mirror up to nature—philosophically and figuratively speaking—holds good; it confirms the human relevance of ethics. For Smith—appreciably more than for Hutcheson and Hume—reference to social existence locks one's moral character in place and locates our social duty. If an individual existed in solitude, Smith asserts, he could

> no more think of his own character, of the propriety or demerit of his own sentiments and conduct, of the beauty or deformity of his own mind, than of the beauty or deformity of his own face. All these are ob-

jects which he cannot easily see, which naturally he does not look at, and upon which he is provided with no mirror to enable him to turn his eyes. Bring him into society, and he is immediately provided with the mirror which he wanted before. It is placed in the countenance and behaviour of those he lives with. (254–55)

This passage immediately follows one of Smith's most forceful delineations of the "impartial spectator," the "supposed equitable judge" who "by sympathy" could place himself or herself "thoroughly . . . into all the passions and motives" (254). The Stoic idea that sympathy is a principle of attraction that coheres society is probably Smith's foundation here—though, as we saw earlier, the need for imaginative projection exceeds such an idea. Yet if the feelings of the man upon the rack cannot be fully identifiable, and the best we can do is to "conceive ourselves enduring all the same torments" (even to the point where we "enter as it were into his body" via the imagination), this lack of complete identification does not entirely undermine the possibility for positing such imaginative acts of sympathy as the basis for action in the social world.

This shift away from religion to sociology and from law to psychology marks the *Theory* as a seminal indicator of wider cultural shifts. Taking the long view, Raymond Williams noted the decisive movement in the century from theoretical models of social conduct to ideas of affective response, whereby a spectator became a "consumer of feelings"; a movement that influenced how the tragic hero was regarded, and also the actors who portrayed him.[35] What is perhaps most remarkable, however, is the need for affective union that Smith is expressing. As David Marshall points out, it was the prospect of anti-social isolation that most motivated his thoughts:

> For Smith, the impossibility of sympathy is founded in a system that insists on the distance between people, depends on that distance, and dreams of making that distance disappear. . . . Smith takes as a presupposition the separateness of other minds, the limitations of our ability to share other people's feelings.[36]

As Marshall's overview implies, the idea of the "impartial spectator" has, in the last analysis, to be an ideal one. And yet, the ideal could also act socially, as a checks-and-balances concept constructed not only out of one's playhouse experiences but out of a broader model of spectatorship. While 'acting' possesses overtones of simulation, the word shades off, in Smith, into a more technical sense of being an agent in the wider world. When Hume's theatre-goer enters the auditorium he expects a communal sensorium, where the whole feels more than the mere sum of its parts.[37] The net effect of the *Theory* is far different. Similarly, Smith did not resort to Hutcheson's moral sense psychology, as he was not persuaded that anyone securely possessed such an intuition. Instead, in 1759, it was habitual—even vigilant—(self-)reflection that provided the emotional ties through which, Smith hoped, egoistical self-absorption might be diluted and turned to a range of valuable social virtues.

If there is a virtue in providing a snapshot view of cultural history centered on just one year, then it is to bring to the fore synchronic preoccupations. By 1790, Smith's more doubtful—or wishful—thoughts became understated, and reliance on his own brand of Stoic principles strengthened. In 1759 itself, the need for a confrontation with social fragmentation and personal isolation was shared by several others. Alexander Gerard, in *An Essay on Taste*, optimistically regarded the "suspense, anxiety, terror" of tragedy as transformed, when "infused by sympathy," into an intense and noble satisfaction. For Gerard, imagination, by an "inexplicable" force aided by sympathy, provided an "associating power" whereby the "rude and indigested chaos" of raw materials was alchemized into "connection."[38] Less optimistically, Johnson's *Rasselas* followed not just his protagonists but also a whole gallery of characters whose aspirations are thwarted by social disconnection: from the philosopher who finds, on the death of his only daughter, that "all human friendship is useless," and that he has become "a lonely being disunited from society" (chapter 18); or the hermit who is laudable in his "perpetual perseverance," yet leaves himself open to the charge of "desertion of duty" by his choice of reclusiveness (chapter 22); to the contemplation of a single life, which is not, in itself, perennially an evil, yet which leads one to the conclusion that "to live without feeling or exciting sympathy, to be fortunate without adding to the felicity of others, or afflicted without tasting the balm of pity" involves one in "a state more gloomy than solitude" (chapter 27).[39] It is perhaps but a small step, though, from this gloomy prospect to Johnson's appreciation (as recorded by Boswell) of a "civilized society" in which "we all depend upon each other, and [where] our happiness is very much owing to the good opinion of mankind."[40] As these Johnsonian examples suggest, even if all human wishes are vain, loneliness, isolation, and solitude only registered as negative from the perspective of the desirable sociability that Smithian sympathy was designed to encourage.

On the other hand, the perspective on the *Theory* that looks no further than the first edition alerts us to its lack of assurance and its merely tentative sense that the (freely chosen) inculcation of moral sentiments will be sufficient. In attempting to surpass Hutcheson's reliance on benevolence with the indispensable check of justice, Smith dwells more than one would expect on the fragility of social consonance:

> Society . . . cannot subsist among those who are at all times ready to hurt and injure one another. The moment that injury begins, the moment that mutual resentment and animosity take place, all the bands of it are broke asunder, and the different members of which it consisted are, as it were, dissipated and scattered abroad by the violence and opposition of their discordant affections. . . . Men, though naturally sympathetic, feel so little for another, with whom they have no particular connexion, in comparison of what they feel for themselves . . . a man would enter an assembly of men as he enters a den of lions. (189–90)

When Frank McLynn finds 1759 a year that marks Britain's self-confident mastery, the evidence he marshals is incontrovertible.[41] Merchant and military adventures paid off abroad; entrepreneurship and invention accelerated at home. At the same time, there was a price: what Smith revealed just as consistently as this exterior assurance was his sense of the frailty of common feeling and the insistent need for it not to be neglected. Take but sympathy away and hark what discord follows. There is some way to go before we reach the protection of the "invisible hand" that promotes an end uncatered-for by human volition in *The Wealth of Nations*.[42]

Notes

1. See Ian Simpson Ross, *The Life of Adam Smith*, 2nd ed. (Oxford: Oxford University Press, 2010), 71, and Nicholas Phillipson, *Adam Smith: An Enlightened Life* (London: Allen Lane, 2010), 65. According to a reviewer later in the century, Smith earned a reprimand from the Heads of Balliol College for reading Hume: "the heads of the college thought proper to visit his chamber, and finding Hume's *Treatise of Human Nature*, then recently published, the reverend inquisitors seized that heretical book, and severely reprimanded the young philosopher" (*Monthly Review*, n. s., 22 [January 1797], 60).

2. *The Correspondence of Adam Smith*, ed. Ernest Campbell Mossner and Ian Simpson Ross, 2nd ed. (Oxford: Oxford University Press, 1987), 40.

3. Adam Smith, *The Theory of Moral Sentiments*, ed. D. D. Raphael and A. L. MacFie (Oxford: Oxford University Press, 1976). References will be to this edition, and will be given parenthetically.

4. See Adam Smith, *Theorie der ethischen Gefühle*, trans. and ed. Walther Eckstein, 2 vols. (Leipzig: Carl Gerolds Sohn, 1926), 1:xlii–xliv.

5. *Spectator* no. 1 (1 March 1711), in *The Spectator*, ed. Donald F. Bond, 5 vols. (Oxford: Clarendon Press, 1965), 1:2–5.

6. *Spectator* no. 274 (14 January 1712), in *The Spectator*, 2:568.

7. *Spectator* no. 564 (7 July 1714), in *The Spectator*, 4:525. See also Addison's projection of himself as an "impartial Spectator" in his dedication of the collection to John Lord Somers, Baron of Evesham: *The Spectator*, 8 vols. (London: Jacob and Richard Tonson, 1757), sig. A.

8. The most succinct description of this process can be found in D. D. Raphael, *The Impartial Spectator: Adam Smith's Moral Philosophy* (Oxford: Clarendon Press, 2007), 34–42.

9. The technical senses of "sympathy" and "imagination" are discussed in Alexander Broadie, "Sympathy and the Impartial Spectator," in *The Cambridge Companion to Adam Smith*, ed. Knud Haakonssen (Cambridge: Cambridge University Press, 2006), 158–88, and Charles L. Griswold, "Imagination: Morals, Sciences, and Arts," in *Cambridge Companion to Adam Smith*, 22–56.

10. Henry Home, Lord Kames, *Essays on the Principles of Morality and Natural Religion*, 2nd ed. (London: C. Hitch, L. Hawes, R. and J. Dodsley, and others, 1758). Kames's view is expressed most clearly in Part I, essay ii, chaps. 3–4 (especially pp. 40–41).

11. Thomas Hobbes, *Leviathan*, ed. Richard Tuck (Cambridge: Cambridge University Press, 1991), 117.

12. Francis Hutcheson, *An Inquiry into the Original of our Ideas of Beauty and Virtue in Two Treatises*, ed. Wolfgang Leidhold (Indianapolis: Liberty Fund, 2008), 168.

13. This is most clearly explained in his "Illustrations upon the MORAL SENSE," in *An Essay on the Nature and Conduct of the Passions and Affections*, ed. Andrew Ward (Manchester: Clinamen Press, 1999), 139–43.

14. David Hume, *An Enquiry concerning the Principles of Morals*, in *Enquiries concerning Human Understanding and concerning the Principles of Morals*, ed. L. A. Selby-Bigge, 3rd ed., rev. and ed. P. H. Nidditch (Oxford: Clarendon Press, 1996), 289 (Appendix 1: "Concerning Moral Sentiment"), 276 (section ix).

15. It should also be noted that, according to Smith, the more that we depend on this internal examination, the more we become capable of autonomous ethical judgments. See Jerry Evensky, *Adam Smith's Moral Philosophy: A Historical and Contemporary Perspective on Markets, Law, Ethics, and Culture* (Cambridge: Cambridge University Press, 2005), 46–47.

16. John Mullan, *Sentiment and Sociability: The Language of Feeling in the Eighteenth Century* (Oxford: Clarendon Press, 1988), 47. Mullan perhaps overstates Hume's postmodernity, as there is a point, for Hume, at which this personal scrutiny determines action.

17. T. D. Campbell traces the necessary semantic alternation between an "empirical ideal type" and the fruits of direct sensitivity to actual observation: *Adam Smith's Science of Morals* (London: George Allen and Unwin, 1971), 127–45. See also Raphael, *Impartial Spectator*, 27–29, 31–34.

18. Mullan, *Sentiment and Sociability*, 47.

19. See Raphael and McFie's introduction to *Theory of Moral Sentiments*, 15–20; Ross, *Life of Adam Smith*, 188–208; and Phillipson, *Adam Smith*, 269–74.

20. See Hume, *A Treatise of Human Nature*, in *A Treatise of Human Nature: A Critical Edition*, ed. David Fate Norton and Mary J. Norton, 2 vols. (Oxford: Clarendon Press, 2007), 1:367–78 (III. iii.1), and *Enquiry concerning the Principles of Morals*, in *Enquiries*, 268–78 (IX.i).

21. There may be a certain disingenuousness in this, for Hume did advance a more sophisticated line of argument in *A Treatise of Human Nature*, III.iii.5, and in his *Enquiry concerning the Principles of Morals*, V.i.1n. See *A Treatise of Human Nature: A Critical Edition*, 1:391–93, and *Enquiries*, 213.

22. This is exemplified at length (in some terms borrowed from Hume) in section I.i.1–4.

23. This was originally inserted between III.1.3 and 4. A revised account of this stage in the argument became III.1.6 from the second edition on. Smith clarifies the possible division of the self into an "examiner and judge" and the "person whose conduct is examined into and judged of," or the division between spectator and agent. One cannot conceive of the self as identical with the judge in this regard: "But that the judge should, in every respect, be the same with the panel [Scots for "the accused"] is as impossible, as that the cause should, in every respect, be the same with the effect" (113).

24. Although Smith would not have recognized the terminology, there is a "dialogism," or lack of final confirmation, at crucial junctures in his *Theory*; see Vivienne Brown, "Dialogism, the Gaze, and the Emergence of Economic Discourse," *New Literary History* 28 (1997): 697–710.

25. Raphael and McFie, introduction to *Theory of Moral Sentiments*, 16.

26. This is succinctly summarised in Ross, *Life of Adam Smith*, 181–85.

27. Cicero, *De Finibus Bonorum et Malorum*, ed. H. Rackham (London: Loeb Library, 1914), 261–63.

28. *Spectator* no. 411 (21 June 1712): "It is but opening the Eye and the Scene enters. The Colours paint themselves on the Fancy, with very little Attention of Thought or Application of Mind in the Beholder" (*The Spectator*, 3:538).

29. Phillipson, *Adam Smith*, 151.

30. John Wilkins, *Of the Principles and Duties of Natural Religion* (1675), 8th ed. (London: R. Bonwicke, W. Freeman, J. Walthoe, and others, 1722), 219–20 (quoting *Enchiridion*, chap. 23).

31. *Epictetus his Morals, with Simplicius his Comment, made English from the Greek*, ed. and trans. George Stanhope (London: Richard Sare and William Hindmarsh, 1694), 414.

32. Smith, *The Theory of Moral Sentiments*, 6th ed. (London: W. Strahan and T. Cadell, 1790), 350.

33. It is worth mentioning here the honorable notice given by Smith to Voltaire's tragedy, *Mahomet* (1741), which portrays the agonies of Seid and Palmira (who are, due to a religious commandment, duped into executing someone who turns out to be their father). Their inner debates and deep remorse are instructive, and thus motivated by a correct ethical concern (313–14).

34. There is a further reservation concerning the possibility that his own direct experience of drama was minimal. There was no public playhouse in Glasgow in 1759. Raphael notes that, in 1762, Smith served on a University committee that actually ruled against the establishment of one: *Impartial Spectator*, 91–92.

35. Raymond Williams, *Modern Tragedy* (London: Hogarth, 1992), 27.

36. David Marshall, *The Figure of Theater: Shaftesbury, Defoe, Adam Smith, and George Eliot* (New York: Columbia University Press, 1986), 180.

37. For Hume, one's entry into a theatre entails a communion in "one common amusement," leading to a "superior sensibility or disposition of being affected with every sentiment, which [one] shares with [one's] fellow-creatures." See *An Enquiry concerning the Principles of Morals*, in *Enquiries*, 221 (V.ii).

38. Alexander Gerard, *An Essay on Taste* (London: A. Millar, A. Kincaid, and J. Bell, 1759), 54, 60, 174, 221.

39. Samuel Johnson, *The History of Rasselas, Prince of Abyssinia*, in *Rasselas and Other Tales*, ed. Gwin J. Kolb, vol. 16 of *The Yale Edition of the Works of Samuel Johnson* (New Haven: Yale University Press, 1990), 75, 84, 98–99.

40. *Boswell's Life of Johnson*, ed. George Birkbeck Hill, rev. L. F. Powell, 6 vols. (Oxford: Clarendon Press, 1934–1950), 1:440 (20 July 1763). For the most succinct account of Johnson's determination to hold faith in social integration (and integrity) during the writing of *Rasselas*, see James L. Clifford, *Dictionary Johnson: The Middle Years of Samuel Johnson* (London: Heinemann, 1979), 204–21.

41. Frank McLynn, *1759: The Year Britain Became Master of the World* (London: Jonathan Cape, 2004).

42. Smith, *An Inquiry into the Nature and Causes of the Wealth of Nations*, ed. R. H. Campbell, A. S. Skinner, and W. B. Todd, 2 vols. (Oxford: Oxford University Press, 1976), 1:456 (IV.ii). There are earlier traces of this notion in Smith's writing, most directly in his *Theory of Moral Sentiments* (IV.i.10), but there the reference is only to the most efficient means of distribution: see Smith, *Theory*, 184–85.

4

ALONGSIDE THE WELL-KNOWN literary masterpieces published in 1759—Sterne's *Tristram Shandy*, Johnson's *Rasselas*, and Voltaire's *Candide*—the public of the day was enthralled by the brilliance, opulence, and intrigues of the lives of the notorious eighteenth-century courtesans, Fanny Murray and Kitty Fisher, which appeared in print that year. According to *The Memoirs of the Celebrated Miss Fanny Murray*, in her heyday "scarce a magazine appeared without an ode, or an acrostic upon Fanny. The portrait painters supplicated it as a favour to have her likeness—and every print-shop window presented you with Fanny in metzotinto."[1] By the time that the *Memoirs* was published in 1759, Fanny was married, and it was Kitty Fisher whose star was in the ascendancy. In the course of 1759, Fisher was the subject of several portraits by Sir Joshua Reynolds and at least three satirical pamphlets or broadsheets, in addition to the biography. It was said of her, indeed, that all "tea-table talk was entirely concerning her, and the female visitor who could not bring in a fresh story about her was scarcely welcome."[2] Such was Fisher's celebrity and the fascination she commanded, that one satirical poem identified her as a uniquely potent threat to the war effort. In "The Stream of Kitty" (1759), Britain is represented as poised on the brink of victory against the French; about to deliver "The last but great, decisive Blow" yet in grave danger of losing the advantage because "her Men of Might, / So famous, and renown'd in Fight" are "Now turn'd Dupes of K---y F----r" and "shun *Bellopra's* dire Alarms / To revel in an Harlot's Arms."[3]

This representation of martial manhood, sapped by the lure of luxury in the guise of a prostitute, derives from the history of the fall of Rome, as handed down to the eighteenth century by classical-republican political theorists such as Sallust and Livy and, later, Machiavelli.[4] As Britain became wealthier and, in the terms of this narrative, more luxurious, it was a history that increasingly exercised the minds of classically educated gentlemen. 'Luxury' in this discourse can be understood broadly as referring to all those things which are not absolutely necessary to existence and, more generally, to the idea of unbounded appetite.[5] The outbreak of the Seven Years' War in 1756 only fuelled this preoccupation, prompting a spate of publications that used the story of the fall of Rome to warn against the potentially disastrous consequences for the nation of allowing luxury a free rein. 1757, for instance, saw the publication of *The Tryal of Lady Allurea Luxury* and John Brown's *Estimate of the Manners and Principles of the Times*; while in 1759, Edward Montagu published *Reflections on the Rise and Fall of the Antient Republicks. Adapted to the Present State of Great Britain*. All of these texts worry at the issue of whether Britain will be sapped of its martial strength as a result of luxury running rampant. In this essay, I want to argue that it is the urgency and prominence of this classical-republican history of the fall of Rome, in the contemporary cultural imagination, which places stories about the lives of prostitutes center stage in 1759. The various versions of these prostitutes' lives, I shall suggest, are freighted with significance far beyond their immediate subject matter. The essay will consider three substantial publications concerning the lives of prostitutes which were all published anonymously in 1759: *The Memoirs of the Celebrated Miss Fanny Murray*; *The Uncommon Adventures of Miss Kitty F****r*; and *The Histories of Some of the Penitents in the Magdalen-House*. I will be concerned to think about the extent to which these narratives engage with the anxieties about the fall of Rome which surrounded their creation, and will argue that they all, to a greater or lesser extent, work to contain these anxieties through a recuperation of the prostitute as a sentimental figure.

Before turning to the works themselves, it will be helpful to trace the contours of the contemporaneous 'fall of Rome' narratives, which provide such a crucial context for understanding the appeal of these prostitute memoirs. For John Brown in the *Estimate of the Manners and Principles of the Times*, "Vanity, Luxury and Effeminacy" had "increased beyond all Belief" within the previous twenty years. In the context of the "Crisis" of war, he is prompted to ask whether the nation has entered that "last Period of *Degeneracy*" as described in Machiavelli's account of declining Rome.[6] In 1759, Edward Montagu is similarly concerned to "compare the present state of our own country with that of Rome and Carthage," quickly concluding that "we shall find that we resemble them most when in their declining period."[7] As these works suggest, during the final years of the decade Brown and Montagu were both preoccupied with the relationship between the increase of commerce (and its bedfellow, luxury) and the decline of nations. It is, though, to *The Tryal of Lady Allurea Luxury* that we need to turn to find an explicit connection between luxury and prostitution.

The Tryal of Lady Allurea Luxury dramatizes the debate about the social, moral, and martial implications of luxury in the form of a legal trial. Luxury, in this dramatization, is played by Lady Allurea; who, we are told, came over to England in the same ship as Charles II at the Restoration: "His Majesty was very fond of her: She lay in the same Cabbin."[8] Allurea was, in other words, a courtesan. The case for the prosecution asserts that:

> for near a Century past, [she] hath most wickedly and maliciously plotted and conspired the Destruction of this Land, by corrupting the Morals of our People, and endeavouring, to the utmost of her Power, to eraze out of their Hearts every Sentiment of Humanity and Religion . . . [that] she hath made use of the most diabolical Arts to bewitch the People to their Ruin—to make them in Love with Sloth and Idleness—to be base, venal, indolent, and cowardly—to give themselves up to empty Amusements, false Pleasures, and the lowest and most unworthy sensualities. (6–7)

Witnesses for the prosecution include representatives from the aristocracy, the city, and the military. The aristocrat, Lord Good-Mind, testifies that his fortune has been ruined after Lady Allurea struck up an acquaintance with his family. Allurea is accused of seducing the Lord into abandoning his country seat and his wife into eating "Frenchified Dishes" and lolling "on a couch most of the Time that she was not in Bed, at Cards or at her Toilet" (13). Three hundred citizens appear next to represent the city, arguing that Lady Allurea has insinuated her way into "most of the trading Families in the great Cities of London and Westminster" and that, in consequence, many of these, to support their pleasures, have abandoned genuine "Trade" for "Stockjobbing and Sharping" (17). Finally, it is the turn of the military to testify against Luxury. First, the army General testifies that Lady Luxury had made so much

> Progress in debauching the *B------ Soldiery,* that if your hardy, young, and Royal G------ had not in our last Campaigns interposed, and ordered her to be drummed out of every Corps, instead of an Army of Soldiers, we should soon have been reduced to an Hospital of Invalids. (23–24)

Next, the naval Captain describes how Luxury seduced all of his men and then set to work on him with her blandishments, contending that she was such a threat that he had to command that she be tied up. The Captain's recommendation is that Luxury should be burnt to death, or else "the wooden Walls of *England* don't signify a Rush" (28). Like the texts by Brown and Montagu, the *Tryal* is suffused with a sense that military crisis is lending a new currency to the 'fall of Rome' narrative. In summing up, the Attorney General argues that

> *Rome* fell by the Devices of the Prisoner—so did *Greece*—and so must ever free State where she is suffered to take up her Residence—She can assume all Shapes—and, by her Blandishments, soften and effeminate the bravest, roughest, and honestest of Mankind—even the *British* Sailors. (75)

Above all, *The Tryal of Lady Allurea Luxury* shows how closely prostitution was associated with luxury, and how closely it was therefore tied up in the public mind with anxiety over the war effort. The *Tryal* fleshes out the substantial history that lurks behind the accusations made in "The Stream of Kitty," and adds substance to the identification of Kitty Fisher as a direct threat to British imperial expansion. In these ways, the *Tryal* suggests how it was that the luxurious lives of prostitutes were such a subject of fascination for the British public in 1759.

If we turn now to the two most prominent prostitute memoirs published in 1759—*The Memoirs of the Celebrated Miss Fanny Murray* and *The Uncommon Adventures of Miss Kitty F****r*—it very soon becomes clear that their heroines function as personifications of luxury. The memoirs chart the vicissitudes of these women's lives, the swinging to-and-fro between abject poverty and extreme opulence. In their periods of greatest success, both women are described as eclipsing all the rest of society in their luxury. As Mistress of Lord Ramble, for instance, Fanny Murray "not only outshone the most brilliant in beauty and dress, but also in retinue" (1:26). This period of luxury is punctuated by Ramble's death, following which Fanny descends rapidly into common prostitution, though not for long— she soon works her way back up to the world of keeping and becomes the mistress of another Lord. At this point, again, her "splendid equipage . . . numerous retinue . . . elegant furnished house . . . handsome allowance . . . wardrobe of the most gorgeous apparel, and . . . casket of . . . valuable jewels" make her "the envy of women, [and] more than ever the object of men's desire" (1:80). Indeed, Fanny is not just the envy of all women; she becomes the standard of what all women, "from the middling station" to "the most elevated," should aspire to. "Whatever she wears is the law of fashion," we are told; "her tyranny in mode is complete"

(1:81). Like Lady Allurea Luxury, Fanny might thus be understood as seducing all the ladies of Great Britain into emulation of her luxuries. In fact, as I will discuss later, *The Memoirs of the Celebrated Miss Fanny Murray* puts a rather different gloss on the idea of Fanny's role as a trend-setter. Elsewhere, though, the story of her corrupting influence is visible. Indeed, in *The Uncommon Adventures of Miss Kitty F****r*, Fanny features precisely as an 'Allurea Luxury' figure.

In *The Uncommon Adventures*, which is set in Madrid as part of a pretence that "Kitty F****r" does not refer to the famous London prostitute (Catherine 'Kitty' Fisher), Kitty is drawn into prostitution by the lure of Fanny Murray's luxury. The success of Murray (here styled Miss Murrio) in "keeping her equipage, and being the general toast of the gay and polite," the text informs us, "operated upon the minds of most of the girls of an ambitious turn in Madrid; those who were handsome, saw every time they looked in the glass all the conquest and grandeur that attended miss Murrio" (1:19). Miss Murrio, we are told, was a "greater incentive . . . to prostitution than all the arts of men, or the force of inclination" (1:19). It is this incentive which finally persuades Kitty F****r to abandon her respectable but dull life as a milliner for the life of a courtesan. Like Murray, Kitty goes on to live in the greatest luxury: "Her equipage was one of the most brilliant in Madrid; her house as elegantly furnished as any in that metropolis, [and] her table as sumptuous" (2:17). The prostitutes in these memoirs, then, are textbook representations of the allure and dangers of luxury. Indeed, the fact that many of the anecdotes told about their respective excesses are similar (and, in at least one case, identical) seems to emphasize the symbolic nature of these figures as representations of luxury.

This symbolic function is borne out, for example, by the anecdote of the bank-note. In *The Memoirs of the Celebrated Miss Fanny Murray*, the editor describes how one of the stories circulating about Fanny's luxurious excess is that she made "her breakfast off bank notes between bread and butter" (1:82). Elsewhere, this anecdote is widely attributed to Kitty Fisher. In his *History of My Life*, which was completed sometime around 1798, for instance, Casanova recounts an anecdote of Kitty Fisher swallowing an "hundred-pound bank note on a slice of buttered bread which [had been given to her by] Sir Richard Atkins, brother to the beautiful Mrs. Pitt."[9] Writing slightly earlier, another foreigner, Johann Wilhelm von Archenholz, described in *A Picture of England* (1789) how the Duke of York, brother to the King, had tried to secure Kitty's attentions by leaving a present of fifty pounds on her toilet. At this point in her career Kitty was commanding a hundred guineas a night, and was so "much offended" by this meager offering that "to show how much she despised his present, she clapt the bank-note between two slices of bread and butter, and ate it for her breakfast."[10] Fanny and Kitty, it seems, are interchangeable symbols of luxurious indulgence.

As the art historian Marcia Pointon argues, the sense of these high class courtesans representing the pinnacle of luxury is underlined, in the autumn of 1759, by Reynolds's decision to paint Kitty Fisher as Cleopatra. In this portrait, Cleopatra is depicted as being about to consume "the largest pearl ever known" as part of a wager with Anthony. In choosing to portray Fisher as Cleopatra, Pointon says, Reynolds "connects a courtesan reputed to have swallowed a bank-note to a quintessential moment of luxurious consumption." Other accounts of Kitty, Pointon argues, take this line further, depicting her as the embodiment of all those phantasmagoric economic practices associated with the liberalization of finance in the 1690s, such as "stock-jobbing" and "usury." Pointon quotes from the *Odd Letter*, a work of 1760, in which the pseudonymous author, "Simon Trusty," describes his incredulity at Kitty's phenomenal capacity for making money without having anything of substance to trade. Addressing Kitty, he says: "You have found the Way of melting down your Youth into Treasure, and converting perishable Beauty into solid Gold." The point, Pointon argues, is that prostitution "generates income without (the inference is) honest toil; its profits seem immeasurably great and its conduct uncontrollable."[11]

In *The Tryal of Lady Allurea Luxury*, as we saw above, luxury is associated precisely with the new forms of finance. Luxury has lured city families away from a genuine trade in things and into a love affair with stock-jobbing, and cast them into the unpredictability and volatility associated with this new practice. The trauma of the South Sea Bubble of 1720, the first ever stock market crash, was still very much part of the cultural memory in 1759, a constant reminder of the insubstantial nature of this trade and of the potentially disastrous consequences of unfettered desire. The Bubble was, as Emma Clery has argued, very much bound up, in the public mind, with the dangerous desires of women.[12] Simon Trusty's description of Kitty Fisher's miraculous accumulation of money seems to lead us directly back to this association. Indeed, both *The Memoirs of the Celebrated Miss Fanny Murray* and *The Uncommon Adventures of Miss Kitty F****r* clearly envisage their protagonists as stocks in the marketplace, whose value is subject to epic fluctuations. Fanny Murray, in particular, veers from nosegay seller, to mistress in high keeping, to fiancée, to common prostitute, to brothel prostitute, then back to high keeping. Twice, she is robbed of a secure situation by untimely bereavement, and twice she has marriage snatched away from under her by fortune. She is, as the *Memoirs* makes very clear, a commodity, whose worth fluctuates wildly with the market and who has no intrinsic value. At one period of her life, the mere fact of her bidding for a particular piece of china at an auction immediately doubles the price; at another, she is beset by creditors and can make no money but by entering into a brothel. Kitty Fisher, likewise, swings between destitution, after her reputation prevents her from gaining the most menial of employment, and a life in which she can command a hundred guineas per night.

Fanny and Kitty, then, figure in these various accounts as personifications of luxury generally and, more specifically, of the new financial practices with which it was associated. To this extent, the lives of these celebrity prostitutes engaged, more or less explicitly, with contemporary anxieties about the parallel between modern commercial Britain and Rome in its declining years; in particular, with anxieties about the proliferation of the new, 'luxurious' forms of speculative accumulation. The fact that the Seven Years' War was funded almost entirely by these intangible modes of finance can only have added a new piquancy to these narratives.

Strikingly, however, the prostitutes' lives published in 1759 are not, ultimately, narratives of decline and fall. Rather, they are narratives of triumph: fairy tales in which the heroines end up happily ever after. The narratives are as reassuring in their own way, to a population in the midst of war, as the sentimental 'weepies' devoured by cinema-goers during the Second World War. At the end of the second volume of the *Memoirs*, Fanny Murray is granted an annuity of two hundred pounds a year by the son of the man who originally seduced her—an annuity that allows her to secure a husband. She has, the narrative tells us, returned to the "path of virtue" and become the "best of wives" (2:119). We leave Kitty Fisher in a slightly more insecure situation. She is not married, but she is at the top of her game, and the *Uncommon Adventures* ends with her receipt of two letters, one from Fanny M----- (presumably Fanny Murray), the other from another high class courtesan, Lucy -----. Both advise her to capitalize on her current good fortune in order to create a stable future for herself. Fanny's letter, for instance, states that "You have still an opportunity of making a handsome provision for yourself. Act prudently for a while, reform, and live virtuous" (2:21–22), while the other letter, from Lucy, advises her to "Take care of your cards now you have so good a hand" (2:23). Fanny's future is assured, and Kitty's all but so. Thus, while both Fanny Murray and Kitty Fisher are embodiments of luxury, whose fate is clearly tied up with the 'fall of Rome' narrative, they do not ultimately fall; rather, they offer a sentimental containment of this narrative. Murray and Fisher are recuperable, or potentially recuperable, I would argue, because they are both framed as fundamentally sentimental figures: they have natural delicacy, good sense, good taste, and compassion, which act to curb the fatal excesses of luxury, and which are sometimes imagined to walk hand-in-hand with luxury.

In this respect, the narratives have more in common with John Brown's *Estimate of the Manners and Principles of the Times* and with *The Tryal of Lady Allurea Luxury* than they do with Edward Montagu's *Reflections on the Rise and Fall of the Antient Republicks*. Montagu is convinced that the current luxury will end in disaster, whereas both the *Estimate* and the *Tryal* hold out the possibility, however grudgingly, that the growth of luxury is in some sense intimately allied with the growth of a moral sense, and that this may ultimately prove to be the salvation of the nation. In the *Estimate*, Brown embraces the traditional classical-republican model of commercial expansion as a three-stage cycle—a model that can be traced back to Plato's *Republic*. Brown argues that, in its first stages, commerce "supplies mutual Necessities . . . extends mutual Knowledge . . . and spreads mutual Humanity." In its middle period, it "provides Conveniences . . . gives Birth to Arts and Science, creates equal Laws, diffuses general Plenty and general Happiness." In its final stage, however, it changes its "Nature and Effects": "It brings in Superfluity and vast Wealth; begets Avarice, gross Luxury, or effeminate Refinement among the higher Ranks, together with general Loss of Principle" (152–53). Mid-eighteenth-century Britain, Brown argues, is showing the symptoms of this third stage—and yet he goes on to reassure his readers that the British will avoid destruction, confident as he is that Britain has been in possession of "the Spirit of *Liberty, Humanity*, and *Equity*, [which] in a *certain Degree* [is] yet left among us" (28). Brown is adamant that by this "Spirit of Humanity" he understands something very different from that which is usually understood by the moral-sense writers of the mid-century. Brown does not, he says, mean "that Smoothness and refined Polish of external Manners, by which the present Age affects to be distinguished." Rather, he means "that Pity for Distress, that Moderation in limiting Punishments by their proper Ends and Measures, by which this Nation hath always been distinguished" (20–21). Yet, as Brown enlarges upon his description of this ancient "humanity" which is to counter the deleterious effects of luxury, it becomes increasingly difficult to maintain the distinction between the humanity produced by "unmanly delicacy"—which is tantamount to refined sensibility—and the traditional "humanity" of a less commercial age. Brown goes on, for example, to suggest that gifts to charity are the greatest indication of the humanity he is describing. Moreover, he is led at one point fleetingly to wonder whether the "humanity" he describes is not itself a product of "effeminacy." This observation, he comments in a candid moment, might well be a "Question more *curious* in its Progress, than *agreeable* in its Solution" (64). In the main, Brown is determined to refute the notion that *his* idea of "humanity" is the "humanity" of sentimentality, for this he associates with the effeminacy attendant on the influence of luxury. Yet he is at a loss to find any other precedent for his idea, and so is forced to conclude that it may indeed have its roots in commerce and luxury.

This reluctant recognition that "humanity" and "moral sentiment" could emerge from luxury is also a feature of *The Tryal of Lady Allurea Luxury*. Although the court ultimately convicts Luxury, the argument for the defense is adamant that the characteristically modern virtue of sentiment, or humanity, is inextricably linked with the growth of luxury. The bishop bearing witness in her defense describes her as:

> one of the best of Women—her whole Life seems to be devoted to the Welfare, the Ease, and the Happiness of Mankind—In short, till this Nation felt the Effects of her Benevolence, we were but so many *Hottentots*.—She has refined our Taste, enlarged our Commerce, and perfected our Politics and Religion. (36)

The defense of Lady Allurea Luxury apparently turns the 'fall of Rome' narrative upside down. It valorizes luxury, not by countering the argument that it is damaging to the masculine attributes that in the classical-republican tradition constitute virtue, but by insisting that virtue is properly characterized by the attributes of femininity. Effeminacy, with all its implications of indolence and unbounded desire, is thus co-opted for virtue, and is newly dressed up as humanity and sensibility.

Neither Brown nor the author of *The Tryal of Lady Allurea Luxury* is sanguine about the true nature of luxury, yet it is clear that neither is able to avoid a dialogue with the ideas of the pro-commercial moral-sense philosophy, which increasingly dominated cultural discourse in the 1750s. It is also clear, as various cultural historians have established, that because moral-sense philosophy was built around the "feminization" of virtue—the re-spinning of effeminacy as a positive characteristic—this dialogue was inevitably inflected by discussion of the nature of femininity.[13] As it emerged in the work of Shaftesbury at the beginning of the eighteenth century—and as it was taken up, built upon, and modified in the subsequent work of Kames, Hume, and Smith—moral-sense philosophy mobilized around two key ideas. The first was that virtue is beautiful and that all men (and, particularly, women) are naturally in possession of an aesthetic sense which can discriminate between good and evil—much as one's taste buds can distinguish between a pleasant and an unpleasant taste. The second is the argument that this moral sense can be refined or blunted by one's commerce with the world. This second argument is central to David Hume's essay, "Of Refinement in the Arts," in which he argues that the ages of refinement—which are the ages of luxury—are both the happiest and the most virtuous, for "The more men refine upon pleasure, the less will they indulge in excesses of any kind."[14] Hume's argument, like Brown's above, is evidently founded on the various classical-republican descriptions of the second stage of commerce, in which commercial activity, and even luxurious desires, are represented as temporarily beneficent. In Plato's *Republic*, by contrast, such desires start to enfeeble the population, requiring a group of self-disciplined "guardians" to emerge in order to defend the state. Yet even this will not be sufficient to contain the deleterious consequences of luxury. Eventually, for Plato, even the guardians will succumb to the desire for material acquisition, so that the Republic will itself become enfeebled through luxurious self-indulgence.[15]

Hume's optimistic reworking of the classical-republican cycle rejects the idea that the second stage of development will end in corruption and decay. For Hume, the cycle of commercial corruption can be arrested, and there is cause for optimism about a future of economic and moral progress. Civilization, it seems, will become ever more refined and ever more benevolent (278). This optimism is founded on the fact that, unlike Plato and the Roman historians, Hume does not stake the continued virtue of the luxurious society in a small group of self-disciplined guardians remaining at a distance from the realities of the world. Rather, Hume's confidence rests on the men of commerce themselves: men who are immersed in the production and consumption of luxurious items. Through commerce in its broadest sense, individuals are refined and improved in their taste and morals, particularly in their "humanity." For this reason, it is the men of the "middling rank" who, in Hume's opinion, are "the best and firmest basis of public liberty" (277). Their "assiduity in honest industry" creates a "new vigour" in the mind, which satisfies the "natural appetites, and prevents the growth of unnatural ones, which commonly spring up, when nourished by ease and idleness" (270).

In this manner, Hume arrests the classical-republican cycle before it fulfils itself in corruption and national decline. Hume does, however, retain the rigid gendering of the classical-republican argument. Luxury is described by Hume with the conventional attributes of effeminacy: it "softens" the tempers of men and leads them to "mildness and moderation." Yet here, this effeminacy is itself described as "the chief characteristic which distinguishes a civilized age from times of barbarity and ignorance" (273–74). The effeminacy attendant upon luxury in the classical-republican account has been re-spun as the "mildness," "softness," and "humanity" necessary to the success of a modern state. The idea of luxury was thus well on its way to being redefined for a modern commercial age as a positive and largely desirable phenomenon, rather than an inevitable catalyst for social disintegration.[16] As we can see in the lives of Kitty Fisher and Fanny Murray, the prostitute—that most traditional bedfellow of luxury in the classical-republican account—follows not far behind.

As they appear in the narratives of 1759, the fairy-tale reformations (or potential reformations) in the lives of Kitty Fisher and Fanny Murray may possibly feel, as Laura Rosenthal has argued, like a "tail-piece" of morality.[17] Yet I would argue that, particularly in the *Memoirs of the Celebrated Miss Fanny Murray*, moral-sense philosophy is deeply embedded, and that these fairy-tale endings represent the increasing dominance of moral-sense ideas in all discussions of luxury at this time.[18] Neither Kitty Fisher nor Fanny Murray appears at any point as a rapacious whore, motivated by insatiable sexual desire. Indeed, generally, as Rosenthal herself has commented, these narratives are strangely uninterested in sexual activity, and much more concerned with "class and economic concerns."[19] Far from being creatures of insatiable desire, both Kitty and Fanny are represented, in the manner of moral-sense discourse, as naturally virtuous. Kitty Fisher, we learn, has a "good heart, and . . . though her ambition and vanity, nurtured in the soil of parental indulgence, had prompted her to a vicious course of life, she had not divested herself of all moral virtue" (2:9). The evidence of this is that, when she is wealthy, she doesn't forget to look after her family. Fanny Murray's 'memoirs' tell the same story, Fanny herself being

> One whose natural disposition was not vicious, but who, having made a false step, found many obstacles to return in the path of virtue—who was neither avaricious, luxurious, or debauched, further than necessity obliged, but animated with sentiments that would have adorned a much more worthy and exalted station. (2:119–20)

Like Kitty, Fanny also uses her wealth to help her family. What is more, the *Memoirs* embeds a narrative about how Fanny's commerce with society has improved her moral and aesthetic taste and has led to a moderation of her luxurious desires. Fanny, we are told, is decidedly improved by her friendship with a seduced gentlewoman: "All the rusticity of a nosegay girl, or a B—th ring seller, was softened into that easy deportment, which is peculiar to those who move in the most elevated sphere, without that levity or audacity" (1:24). Fanny's manners improve, but so, the text suggests, do her morals. By the end of volume one, Fanny is in high keeping with Sir Richard: "She lived at ease without immerging into any luxurious dissipations or expensive frolicks . . . her mind embellished by learning and experience" (1:108). Indeed, we are told that Fanny lived with such "prudence and oeconomy" that the world was induced to believe she was a wife (1:108). While Fanny is most certainly an embodiment of luxury, then, she is an embodiment of luxury as reworked from the classical-republican model by Hume. She has benefitted from the improvement and refinements attendant on a life of commerce and luxury; indeed, she is a bulwark against its excesses. Her refined tastes are sufficient to make the reader sanguine about her future and, implicitly, about the future of the nation as a whole. Indeed, Fanny becomes a model of luxurious restraint, whose taste is emulated by the polite world at large, and unmatched even by the most respectable aristocrats: "the countess of --- in vain pretended to supplant her. Fanny was never gaudy in dress and but seldom expensive, yet she always gained the victory over her ladyship's extravagant novelties" (2:108–9).

This last point takes us to the heart of the consolatory nature of the *Memoirs*, particularly for an audience in 1759; the idea that the British may be victorious in despite of their luxury, because their luxury is absolutely a luxury of trade and commerce, rather than of indolence. There is a fascinating passage in the *Memoirs* in which Fanny goes to France and is shocked by the luxurious excesses of the French: the way in which they indulge in splendor and extravagance without any recourse to the restraint and economy which constitutes good taste in England. Fanny is shocked by the unnatural manners of the court, where all women, regardless of their health, are forced to wear rouge. Yet she is more shocked by the dozens of fallen aristocrats she encounters, who are penniless but nonetheless starving themselves to maintain a luxurious appearance and lifestyle:

> Many of them rose at six in the morning to have their hair dressed fit for a ball, in order to go to the coffee-house; there caper, sing and babille 'till dinner time; when, instead of following the mechanical way of eating, they would take a walk in the *Thuilleries* or the *Palace-royal*; from thence to the Caffe, and from the Caffe back again, 'till the play or opera was over, where they were to shew themselves—for nothing—in every sense of the word. (1:90–91)

The values of these "noble beggars" are, to Fanny, all out of kilter, and when she asks them why they don't think of setting up in trade she is told that in France "to be a merchant is an absolute disgrace" (1:88). For readers in Britain, there must surely have been something very consoling in the idea that French luxury was not subjected to the restraints naturally imposed by an active involvement in trading and commerce, and an intercourse with all of its productions.

This humane, commercial, moral-sense reworking of luxury is also very evident in the discourse surrounding the establishment of the first Magdalen Hospital for Penitent Prostitutes in London, in August 1758. I have argued elsewhere that the establishment of this Hospital marked the high point of the Whiggish, moral-sense discourse in British culture.[20] The Magdalen Hospital represented a significant ideological departure from earlier social schemes to manage prostitution, due to the predominance of its sentimental commitment to the idea that prostitutes were naturally virtuous but unfortunately corrupted. In the words of William Dodd, the notoriously sentimental preacher at the Magdalen House chapel:

> the nobleness of virtue, and the delicacy of sentiment, have been rather canker'd over, than blotted out: and upon the first remove of the filth, have shewn themselves in particulars, which would do honour to the most exalted state and ideas.[21]

The Magdalen Hospital committed to take in these fallen women and to remove the filth; to recuperate them through a regime of prayer and work, and to send them back out into the world as useful citizens. To this extent, the Hospital was a real world attempt to prove that luxury need not be destructive, even in the midst of war. Indeed, as Jennie Batchelor and Megan Hiatt note, Jonas Hanway, one of the founding fathers of the Hospital, explicitly identified the idea of the rehabilitation of prostitutes as "a vital part of the war effort, as vital even, in Hanway's words, as 'the *arduous* affairs of war.'"[22] It was at least partly this aspect of the charity, I would suggest, which captured the contemporary public's imagination, and its generosity, more successfully than any of its rival institutions. Where the Magdalen Hospital raised £3114.17s for its initial appeal, John Fielding's similar (though much more pragmatic) Asylum for the reception of orphaned girls, which also opened in 1758, raised only just over a thousand pounds.[23] Within months of opening, the Sunday sermons at the Magdalen had become so popular that the public had to be requested not to come earlier than 5pm for the 5.30pm service, and by the 1760s they were so fashionable that a system of tickets had to be introduced.[24] It seems likely that at least part of the appeal of the institution was the implicit promise that it held out of being able to recuperate that traditional personification of luxurious desire: the prostitute.

The memoirs of Fanny Murray and Kitty Fisher, which were published in the year following the establishment of the Hospital, clearly relate to, and might be seen as trading on, the popularity of the Magdalen charity. Indeed, the ending of the second volume of the *Memoirs* of Fanny Murray carries distinct echoes of the sermon by William Dodd quoted above, when it states that Fanny's "natural disposition was not vicious" and that she was always "animated by sentiments that would have adorned a much more worthy and exalted station" (2:119–20). Yet there are significant differences between these memoirs and the literature concerning the Magdalen charity more specifically. These differences lie, I would suggest, in the anxiety, constantly present in the Magdalen Hospital literature, that a refined moral sense is not, on its own, a sufficient bulwark against future destruction. This is very clearly the case in the anonymous *Histories of Some of the Penitents in the Magdalen-House*, a novel first published in 1759 in order to promote the cause of the charity. The novel, like the charity itself, proceeds from the sentimental premise that prostitutes are victims of society and explicitly invokes moral-sense theory. The reader is invited to understand the institution as a tribute to the compassion which it is imagined that commerce and refinement have generated in the modern age. The Magdalen Hospital is described, for instance, as the product of commercial men who are "noble, if not by blood or descent, intrinsically so from the generous benevolence of their worthy hearts."[25] As such, it is "an institution which does so much honour to the present age; [and] which will reflect never-fading glory on those who instituted it" (4). The supreme characteristic of the four Magdalens whose stories are given in the *Histories* is delicacy of sensibility. Of the first penitent, Emily, we are told from the outset that her "nature is superior" to any offences against "honesty, or sincerity," and that she has a "tenderness of heart" which may make her susceptible to the snares of the world (13). The second penitent has a delicacy of sentiment which makes her an outsider and a victim in the worldly aristocratic household in which she finds herself. The third penitent, like Emily, has a sensibility which naturally leads her to shy away from the moral laxity of the brothel she is staying in; while the fourth is a thoroughly Romantic soul whose sensibility shudders at the mercenary marriage proposed to her by her father. All three of the penitents who bear children are also shown to have an acute maternal sensibility; and all display a delicacy of taste which prefers elegant simplicity to decadent display.

Sensibility, then, is undoubtedly a highly prized moral attribute in this text. Yet it is also clear that we are not to understand it as a virtue sufficient in itself, at least in terms of this world. Indeed, in the case of these penitents, sensibility is most frequently a contributing factor in their fall. For the three mothers, it is the extent of their maternal sensibility which forces them into prostitution; moreover, the refined sensibilities of these women leave them prey to the machinations of selfish plotters. When Emily, for example, is spontaneously lent money to pay off her debts by an old woman (who turns out to be a bawd), she says "I thought that, in the same situation, I should have done like her; and therefore was grateful, but not surprised" (37). Emily's sister thus turns out to have been correct in her prediction that Emily will be as much in danger from the "tenderness" of her heart as from "the snares that will be laid in her way" (13). Sensibility, moreover, is shown in itself to be very little different to amorous love. When the third penitent, Fanny, goes to live with the Lafew family, she is inspired, by her love for the husband, into the most extravagant acts of benevolence to the family. Among other things, her love for Mr Lafew causes her to risk her life to save one of his children. Here, also, the tender sensibilities of both parties lead them very swiftly into the bedroom. While sensibility may be an exquisite moral attribute (and one cannot be esteemed, in this novel, without it), then, it is not sufficient, in its own right, as an instrument for guiding one through the world. For this, one needs religion. When Emily is forced to choose between becoming a prostitute in a brothel or having her child taken away from her, her moral "delicacy" does not, as it should, lead her to the 'right' decision. Emily prefers prostitution to losing her child, and the reader is made very clearly aware that this is because her actions are dictated by sentimental delicacy and not, as she calls it, the "sacred . . . virtue" (42).

The 1759 memoirs of the courtesans Kitty Fisher and Fanny Murray, and *The Histories of Some of the Penitents in the Magdalen-House*, all share the reassuring moral-sense commitment to the reformability of prostitutes and, implicitly, luxury; they are all more-or-less consoling narratives for a luxurious society in the midst of war. Yet where the courtesan narratives, particularly the *Memoirs of the Celebrated Miss Fanny Murray*, offer fairy-tale faith in the ability of luxury actually to promote virtue in society, the *Histories* signals the limits of this consoling narrative. In this manner, *The Histories of Some of the Penitents in the Magdalen-House* prefigures both the abandonment of the Enlightenment attempt to reconcile virtue and commerce—which is marked most starkly by the publication of Adam Smith's *Wealth of Nations* in 1776—and the almost simultaneous abandonment by the Magdalen charity of the idea that prostitutes could, and should, be recuperated and returned to the world as useful citizens.

Notes

1. *The Memoirs of the Celebrated Miss Fanny Murray, Interspersed with the Intrigues and Amours of Several Eminent Personages, Founded on Real Facts*, 2 vols. (Dublin: S. Smith, 1759), 2:53. Further references will be given parenthetically. The quotation in the title to this essay is taken from Edward Young, *The Centaur not Fabulous. In Five Letters to a Friend, on the Life in Vogue* (London: A. Millar and R. and J. Dodsley, 1755), 60.

2. *The Uncommon Adventures of Miss Kitty F****r*, 2 vols. (London: Thomas Bailey, 1759), 2:17–18. Further references will be given parenthetically.

3. "The Stream of Kitty," in *Uncommon Adventures*, 2:24.

4. For a discussion of the traditions of classical-republican thought, see J. G. A. Pocock, *The Machiavellian Moment: Florentine Political Thought and the Atlantic Republican Tradition* (Princeton: Princeton University Press, 1975).

5. Christopher Berry, *The Idea of Luxury: A Conceptual and Historical Investigation* (Cambridge: Cambridge University Press, 1994), 49.

6. John Brown, *An Estimate of the Manners and Principles of the Times*, vol. 1 (London: L. Davis and C. Reymers, 1757), 117, 28. Further references will be given parenthetically.

7. E. W. Montagu, junior, Esq., *Reflections on the Rise and Fall of the Antient Republicks. Adapted to the Present State of Great Britain* (London: A. Millar, 1759), 373.

8. *The Tryal of Lady Allurea Luxury, Before the Lord Chief-Justice Upright, on an Information for a Conspiracy* (London: F. Noble, 1757), 9. Further references will be given parenthetically.

9. G. Casanova, Chevalier de Seingalt, *History of My Life*, trans. W. R. Trask (New York: Harcourt, 1970), 308.

10. Johann Wilhelm von Archenholz, *A Picture of England: Containing a Description of the Laws, Customs, and Manners of England*, 2 vols. (London: Edward Jeffery, 1789), 2:92–93.

11. Marcia Pointon, "The Lives of Kitty Fisher," *British Journal for Eighteenth-Century Studies* 27 (2004): 82, 88.

12. Emma Clery, *The Feminization Debate in Eighteenth-Century England: Literature, Commerce and Luxury* (London: Palgrave, 2004), 56.

13. For an extremely useful discussion of the idea of "feminization" see Clery, *Feminization Debate*, 1–12.

14. David Hume, "Of Refinement in the Arts," in *Essays Moral, Political and Literary*, ed. Eugene F. Miller (Indianapolis: Liberty Classics, 1987), 269, 271. Further references will be given parenthetically.

15. *The Republic of Plato*, trans. Francis Macdonald Cornford (Oxford: Clarendon Press, 1941), 61, 109.

16. For a discussion of the demoralization caused by luxury see Berry, *Idea of Luxury*, 101–76.

17. Laura J. Rosenthal, *Infamous Commerce: Prostitution in Eighteenth-Century British Literature and Culture* (Ithaca: Cornell University Press, 2006), 105.

18. In this respect, I would argue that these narratives are different to John Cleland's *Memoirs of a Woman of Pleasure* (1748–1749), from which the phrase "tail-piece of morality" derives, and in which sentimentality is really just a gloss.

19. Rosenthal, *Infamous Commerce*, 198.

20. Mary V. Peace, "The Magdalen Hospital and the Fortunes of Whiggish Sentimentality in Mid-Eighteenth-Century Britain: 'Well-Grounded' Exemplarity vs. 'Romantic' Exceptionality," *Eighteenth Century* 48 (2007): 125–48.

21. William Dodd, *A Sermon on St. Matthew, Chap. IX. Ver. 12, 13* (London: L. Davis and C. Reymers, [1759?]), ii. As the subtitle to the printed version indicates, this sermon was "*Preach'd at the Parish Church of St. Laurence, near Guild-Hall, April the 26th, 1759, before the President, Vice-Presidents, Treasurer and Governors of the Magdalen House for the Reception of Penitent Prostitutes.*"

22. Jennie Batchelor and Megan Hiatt, introduction to *The Histories of Some of the Penitents in the Magdalen-House, As supposed to be Related by Themselves*, ed. Batchelor and Hiatt (London: Pickering and Chatto, 2007), xii.

23. H. F. B. Compson, *The Story of a Great Charity* (London: Society for Promoting Christian Knowledge, 1917), 42.

24. Compson, *Great Charity*, 150; Sarah Lloyd, "Pleasure's Golden Bait: Prostitution, Poverty and the Magdalen Hospital," *History Workshop Journal* 41 (1996): 56.

25. *Histories of Some of the Penitents*, 10. Further references will be given parenthetically.

Part III

T O INVESTIGATE WHAT WAS MEANT by an 'author'
in 1759 is to encounter, from the outset, some obvious contradictions—chiefly
that between the abstracted and rarefied figure of the artist, and the more workaday, and far less exalted practical experience of the writer. If 1759 is a pivotal
moment in eighteenth-century literature and culture, it is also a representative
example of this contradiction in action, given the publication during the year of
three works in which these disparate notions of authorship played a significant
part, whether directly or implicitly. That the idea of authorship was in a state of
flux at this time can be demonstrated by an examination of these well-known
works, and their different slants on the status of authorship and the conditions of
writing. Although their apparent ambitions are very different, Oliver Goldsmith's
Enquiry into the Present State of Polite Learning in Europe and Edward Young's *Conjectures on Original Composition* have more in common than is usually considered.
Furthermore, while the issue of authorship is more submerged in Samuel Johnson's
Rasselas, the idea of the artist plays a minor but not unimportant role in the story,
in the example and contributions of Imlac and his disquisitions on his chosen vocation as poet (which are often, and sometimes too readily regarded as indicative
of Johnson's own critical theory).[1] The background to these works is a shift in the
understanding of authorship during this period, from something approaching a
vocation (or at least a necessary undertaking), usually supported by patronage, to
the conflicting status of a commercial trade, which opened the author to all the
exigencies that this entailed.

Almost everything about the idea of the eighteenth-century British author
has been questioned in recent decades. The more aesthetic argument concerns

the role of the author as artist, which encompasses a change described (somewhat proto-Romantically) by Martha Woodmansee, who begins with the Renaissance idea of the author as an "unstable marriage of two distinct concepts," being both a "craftsman"—a "master of a body of rules, or techniques, preserved and handed down in rhetoric and poetics"—and a figure who is "inspired," whether by muses or by God. Here, the change that takes place in the works of eighteenth-century theorists is that they "minimized the element of craftsmanship . . . and they internalized the source of that inspiration."[2] As Woodmansee goes on to point out, a related but greater change during the period lay in the material conditions of authorship. Yet the traditional narrative that found (or more often assumed) in the eighteenth century an orderly movement from patronage to professionalism has itself been criticized as overly teleological and Whiggish. Notably, Dustin Griffin has suggested that "there was no rapid or complete changeover during the century from an aristocratic culture to a commercial culture, no sudden change from a patronage economy to a literary marketplace."[3] Instead, Griffin suggests, there was a gradual, complex, and often uneasy movement, in which patronage continued alongside the increasing attempts of professional authors to earn a commercial living.

In an influential work, Brean Hammond has examined how, during this period, "conflicts between an older, patronage-based model of authorship as the result of prolonged study and immersion in the classics, and a newer model of professionalism gradually being constituted, are at their most dramatic." Specifically, this drama is concerned with the struggles of commercial literary authorship to become accepted and viable; as Hammond puts it, authorship could "only develop as a profession when it became respectable for individuals to live off their wits."[4] Hence Hammond's investigation of the ways in which, from the Restoration onwards, the fight to own (and to be rewarded for selling) literary property became central to the profession of authorship. As Mark Rose outlines in *Authors and Owners* (1993), the prolonged arguments over copyright during the period are fundamental to our modern understanding of the authorial role: "the representation of the author as a creator who is entitled to profit from his intellectual labor came into being through a blending of literary and legal discourses in the context of the contest over perpetual copyright." From this viewpoint, it is futile to attempt to separate the idea of the writer, in purely aesthetic terms, from the material substance of their creations. Rather, as Rose observes, "the sense of the commodity value of writing is often just beneath the surface of eighteenth-century discussions of literary worth."[5]

Rose relates the mid-eighteenth-century contrast between genius and mechanical writing to the contemporary copyright debates, where "the task was to differentiate true authorship from mechanical invention and to mystify and valorize the former."[6] In a manner akin to Hammond, Linda Zionkowski has argued pointedly that this process of differentiation was very actively pursued by figures who have been accepted by posterity as standing at the center of literary culture at this time. For Zionkowski, "instead of developing as a natural result of writers' financial independence, the idea of a literary profession was devised amid a context of debate . . . on the formation of a literary canon." The emergence of the literary profession thus "had its roots in exclusionary concepts of literary labor and value[,] concepts resting on the denial of certain features inherent to commodified print."[7] Zionkowski's somewhat uncomplicated argument is that the writings of Henry Fielding, Johnson, and Goldsmith concerning modern authorship were conscious "attempts to institute a guardianship over print." What this argument neglects is the material and sometimes intellectual insecurity of these writers at different times, which makes it hard to view their plans as so deliberately designed to further their ideological ends. Similarly, Zionkowski's blanket description of "theories of writing that restrict or limit composition" reduces and simplifies the mixture of observation, worry, and genuine bemusement about the burgeoning number of authors that was expressed by Goldsmith, Johnson, and others in the mid-century period.[8] It is with this mixture of responses that the present essay is concerned, beginning with a figure whose almost pointed avoidance of these crucial ongoing developments in the commercial status of authorship makes him such an interesting case for analysis.

Edward Young's *Conjectures on Original Composition* is usually viewed from the perspective of its subsequent influence on Romanticism, both British and European, and of the movement away from the model of Popean imitation, towards a more organic sense of artistic form. As one critic summarizes, Young's argument is "a showcase for emerging ideas, a mileage-marker on the road from Neoclassicism to Romanticism."[9] It is also useful, though, to look at this important critical treatise from a different angle. It should be remembered that the work was a product of advanced years: not only was the venerable Young seventy-six at the time of its publication, he had also changed in many respects from the poet who, three decades earlier, had written satires such as *The Universal Passion* alongside (and in some ways in dialogue with) those of Pope.[10] In contradistinction to the Popean tone of his earlier satires, the critical thesis put forward in the *Conjectures* is entirely removed from the smoke of the marketplace. In discussing originality, Young rarely acknowledges the more mundane aspects of the process of composition and the retailing of creative goods. When Young does have to touch on the quantity, rather than the quality, of contemporary literary production, he puts forward a peculiar solution for controlling its fecundity:

> first, a few Thoughts on Composition in general. Some are of Opinion, that its Growth, at present, is too luxuriant; and that the Press is over-charged. Overcharged, I think, it could never be, if none were admitted, but such as brought their Imprimatur from sound Understanding, and the Public Good. Wit, indeed, however brilliant, should not be permit-ted to gaze self-enamour'd on its useless Charms, in that Fountain of Fame (if so I may call the Press), if Beauty is all that it has to boast; but, like the first Brutus, it should sacrifice its most darling Offspring to the sacred interests of Virtue, and real Service of mankind.[11]

The reference to Lucius Junius Brutus—that founder of the Roman Republic, prepared even to condemn his sons to death for treason in the service of the state—reveals Young's idea of authorship: it is a voluntary act, undertaken by those whose talents are worthy of exhibition, not by writers wishing to bask in their wit for its own sake. Both aesthetic pleasure and fulfillment have to be sacrificed to public service, and those wanting only to please themselves should withdraw from writing (or publishing—the two are conflated by Young). Even setting aside the considerable difficulty involved in separating merely frivolous and self-indulgent authors from those serving the higher cause of moral improvement, Young's gentlemanly prescription remains thankless and futile. In forbidding all but pre-cise sorts of literature (essentially those that are of a high standard, and virtuous), Young seems somehow to expect the majority of aspiring authors to accept their lack of talent or moral fiber, and simply withdraw into obscurity.

Given that the production of literature written mainly for money, rather than edification, was perceived to be increasing at this time, Young's wish for au-thorship to become self-filtering reveals itself as Canute-like. The distance between the traditional ideal of literature as a species of learning, and the pragmatic school associated with Grub Street, that saw writing purely in terms of material remu-neration, is captured by Young's description of the attractions of composition:

> To Men of Letters, and Leisure, it is not only a noble Amusement, but a sweet Refuge; it improves their Parts, and promotes their Peace: It opens a back-door out of the Bustle of this busy, and idle world, into a

delicious Garden of Moral and Intellectual fruits and flowers; the Key of which is denied to the rest of mankind. (4–5)

This language of recuperation, peace, sweetness, and retreat from the bustle of the busy world suggests that literature should be a fantasy, a pleasant idyll, and type of pastoral. Here, authorship is neither a livelihood nor a burden, but something performed because of innate, vocational talent, and directed towards edification. Besides ethical improvement, its only value, and required justification, lies in its own performance, which shuts the door on the more humdrum world.

It is possible to find something unconsciously defensive in Young's deliberate eschewal of the mundane practicalities of authorship and publishing. It is also an odd attitude, given that Young's long literary career was no less subject to the exigencies of making a living than the careers of other writers of his time. Young had, in fact, been active and successful in seeking and gaining the patronage and preferment that would sustain his writing. In Dustin Griffin's words, "Young seems to have understood that the economics of literature depended on a network of friends and supporters, who could defend your reputation, introduce you to a patron or a bookseller, and sign up subscribers."[12] As Griffin points out, Young utilized this understanding more effectively than did many of his contemporaries. In the *Conjectures*, though, this awareness of the material conditions of authorship is obscured; replaced by an ideal sense of what authorship ought to be, rather than what it is. This abstract ideal underpins the main burden of Young's argument— the need for originality in literature, and the potential to emulate the past. Young's nagging sense that such emulation could not be achieved finds expression in the familiar comparison of past with present, to the detriment of the latter:

> Quite clear of the dispute concerning *antient and modern Learning*, we speak not of Performance, but Powers. The modern powers are equal to those before them; modern performance in general is deplorably short. How great are the names just mentioned? [Thucydides, Herodotus, Livy, and Demosthenes] Yet who will dare affirm, that as great may not rise up in some future, or even in the present age? Reasons there are why talents may not appear, none why they may not exist, as much in one period as another. An Evocation of vegetable fruits depends on rain, air, and sun; an Evocation of the fruits of Genius no less depends on Externals. What a marvellous crop bore it in Greece, and Rome? And what a marvellous sunshine did it there enjoy? What encouragement from the nature of their governments, and the spirit of their people? Virgil and Horace

owed their divine talents to Heaven; their immortal works, to men; thank Mæcenas, and Augustus for them. Had it not been for these, the genius of those poets had lain buried in their ashes. (46–47)

The same amount of talent and potential exists as in the past, but it cannot be brought to fruition because of the inability of the present to match the illustrious classics, to provide sufficient contributions towards the artistic upkeep of modern authors. It is, of course, not a new argument to festoon the past with garlands for being kinder to its artists than the present. Yet, even if there is something rose-tinted in it, Young's line of thought remains tentative: he does not in fact say that the modern system of patronage is so inferior as to be dangerously useless by comparison. His own example showed that it was not the case that patronage had disappeared in the face of the burgeoning literary marketplace; instead, it had stopped being the necessary fulcrum of an author's career. In the *Conjectures*, Young seems to expect patronage to be the sort of defining measure that it supposedly had been in previous ages, when it could serve as an index of artistic talent and a way of rewarding works of genius and virtue. The not insignificant problem with this argument is that it overlooks the eternally capricious nature of such patronage. Young had succeeded, to a degree beyond most writers, in gaining recognition and income from patrons, but the patronage system of any artistic era in European culture had never been the foolproof estimation of talent and worth that he intimates in the *Conjectures*. Instead, patronage had let down or marred as many careers as it had aided, and a more appropriate summary of its arbitrary workings is Burns's comment on the travails of James Thomson, and his "axiom undoubted—/ 'Wouldst thou hae Nobles' patronage, / First learn to live without it!'"[13]

Young's *Conjectures*, then, exhibits a marked ambivalence towards the idea of modern authorship. Young places his faith in patronage as the most efficient and just form of literary support, but he cannot admit to any of its difficulties. He wants the most important and most virtuous authors to be confident in their abilities and sure of their own judgments—he warns the prospective writer of the necessity to "*know thyself*" (52)—but he also registers that such a contemporary pantheon is self-selecting:

The man who thus reverences himself, will soon find the world's reverence to follow his own. His works will stand distinguished; his the sole Property of them; which Property alone can confer the noble title of an Author, that is, of one who (to speak accurately) thinks, and composes;

while other invaders of the Press, how voluminous, and learned soever, (with due respect be it spoken) only read, and write. (53–54)

The distinction is thus between a solid notion of lasting, "distinguished" authorship, and the ephemera of the "invaders of the Press"—those who only scribble for the present, without sufficient depth of thought or true expression. Again, it is not easy to see how such invaders might be persuaded of their trespass, and made to leave. Young's distinction posits a clear sense that talent, like virtue, is easily recognizable in consensual fashion, while the self-subordination of inferior talents, it seems, will naturally ensure their exclusion from the literary pantheon. He was far from alone in thinking thus. In 1783, James Beattie would remark on the natural justice of artistic merit not being equally distributed, as all do not all things well: "All men are teachable; but few possess the power of useful invention. Such is the will of our Creator. And it is right that it should be so."[14] There is little point in criticizing Beattie, or Young, for presupposing that a hierarchical system of artistic value would render some appropriate candidates for literary honors, whilst relieving others of their pretensions. What is more questionable is the point that Young's thesis repeatedly moves away from answering: who is to decide on the pragmatic division of such allocations of invention, to reward the worthy recipients while ignoring those who are, at best, merely meretricious?

The attitude of Young towards the material conditions of authorship in 1759 was, then, markedly contradictory. From his own experience, he must have been well aware of the lack of resemblance between his idealistic republic of letters and the more troubling reality, in which struggling writers were often denied the luxury of viewing their works as contributions to the store of artistic genius and moral virtue. Yet such questions and contradictions lurk in the margins of the elderly Young's ringing and radiant argument for originality. A very different perspective emerges from another work on modern authorship published in 1759. The problems of living authors, who find very little reason to reverence themselves, recur (and, in some ways, dominate) in Goldsmith's *Enquiry into the Present State of Polite Learning in Europe*. Despite its ostensibly august subject, financial questions relating to artists are continually breaking through into Goldsmith's treatise, rendering its title somewhat anomalous: John Forster, in his famous biography of Goldsmith, suggested that it was "so far a misnomer that to substitute *Mr. Griffiths's Shop* for *Europe* would perhaps more correctly describe the polite learning it enquires into."[15] There is, indeed, a marked contrast between Young's

Olympian calm and detachment, and Goldsmith's often angry denunciation of the injustices of the modern literary world. Yet, far from comprising the grumblings of a far less successful author than Young, the *Enquiry* contains a series of pertinent and valuable observations about the state of British literary culture in 1759.

One of Goldsmith's models for the *Enquiry* was a text by an author who had written for his livelihood for years, with diminishing returns. The main focus of James Ralph's *The Case of Authors by Profession or Trade* (1758) is the status of the author: how the professional writer is looked down upon and expected to live like an amateur or, alternatively, to be at the mercy of a market shaped by booksellers and theatre-managers. Ralph's argument shows considerable disillusionment with the continual lack of respect or remuneration he had received, and the process he describes is systematic. In Ralph's view, the literary market grinds authors down not because of some natural antipathy or deliberate lack of justice, but simply because it is in its nature to do so:

> Authors do not come as wise into the world, as they go out of it—Raw from the Schools, esteeming Virgil a far greater Man than Augustus, Caesar the Writer than Caesar the Dictator, and eager to inrol themselves on the same List, in Hope to be consider'd accordingly, they write, are flatter'd by their Friends; publish and are undone—Undone good and bad alike—These with Contempt, Those with Neglect, which is all the Difference between them.[16]

In comparison with Young's hymn to the invariable timelessness of true literary genius and the seamless recognition of it in any era, this is an outburst from a literary Trade Unionist, arguing over conditions which are by nature unfair and destructive of talent. Ralph's palette is not extensive: he makes an important claim for the dignity of professional authorship, but his idea of an author is of a pure soul compelled to write, and singularly unprepared to deal with the amassed, cynical forces of commerce and criticism. Yet the value of Ralph's text is in showing the problem with a line of thought like Young's, which expects that unwanted writers should instinctively realize their superfluity, give up the game, and retreat from view:

> We are Writers; consequently incapable of taking up any other Trade; and consequently, instead of Examples, can only bequeath our Advices and Warnings to others. And, if Advice had any Power to convince or Warnings to deter, the Glut of Writing which has cloy'd the present Age,

should be follow'd, like *Pharaohs* Years of Abundance, with a Dearth as durable.[17]

As well as pointing out the inefficacy of such thinking with regard to different types of writers (a playwright can be commercially successful but artistically and critically negligible, a poet the reverse), Ralph here anticipates the folly of those, like Young, who suggest whittling down the over-crowded literary market by warning off aspiring authors, as though nobody had thought of doing so before. More generally, *The Case of Authors* provided the basic critique of a system that treated writers as commercial tokens, and cared little about them beyond their earning capacity.

In his *Enquiry into the Present State of Polite Learning*, Goldsmith nuances Ralph's advocacy of the professional writer, and offers a broader range of potential reasons for the perceived problems of authorship. He does this in part by arguing for the subjectivity of experience, suggesting that complaints about the barbarism of contemporary literary culture might well originate in very personal factors:

> To deplore the prostitution of learning, and despise contemporary merit, it must be owned, have too often been the resource of the envious or disappointed, the dictates of resentment not impartiality. The writer, possessed of fame, is willing to enjoy it without a rival, by lessening every competitor; the unsuccessful author is desirous to turn upon others the contempt which is levelled at himself, and being convicted at the bar of literary justice, vainly hopes for pardon by accusing every brother of the same profession.[18]

Goldsmith here adroitly identifies the motives behind grievances about the travails of the literary life. The passage evinces a belief in an absolute and (relatively) fair idea of evaluative literary jurisdiction, and an awareness that the actions of authors are not always high-minded, being often compromised by their own problems of status, or their bitter past experience. Yet alongside this rational assessment of the troubles of authorship is an anger that reflects Goldsmith's own troubled career as an indigent author. The result is an odd work that mingles a dispassionate, accessible account of artistic and literary history with far more immediate (and hardly dispassionate) concerns:

> The poet's poverty is a standing topic of contempt. His writing for bread is an unpardonable offence. Perhaps of all mankind an author in these

> times is used most hardly. We keep him poor, and yet revile his poverty.
> Like angry parents who correct their children till they cry, and then cor-
> rect them for crying, we reproach him for living by his wit, and yet allow
> him no other means to live. (1:314)

This is telling of the double standard that expected writers to live and work like bohemian caricatures, yet then homiletically condemned them for their childish folly, extravagance, and immorality. This double standard was an effect of the melodrama that had become attached to Grub Street culture, whereby the works of hapless writers had become of increasing irrelevance in comparison with the notoriety of their lives. The result of this was what Pat Rogers describes as "a picturesque story masquerading as truth," in which authors themselves served as vehicles for the thinly submerged voyeurism of readers and moralizing critics.[19] It is an unfortunate paradox that the literary culture of mid-eighteenth-century Britain needed authors, but also needed quite a few of them to fail—whether laughably, tragically, or sometimes both—in order to service its own requirements for entertainment and for (supposed) instruction at their expense. With regard to Goldsmith, outbursts such as the above were also indicative of a peculiar contra-diction in the logic of his argument, which informed his discussion of contem-porary authors as being naturally a part of the established and venerated history of learning that he was supposed to be detailing. From this perspective, modern authors, many of whom remain to fortune and to fame unknown, were assumed to be worthy of literary distinction by virtue of their mere existence.

In the *Enquiry*, the problems of all of European scholarship are made syn-onymous with the inequalities of contemporary British literary culture. In this equation of learning and authorship, Goldsmith's *Enquiry* is no less at odds with the true state of literary culture in 1759 than was Young's *Conjectures*. Forster's summary of this uneven work hints as much: "Manifest throughout the book is one over-ruling feeling, under various forms; the conviction that, in bad critics and sordid booksellers, learning has to contend with her worst enemies."[20] If both writers saw contemporary authorship as incommensurate with the fulfillment of their ideals, though, then this was for widely different reasons: Young desired the apotheosis of literary genius, and preferred to ignore, or to avoid, monetary considerations, whereas Goldsmith fused uneasily the contemporary decadence of European letters with the inability of struggling writers to make a living. Where Young shuns the practical, Goldsmith immerses himself in its details, to show its injustices. Forgetting his own caveat about the personal prejudices of those who lament the evils of the literary world, for instance, Goldsmith waxes romantic, and lays into the establishment:

> It is enough, that the age has already yielded instances of men pressing foremost in the lists of fame, and worthy of better times, schooled by continual adversity in an hatred of their kind, flying from thought to drunkenness, yielding to the united pressure of labour, penury, and sorrow, sinking unheeded, without one friend to drop a tear on their unattended obsequies, and indebted to charity for a grave, among the dregs of mankind. (1:315–16)

Such melodramatic and sentimental invoking of tragedy and waste eschews the complex moral discussions of a work such as Johnson's *Life of Savage* (1744), in which questions of responsibility and culpability are made part of the reader's experience. Johnson's work was designed to challenge its audience's stock responses to the often absurd and ultimately tragic life of its subject.[21] Goldsmith's *Enquiry* presents instead a broken-backed narrative, where substantial and distanced criticism concerning learning and literature is mixed with highly subjective passages on the woes of authorship, aptly summarized by Zionkowski's description of Goldsmith's wider tendency to "waver between nostalgia for a literature managed by the Great and a defense of authors' reliance on commercial publishing."[22] As in Ralph's *Case of Authors*, the assumption in these latter parts of the *Enquiry* is that an author is naturally alienated by cruelty of commercial circumstance in an unjust world: Mammon (in the form of the bookseller) ruins what ought to be left for posterity.

How, though, should the deathless musings of authors be funded, and how can it be decided which amongst the increasing multitude of aspirants are worth the effort and expenditure? Goldsmith falls back, like Young, on patronage:

> Thus the man, who under the protection of the Great, might have done honour to human nature, when only patronized by the bookseller, becomes a thing little superior to the fellow who works at the press. (1:316)

As with Young's *Conjectures*, Goldsmith's praise of patronage as the best support for the artist is undermined by nostalgia and wish-fulfillment: the burden of the sentence falls on the "might have," given the considerable contemporary evidence of "the Great" offering next to no protection when it was most needed or deserved (as with Lord Chesterfield's notorious failure to support Johnson's *Dictionary*). From a modern perspective, it might also be asked why authors should instinctively be thought of as naturally superior to the typesetter. To put it another way, almost all writers produced to make money, and not all could quibble with their artisan status. Why, moreover, should patrons have offered their 'protection' to the assorted writers of the age, when, as in any age, these ranged from figures of genius and great talent to the ineffectual and mediocre? A particular problem here is Goldsmith's stretching of the idea of 'learning', which he uses to cover all cultural ground, and all writers, regardless of their actual achievements. In this bullish defense of the idea of literature, the works of contemporary professional authors are rendered equal with timeless masterpieces of art. Distinctions between learning and authorship, and between past and present, are thus blurred, to the extent that authorship in the present becomes a natural extension of the achievements of the past.

Taken together, Young's *Conjectures* and Goldsmith's *Enquiry* reveal a genuine contemporary confusion over the nature and status of authorship; over whether writers were to be treated as the sort of detached artists that Young's pastoral vision idealizes, or as more immediate workers, writing foremost for financial reward. Goldsmith finds the latter status insulting—hence his contempt for the way in which the literary marketplace has betrayed so many writers of genius—but for all his vitriol, he is as unable as Young is to offer any formula which would help to evaluate the qualities of a real author of genius that the literary culture of the period should help and cherish, rather than degrade and destroy. An illuminating example here is the career of Christopher Smart (discussed in this volume by Rosalind Powell), which in its peculiar move from literary journalism to a poetry of religious exaltation (at the price of incarceration) could not be accommodated to any contemporary model of patronage or commercial support. A further complication, not addressed by Goldsmith, is that authors could now seek and receive critical praise, literary fame, and financial reward from and through booksellers, and could hardly be judged as blameworthy for doing so, given the arbitrary injustices that both Goldsmith and Ralph dwelt upon in their troubled reflections on the contemporary conditions of authorship.

A related but differently positioned perspective on these wider arguments about the nature of the contemporary author is provided by Johnson's *Rasselas* and its most designedly creative character, Imlac. When removed from their immediate context in Johnson's narrative, Imlac's strictures about the poetic art are in many ways surprisingly similar to the preoccupations of Goldsmith and Young. It will be recalled that Imlac presents the poetic vocation as an apex of human achievement, in its rare demands of breadth and depth of knowledge and experience:

> Being now resolved to be a poet, I saw everything with a new purpose;
> my sphere of attention was suddenly magnified: no kind of knowledge
> was to be overlooked. . . . To a poet nothing can be useless. Whatever is
> beautiful, and whatever is dreadful, must be familiar to his imagination:
> he must be conversant with all that is awfully vast or elegantly little.[23]

This strain of poetic enthusiasm exasperates even the naïve Rasselas (no mean
feat): "Imlac now felt the enthusiastic fit, and was proceeding to aggrandise his
own profession, when the Prince cried out: 'Enough! Thou hast convinced me,
that no human being can ever be a poet'" (46).[24] As Imlac observes, the difficulty
of mastering poetry is indicated by the regard in which it is held:

> Wherever I went, I found that poetry was considered as the highest
> learning, and regarded with a veneration somewhat approaching to that
> which man would pay to angelick nature. And yet it fills me with won-
> der, that, in almost all countries, the most ancient poets are considered
> as the best. (39)

Here, poetry is so exalted as to be nearer the divine than the human, with the
angelic comparison tilting at the fixed boundaries of the chain of being. There is
also a glancing reference here to the eternal battle between the ancients and the
moderns, which can be aligned with the central thesis (and arguable neurosis) of
Young's *Conjectures*, concerning the need to move away from merely emulating the
writers of the illustrious past.

Less often noted, amidst these enthusiasms, are Imlac's more mordant reflections on the relationship between authorship and posterity: poetry is the most
exalted of artistic vocations for its practitioners, yet its rewards are neither tangible
nor necessarily to be enjoyed in this life. As Imlac explains, the poet must "content
himself with the slow progress of his name, condemn the praise of his own time,
and commit his claims to the justice of posterity. He must write as the interpreter
of nature and the legislator of mankind, and consider himself as presiding over
the thoughts and manners of future generations, as a being superior to time and
place" (43). It is significant (and rarely remarked upon) that the ideal poet must
accept that they are likely to be a prophet without honor, and that their artistic
value and precepts are more concerned with the future than with the present,
which will (almost inevitably, it seems) either ignore or disregard both themselves
and their ideas. It is to be expected that such legislature will be unacknowledged,
given Imlac's earlier description of the obscurity of the pursuit of scholarship,

its distance from public renown, or even recognition: "the life that is devoted to knowledge passes silently away, and is very little diversified by events. To talk in public, to think in solitude, to read and to hear, to inquire, and answer inquiries, is the business of a scholar. He wanders about the world without pomp or terrour, and is neither known nor valued but by men like himself" (31). This scholarly version of authorship is a world of relative silence and obscurity, with little or no reward beyond the virtue of its own accomplishment; an austere, monastic life of knowledge for its own sake. In Imlac's terms, the very desire for public recognition suggests a sort of vanity that would render the aspirant a failure in this milieu. Yet if to be a scholar or a poet is indeed so difficult and unrewarding, then we might also ask: why does Imlac stay in the job?

The answer is that he has no choice: it is his vocation. At the end of *Rasselas*, Imlac and his new comrade in existential arms, the astronomer, are "contented to be driven along the stream of life without directing their course to any particular port" (176). Yet whatever happens, Imlac will still be a poet, by virtue of his being fitted for this difficult task at which he has worked so hard. Imlac's vision of the poet echoes a central Johnsonian theme: an understanding of the limits of what can be humanly achieved, and of what is inevitably lost between conception and final result, coupled with the need to accept such imperfection with patience, and not to allow the impossibility of complete fulfillment to undermine the process of striving. It is perhaps unsurprising that this idealistic scholar-poet within an Oriental tale bears little immediate resemblance to the typical author of the time, yet it is instructive to observe how Johnson positions this ideal against more recent notions of authorship: Imlac is a poet, not a writer of fiction (even if he appears in one) or a writer of other prose forms or of drama. Indeed, not the least of the confusions surrounding the idea of authorship in 1759 relates to the many sorts of career that it could represent. Johnson, like Young and (to a lesser extent) Goldsmith, assumes that poetry is the first aim of literary production and thus of authorship, being the most exacting and exalted form of literary composition. The difficulty that arises from this is that conflicting models of authorship, such as the writing of prose fiction for commercial reward, were becoming increasingly prevalent at this time.[25]

Johnson's example highlights this difference: Imlac is the very type of the creative artist making art, rather than an artisan attempting to make money. Given the presence, in 1759, of a growing number of aspiring authors of various kinds of writing who were trying to tap into the potential rewards of the literary market, this distinction, whilst crude, allows us to understand something more of the context of Goldsmith and Young's discussions of authorship. The alleged immediate impetus to the production of *Rasselas* itself leads into such debates. As is well known, Boswell was told by the bookseller, William Strahan, that "Johnson wrote it, that with the profits he might defray the expence of his mother's funeral, and pay some little debts which she had left."[26] It is a minor irony in the larger centrality of *Rasselas* to Johnson's canon that the apparent reasons behind its creation conflict very obviously with Imlac's vision of the artist as scholar-poet. Rather than being abstracted from the world, and pursuing knowledge and the life of the mind as part of a vocation, Johnson the author had pressing material needs to inspire his composition. Here is an authorial variation on the paradox that was cited more broadly earlier—the paradox of being able to delineate very precisely the value of art and artistry, whilst knowing full well the shortcomings of such abstractions in a market stimulated precisely by want and need. Or, as another familiar part of Boswell's narrative explains it, Johnson "uniformly adhered to that strange opinion, which his indolent disposition made him utter: 'No man but a blockhead ever wrote, except for money.' Numerous instances to refute this will occur to all who are versed in the history of literature."[27] Such instances, though, are not really the point: it was not just Johnson's guilt at his own perceived indolence that reminded him of the very real pressures that generated art, and that could not be reconciled with the aesthetic detachment of the scholar-poet, Imlac.

As part of his wider argument that Johnson's whole career was both a product of and a shaping force behind eighteenth-century print culture (particularly in his personal contributions towards biography, as both author and subject), Alvin Kernan has described how Johnson "accepted and arranged the real situation that print offered in the most attractive manner possible." Such acceptance can be seen, Kernan argues, in the manner in which Johnson's great literary undertakings "were all either commissioned by the printers and publishers, or planned by Johnson himself as commercial publishing ventures."[28] Johnson knew that the author and their work could almost never be separated from the nexus of channels that brought that work to the world, and that such quotidian concerns as making a living were more immediately relevant than broader conceptualizations of authorship. That such an attitude could co-exist alongside the unattainable (but nonetheless deeply held) ideal of the poet espoused by Imlac is one proof of Johnson's greater sense of perspective about the nature of authorship, when placed alongside contemporaries such as Young and Goldsmith. Mark Wildermuth has recently described this attitude as Johnson's "uniquely double perspective; he is a refined man of taste and a scholar who also knows the street reality of the publishing world from his experience at this time as a Grub Street writer." Johnson could thus "create a kind of practical criticism adapted to the needs of virtually any member of the literate culture who might be inclined to consider" his arguments.[29] By creating the possibility for flexibility in his writings, this adaptability, borne of his "double perspective" on the contemporary cultural scene, is also what prevents Johnson from being easily positioned by modern critics within a particular literary movement—of taste, or canon-formation—in any simple or homogenized sense.

If it is possible to argue that there is a fundamental difficulty, in writers from more than one literary generation, in understanding the role of the author in 1759, then this can also be connected to emerging literary trends, such as the blasé self-consciousness of Shandyism, or the calculated nostalgia and veneration of virtues such as heightened emotional response (artistic and otherwise) inherent in sentimentality.[30] These are authorial strategies that allow for the ambivalent status of the writer: whether mocking acknowledgement of the oddities of posterity, pretended self-depreciation, or deliberate use of the pure past against the impure present. They are symptoms of the same problem that Young and Goldsmith could not solve, and of which Johnson too, in his material needs and distance from the ideal poetic role of Imlac, was acutely aware: how to define the role and purpose of authorship at a time when fewer patrons were protecting people to write (whether for the sake of virtue, the good of the world, or sheer aesthetic pleasure), and when many more people were attempting to be paid for writing, whether or not their talents were suited to such an end.

When, in 1753, Johnson in *Adventurer* 115 styled the present as "*The Age of Authors*," he was in one sense only describing the truth that "perhaps, there never was a time, in which men of all degrees of ability, of every kind of education, of every profession and employment, were posting with ardour so general to the press." This is what he describes as an endless search for "literary praise," and it has a clear drawback: "at all times more have been willing than have been able to write," and the "dogmatical legions of the present race" seem to outnumber those of the past.[31] By 1759, there was more willingness in proportion to ability than ever before; the concomitant effect was that authorship took on so many different aspects as to be near impossible to define, at least within the compasses used by Young and Goldsmith. Yet, like Johnson's impossibly distant ideal of authorship in *Rasselas*, such compasses indicate much about the authorial temper of the moment, which was one of contradictory veneration of the past and acknowledgement of the shifting present. This vexed vision was perhaps inevitable, given the transitions that were taking place—not least the rise in the popularity of narrative fiction—within contemporary British literature.

Notes

1. For a thorough attempt at mapping Imlac's ideas onto Johnson's wider aesthetic, see Martin Kallich, "Samuel Johnson's Principles of Criticism and Imlac's 'Dissertation upon Poetry,'" *Journal of Aesthetics and Art Criticism* 25 (1966): 71–82.

2. Martha Woodmansee, *The Author, Art, and the Market: Rereading the History of Aesthetics* (New York: Columbia University Press, 1994), 36, 37. These references from Woodmansee are part of a longer discussion of individual genius and its relationship to emergent ideas of copyright, as applicable to German culture (35–55).

3. Dustin Griffin, *Literary Patronage in England, 1650–1800* (Cambridge: Cambridge University Press, 1996), 10.

4. Brean S. Hammond, *Professional Imaginative Writing in England, 1670–1740: "Hackney for Bread"* (Oxford: Clarendon Press, 1997), 5, 23.

5. Mark Rose, *Authors and Owners: The Invention of Copyright* (Cambridge, MA: Harvard University Press, 1993), 6, 118, 119. For a more local discussion of copyright and literary ownership in the mid-century, and the differing conceptions of Johnson and Young regarding such ownership, see Linda Zionkowski, "Aesthetics, Copyright, and 'The Goods of the Mind,'" *British Journal for Eighteenth-Century Studies* 15 (1992): 163–74.

6. Rose, *Authors and Owners*, 119.

7. Zionkowski, "Territorial Disputes in the Republic of Letters: Canon Formation and the Literary Profession," *Eighteenth Century* 31 (1990): 4, 5.

8. Zionkowski, "Territorial Disputes," 13, 17.

9. Robert L. Chibka, "The Stranger within Young's *Conjectures*," *ELH* 53 (1986): 541. Chibka's article provides a good modern overview of Young's enterprise. For more on the context and possible meanings of the *Conjectures*, see Alan D. McKillop, "Richardson, Young, and the *Conjectures*," *Modern Philology* 22 (1925): 391–404; Joel Weinsheimer, "Conjectures on Unoriginal Composition," *Eighteenth Century* 22 (1981): 58–73; and D. W. Odell, "The Argument of Young's *Conjectures on Original Composition*," *Studies in Philology* 78 (1981): 87–106.

10. The seven parts of *The Universal Passion* were first published separately, before appearing together in a collected edition in 1728.

11. Edward Young, *Conjectures on Original Composition: In a Letter to the Author of "Sir Charles Grandison"* (London: A. Millar and R. and J. Dodsley, 1759), 5. Subsequent references are given parenthetically.

12. Griffin, *Literary Patronage*, 158. For Griffin's general account of Young's dealings with patronage, see pp. 155–69 of his study.

13. Robert Burns, "Extempore–on some Commemorations of Thomson," in *The Poems and Songs of Robert Burns*, ed. James Kinsley (London: Oxford University Press, 1969), 459.

14. James Beattie, *Dissertations Moral and Critical* (London and Edinburgh: W. Strahan, T. Cadell, and W. Creech, 1783), 146.

15. John Forster, *The Life and Times of Oliver Goldsmith* (1848), 3rd ed. (London: Ward, Lock and Co., 1890), 114. The reference is to Ralph Griffiths (1720?–1803), bookseller and (as editor of the *Monthly Review*) Goldsmith's repeated source of employment and often much-needed funds.

16. James Ralph, *The Case of Authors by Profession or Trade, Stated* (London: R. Griffiths, 1758), 71. For two different accounts of Ralph, see Robert W. Kenny, "Ralph's *Case of Authors*: Its Influence on Goldsmith and Isaac D'Israeli," *PMLA* 52 (1937): 104–13, and Zionkowski, "Territorial Disputes," 13–17. Zionkowski views *The Case of Authors* as "an important analysis of authorial labour and a theory of literary value" which to some extent "demystifies" the views advanced by Goldsmith, amongst others (13).

17. Ralph, *Case of Authors*, 64–65.

18. Oliver Goldsmith, *An Enquiry into the Present State of Polite Learning in Europe*, in *The Collected Works of Oliver Goldsmith*, ed. Arthur Friedman, 5 vols. (Oxford: Clarendon Press, 1966), 1:258. Subsequent references are given parenthetically.

19. Pat Rogers, *Grub Street: Studies in a Subculture* (London: Methuen, 1972), 377.

20. Forster, *Life and Times*, 114.

21. For the purpose of Johnson's *Life of Savage*, see Robert Folkenflik, *Samuel Johnson, Biographer* (Ithaca: Cornell University Press, 1978), 213, and Paul K. Alkon, "The Intention and Reception of Johnson's *Life of Savage*," *Modern Philology* 72 (1974): 139–50.

22. Zionkowski, "Territorial Disputes," 7.

23. Samuel Johnson, *The History of Rasselas, Prince of Abyssinia*, in *Rasselas and Other Tales*, ed. Gwin J. Kolb, vol. 16 of *The Yale Edition of the Works of Samuel Johnson* (New Haven: Yale University Press, 1990), 41–42. Subsequent references are given parenthetically.

24. On this passage, see also James Watt's essay in this volume.

25. On Young's *Conjectures* and the contemporary novel, see Moyra Haslett's essay in this volume.

26. *Boswell's Life of Johnson*, ed. George Birkbeck Hill, rev. L. F. Powell, 6 vols. (Oxford: Clarendon Press, 1934–1950), 1:341. It is unlikely that the motives behind the writing of *Rasselas* were so single-minded. For discussion of the evidence regarding its composition, see Kolb's introduction to *Rasselas and Other Tales*, xix–xxvi.

27. *Boswell's Life of Johnson*, 3:19–20.

28. Alvin Kernan, *Printing Technology, Letters and Samuel Johnson* (Princeton: Princeton University Press, 1987), 97, 94.

29. Mark E. Wildermuth, *Print, Chaos, and Complexity: Samuel Johnson and Eighteenth-Century Media Culture* (Newark: University of Delaware Press, 2008), 94.

30. See Maureen Harkin, "Mackenzie's *Man of Feeling*: Embalming Sensibility," *ELH* 61 (1994): 336, and Paul Goring, *The Rhetoric of Sensibility in Eighteenth-Century Culture* (Cambridge: Cambridge University Press, 2005), 142–81.

31. Johnson, *Adventurer* no. 115 (11 December 1753), in *The Idler and The Adventurer*, ed. W. J. Bate, John M. Bullitt, and L. F. Powell, vol. 2 of *Works* (New Haven: Yale University Press, 1963), 457.

6

TOWARDS A NEW LANGUAGE: SUBLIME

AESTHETICS IN SMART'S *JUBILATE AGNO*

ROSALIND POWELL

I

N 1759, CHRISTOPHER SMART was writing the most varied
and interesting fragment of his incomplete work of enthusiastic praise, *Jubilate
Agno* (1758–1763). In the same year, Edmund Burke published the second (revised) edition of *A Philosophical Enquiry into the Origin of our Ideas of the Sublime
and Beautiful*. A significant departure from the first edition of the *Philosophical
Enquiry* was that Burke made an explicit connection between his idea of the
sublime and the notion of the divine, producing a conceptual intertwining that
is important to any consideration of religious writing during the mid-eighteenth
century. As Burke now observed:

> I know some people are of opinion, that no awe, no degree of terror, ac-
> companies the idea of power, and have hazarded to affirm, that we can
> contemplate the idea of God himself without any such emotion. I pur-
> posely avoided when I first considered this subject, to introduce the idea of
> that great and tremendous being, as an example in an argument so light as
> this; though it frequently occurred to me, not as an objection to, but as a
> strong confirmation of my notions in this matter. . . . But whilst we con-
> template so vast an object, under the arm, as it were, of almighty power,
> and invested on every side with omnipresence, we shrink into the minute-
> ness of our own nature, and are, in a manner, annihilated before him.[1]

Burke's account of the sublime, which emphasizes obscurity, power, infinite-
ness, and other qualities of grandeur, bears a striking resemblance to elements of
Smart's early verse that describe the divine, in particular his winning entries for
the Seatonian Prize at Cambridge University, written between 1750 and 1756 on

the themes of "Goodness," "Eternity," "Omniscience," "Immensity," and "Power." The definition of the sublime in Burke's *Enquiry* points towards a particular view of God as unknowable and terrifying:

> Whatever is fitted in any sort to excite the ideas of pain, and danger, that is to say, whatever is in any sort terrible, or is conversant about terrible objects, or operates in a manner analogous to terror, is a source of the *sublime*. (39)

With the direct application of these sublime attributes to the divine promoted in the 1759 edition of the *Philosophical Enquiry*, their resonance with Smart's characteristic portrait of thunder as the "terrific voice" of God is striking.[2] The connection between Smart's translation work and the sublime has been made previously by Donald Davie.[3] By revising this connection in terms of the restriction placed on language by an inability to describe God, this essay will provide a reading of Smart's original verse of 1759 to present a reassessment, rather than a reinforcement, of the Burkean sublime.

Previous discussions of Smart's sublime poetics have drawn stylistic connections between *Jubilate Agno* and Robert Lowth's account of Old Testament poetry in his 1754 work, *Praelectiones Academicae de Sacra Poesi Hebraeorum*. Jeanne Murray Walker's structural analysis of Smart's poem as a fragmented kind of psalm, for example, refers to Lowth's identification of parallelism in biblical verses.[4] Similarly, Tom Keymer associates Lowth's description of the *Mashal* style of forceful Hebrew poetry with the "spare, rigorous, yet intensely plangent style" of *Jubilate Agno*.[5] However, Lowth's account of the religious sublime is limiting with regard to the present investigation, because it is focused solely on Hebrew poetic diction and the subject matter of biblical verses. Lowth follows Longinus in describing the sublime as "that force of composition, whatever it be, which strikes and overpowers the mind, which excites the passions, and which expresses ideas at once with perspicuity and elevation; not solicitous whether the language be plain or ornamented, refined or familiar."[6] By contrast, Burke's account of the sublime looks beyond this "force of composition" to the existence of the sublime in nature. Furthermore, his comparison between the sublime and the beautiful is better suited to the current investigation of artistic forms.

Burke's sublime element of unknowable terror is a key theme in the Seatonian Poems, yet it is surmounted in Smart's later verse. In this essay, I want to examine the development of Smart's writing away from such a sense of a distant divinity, especially in the *Jubilate*, in which the poet explicitly explores how God might be addressed. In particular, I will consider how Smart forms a connection between God's language and the most beautiful expressions that man can achieve through his creative and artistic works. Considering that Smart wrote the fragments of *Jubilate Agno* whilst incarcerated in the madhouse, it is difficult to ascertain whether he might have been directly influenced by works published in 1759. Nevertheless, the possible connection with the ideas of the sublime and the beautiful in Burke's treatise merits further examination, particularly in terms of how Smart's account of divinity moves beyond the restrictions on expression that are voiced in the *Philosophical Enquiry*. An important critical starting-point for this investigation is Geoffrey Hartman's essay on "Christopher Smart's 'Magnificat,'" which addresses many of the central themes in *Jubilate Agno*.[7] Hartman's inspection of Smart's religious expression unearths two sources of difficulty: the ineffability of God, and the limitation of language. These two problems form the basis of my own reading of Smart's poem, which attempts to explore and to move beyond the themes set out in the earlier critic's short article. By looking at the second fragment (fragment B) of *Jubilate Agno*, which was written during 1759 and 1760, I want to consider Smart's reaction against the idea of the sublime as represented by authors such as Burke. In particular, I shall explore how Smart uses the language of aesthetic communication through sight and sound. To begin with, the essay will focus on Smart's manipulation of individual letters as a means of creating new modes of expression. The discussion will then move on to investigate how art and colors suggest the visual expression of beauty as a reflection of divine sublimity that is within the grasp of man's comprehension. Finally, I will shift the focus to music, which Smart identifies as especially significant in terms of both signification and setting in his stipulation that, in order to present the dual importance of purity and beauty in *Jubilate Agno*, "it would be better if the LITURGY were musically performed."[8] At least in the context of *Jubilate Agno*, which can be characterized as a private praise-poem (and which was never published during Smart's lifetime), it will be apparent that I am considering a writer who approaches to the status of rarefied artist described by Adam Rounce in this volume. At this essay will show, Smart's manipulation of language in the *Jubilate* reflects the endeavors of a poet who, above all else, wrote to be "the Reviver of ADORATION amongst ENGLISH-MEN" (B332).

We can begin by considering Smart's reference to sublime language in his first Seatonian Poem, "On the Eternity of the Supreme Being" (1750), where he asks:

"May then the youthful, uninspired Bard / Presume to hymn th'Eternal[?]"[9] The poet's expression of the religious sublime appears here between limits and boundaries; between the idea of divine intent and the portrayal of human act. As he goes on to indicate in "On the Immensity of the Supreme Being" (1751), God's attributes are only reflected through the poet's awed response: "I thy servant, like the still profound, / Astonish'd into silence muse thy praise!"[10] Indeed, in his early verse, Smart reflects constantly upon the power of God and the comparative littleness of anything mortal. As he tries to evoke the unimaginable greatness of the deity, the poet calls upon his reader to imagine the most powerful aspect of nature and to magnify it to an inconceivable degree:

> What, Aetna, are thy flames to these?—No more
> Than the poor glow-worm to the golden Sun.[11]

Here, the rhetorical question and its negative response stress the limitations of both imagination and description for a poet attempting to comprehend the scale and power of the divine.

Smart also emphasizes the futility of human expression and the limits imposed upon human language. Words, "the weak interpreters of mortal thoughts," are not sufficient to translate God into something comprehensible.[12] Smart thus registers limits on expression that echo Augustine's *Confessions*:

> What has anyone achieved in words when he speaks about you? Yet woe to those who are silent about you, because, though loquacious with verbosity, they have nothing to say.[13]

The traditional Augustinian viewpoint is also wielded by Burke in his account of the sublime, where he warns that "when we define, we seem in danger of circumscribing nature within the bounds of our own notions" (12). This sense of verbal and conceptual restriction is central to Smart's voicing of the impossibility of writing about the divine (beyond general references to infinite, powerful attributes) in his Seatonian Poems. However, a change occurs in his later verse, and the idea of God is communicated in *Jubilate Agno* through tropes that refer to another language, "the poetry of Christ," beyond that which is used for mortal expression (B506). The concept of the religious sublime, which is the linguistic response to the divine, is integral to the present study of Smart's language. This concept explains why it is necessary for Smart to overcome the expressive anxiety of the Seatonian Poems and to use a special kind of language to describe and address the divine in *Jubilate Agno*. While Burke provides a broad starting-point for considering the religious sublime, my approach to *Jubilate Agno* also moves away from the Burkean perspective and involves the working out of an innate paradox of religious poetry, whereby the inability to articulate ideas of the divine is confronted by the necessity of so doing.

The possibility of a linguistic conception of God is envisaged in *Jubilate Agno* through reference to "uncommunicated letters," which "are signs of speech too precious to be communicated for ever" (C44–45). Importantly, this mystery is a matter for celebration, signifying as it does the worth of things "too precious to be communicated." Burke insisted that poetry was not just "the power of raising sensible images" that could be seen or felt (170). Because it might be able to reach beyond sensory experience, poetry is the ideal medium for religious writing, as this form of composition reaches beyond images that can be described or written in full. Alongside the purely linguistic elements of *Jubilate Agno*, therefore, Smart refers to other modes of communication that might reflect divinity in a way that extends beyond the limitations of language. Throughout the Old Testament, men communicate to God in their own languages, with the response coming through signs, actions, and sounds (such as the whirlwind in Job, the burning bush in Exodus, and the recurring use of significant numbers throughout Scripture). In *Jubilate Agno*, Smart adopts his own system of signs: Latin and Hebrew letters, a detailed spectrum of colors, and a special language of musical sounds. For Smart, the inclusion of such signs goes some way towards overcoming the paradox of communication in religious poetry.

The language that Smart uses to approach God is reached via a negotiation of boundaries that both protect divinity and limit expression. The use of pure language is especially important for Smart because it suggests freedom from corruption and the suitability of that language for praising God. Importantly, it is through language itself that God is addressed and the purification of language stands as a purification of the people because it creates a new channel to God, as "the AIR is purified by prayer which is made aloud and with all our might" (B224). The poet echoes the prophecies of Zephaniah that pure language shall be restored: "For then I will turn to the people a pure language, that they may all call upon the name of the LORD."[14] The distinctive language to be used for prayer is described in the *Jubilate* as Smart indicates the verbal circumspection required to praise God: "For all good words are from GOD, and all others are cant" (B85). This use of the word "cant" to describe the wrong sort of language relates to the *OED* definition of cant as "affected or unreal use of religious or pietistic phraseology." This meaning of insincere, unholy language is intensified in Smart's poetry to refer to all language with which it is improper to address God. The use of the word "cant" in opposition to purity is also significant as, in conjunction with a further *OED* definition—"singing, musical sound"—cant may suggest jarring notes that clash with "God's natural key" (B364), upsetting the desired harmony of joyful praise. In his poem, Smart places "purity" between goodness and sublimity as one of the twelve "cardinal virtues," bringing with it connotations of cleanliness in the Hebrew law outlined in Leviticus and Numbers. Smart presents this virtue within the realm of language to suggest that we should, like Eleazar, "serve the Lord decently and in purity" (A17). Only "good words" are suitable for the new verse that Smart aims to present, as he wishes to approach God in a language of divine origin, not one of impure manufacture. Smart is not only concerned, though, with the purgation of polluted language and the impossibility of human expression. This purgation is the precondition for the transcription of other divine languages—represented by art, music, hidden signatures, and special letters—into the best possible form of human language. In this search for a special language, the poet seeks to create a liturgical canticle—which he calls "my MAGNIFICAT" (B4)—that not only describes God but that also reflects its own origin in divine creation.

The first poetic method that Smart employs to extend the possibility of expression in *Jubilate Agno* is the use of symbolic letters and signs. In the Burkean model of the sublime, the human interpretation of nature is described through the familiar trope of the *liber naturae*:

> The characters of nature are legible it is true; but they are not plain enough to enable those who run, to read them. We must make use of a cautious, I had almost said, a timorous manner of proceeding. (4)

For Burke, the book of nature is readable only in part. Against this, Smart reduces the large scales and incomprehensibility that Burke identifies as sources of the sublime down to miniature signs that symbolize grandeur. In the second fragment of the *Jubilate*, Smart presents alphabetical lists that might be read as a presentation of elements from the *liber naturae*, categorized for comprehension:

> For A is the beginning of learning and the door of heaven.
> For B is a creature busy and bustling.
> . . .
> For E is eternity—such is the power of the English letters taken singly.
> For F is faith. (B513–18)

The "power of the English letters" seems to exist both in communicating ideas otherwise incomprehensible to man and in ordering them in his mind through a kind of onomatopoeic catalogue. In *Jubilate Agno*, all letters have a divine significance. This significance is reinforced by reference to further letters that are beyond the current capacity of human language: "For there are more letters in all languages not communicated" (C40). Smart suggests that letters taken individually are significant entities in themselves, and not just the building blocks for linguistic communication. Kabbalistic theory reinforces this heightened significance because, in the terms of this theory, the divine origin of characters signals subsequent divine possibility. Smart's positing of the existence of more letters, beyond the twenty-four that are spoken and written, likewise refers to a mysterious symbolism, a further language of praise. In this way, the original letters exist as a transliteration of more letters, translated for the comprehension of Smart and his readers.

The new reading of letters proposed by Smart might refer to a new system whereby anybody who reads carefully (that is, prayerfully) enough will locate an otherwise unseen language of divine communication. The beginning of the search for divine language is thus carried out through the adoption and transcription of known letters. Letters and numbers form a structural basis for much of Smart's poem, in which he utilizes such symbols to perform an exegesis of God's signatures upon nature. As Clement Hawes recognizes, this exegesis creates boundless possibilities:

> [A]ttempting to read the *Jubilate* with a full awareness of its echoes and puns, its miraculous casts into Scripture and other texts, induces something like a "reader's sublime," a state of absolute metaphor in which anything can potentially stand for anything else.[15]

In reading this new language of divine signification we are drawn into a new realm of interpretation, where the possibility of portraying the pure Word is knit into the poem's structure. It may be conjectured from this that Smart's references to divine language expand upon Burke's analysis of words that, "whatever power they may have on the passions, they do not derive it from any representation raised in the mind of the things for which they stand" (164).

In the description of flowers in *Jubilate Agno*, Smart introduces what might seem to be an inventive metaphor that reaches beyond the expressive possibilities of language:

> For elegant phrases are nothing but flowers.
> For flowers are peculiarly the poetry of Christ. (B505–6)

However, Smart may envision the "poetry of Christ" to be something that is in fact real and only symbolized by the flowers as a kind of tangible explanation. I would suggest that the real content of this extraordinary divine language (incarnated in poetry) is a certain phrasing, vocabulary, and system of signs. The extended meanings and puns on the alphabet in *Jubilate Agno* are authorized by Kabbalistic and Pythagorean theories, which structure the "reader's sublime" into an already accepted form of human language. Letters and numbers take on specific properties whatever their actual context within the poem, and they add another layer of meaning onto the words of ordinary expression. Alun Morris David identifies this as a peculiar phenomenon of the eighteenth century, whereby, "In a manoeuvre familiar from Christian Kabbalism, Jewish mystical practice is assimilated into the orthodox identification of Christ with *logos*."[16] Just as Smart Christianizes the Psalms in his translation, so he utilizes the symbolism and language of Judaism and Ancient Greece in the articulation of praise for a specifically Christian God.

A precedent for this can be found in Henry More's *Conjectura Cabbalistica* of 1653, which also combines the Mosaic with the Christian. This earlier work provides a deeper explanation than the *Jubilate*, as More carries out a threefold exegesis of Genesis to demonstrate that man is a microcosm of the created world. More's text offers an interpretation based not on numbers and signs but upon introspective reading and the allegory of God's signature as "a certain Key to enter Man into the knowledge and use of the Treasures of Nature."[17] In *Jubilate Agno*, Smart depicts the divine through his own system of reading, in which things are both what they seem—"For I is the organ of vision" (B546)—and, as he counters in "On the Eternity of the Supreme Being," totally "INCOMPREHENSIBLE!": obscure to sense and dependent upon divining signs through a kind of Christian Kabbalah.[18] In his summary of "the ways of Smart with language," Hartman notes that each letter of *Jubilate Agno* is resonant with meaning because it can be linked to any signifier through poetic punning, whereby linguistic similarity suggests an essential parallel.[19] In the original Kabbalistic tradition, Creation, both as action and outcome, figures as a combination of the "twenty-two elemental letters."[20] Smart adopts this idea of letters throughout the poem, presenting the *systema naturae* as a code of expression and understanding. The image of the Hebrew *lamed* (ל) inscribed "on the fibre of some leaf in every tree" (B477) presents a literalized version of notaricon, the system by which individual letters signify entire words. More than merely adopting Jewish mysticism, Smart sought to translate it into his own experience of the vernacular, reveling in "the power of the English letters taken singly" (B517). In *Jubilate Agno*, Smart thus presents English as a divine tongue that carries innate spiritual meaning. This peculiar focus shadows the search for the origins of language during the seventeenth century, as the poet writes to rekindle the possibility that "man would know the nature of things by learning to speak and write" a language of direct signification.[21]

In *Jubilate Agno*, then, the introduction of the alphabet as "the beginning of learning" (B513) focuses upon the mystical and infinitely possible significance of letters. This subject turns eighteenth-century linguistic theory upon its head: the focus is reverted from syntax to characters, from discourse to writing, and from instruction to interpretation. In Smart's poem, Creation is structured by linguistic puns and significant characters that lead back to the Creator. An exegesis of the innate meaning of language is found in Fragment B, where Smart asserts that "the power of some animal is predominant in every language" (B625) as a secondary sign of God's own creation of language. The poet thus finds a basis for language in the creatures of creation, and words are directed back to the divine:

> For the Mouse (Mus) prevails in the Latin.
> For Edi-mus, bibi-mus, vivi-mus—ore-mus. (B636–37)

In the second line here, the mouse's appearance as creature is of no consequence, it is simply a vehicle for linguistic play. The word-play carries Smart's informative dissection of the book of nature from single letters to formed phonemes. The stems of the verbs in the second line are more important than the grammatical ending that defines their subject(s). Simple, universal actions—eating, drinking, living—are resolved into the all-encompassing action of the poet's vision: *oremus*, "let us pray." Likewise, Smart identifies a comparable rule as "the Bull and the Dog prevail in the English / For all the words ending in –ble are in the creature. Invisible, Incomprehensi-ble, ineffa-ble, A-ble. . . . For can is (canis) is cause and effect a dog" (B643–46). Again, the theme of the second line refers to God through his attributes. This theory might be extended through the rest of Smart's poem as a new way of reading, whereby words such as "bless" and "invincible" carry the extra weight of God's presence. Throughout the *Jubilate*, Smart manipulated this special kind of reading to extend the reach of language beyond the limitations posed by a Burkean concept of sublime divinity.

An important part of this construction of a new kind of language was Smart's manipulation of other artistic forms as part of his extralingual representation of God. The "signs of speech too precious to be communicated" to which the poet alludes in Fragment C of *Jubilate Agno* are not necessarily verbal in origin. The poem develops the suggestion that language might exist beyond words in a form akin to the powerful communication of music and art. In Fragment B, the poetry of Christ is illustrated as "flowers musical in ocular harmony" (B508), and the senses are important entry points for the comprehension of divine language. Where the human language of religious poetry is inevitably concerned with goodness, eternity, omniscience, immensity, and power, all themes closely knit with the Burkean sublime, divine language that is transcribed into artistic expression is automatically associated by Smart with the idea of beauty. Beautiful objects, distinguished by Burke as small, smooth, not angular, delicate, and beautiful in color, might be identified as the approachable counterparts to sublime ones (113–17). With this in mind, it is worth noting Smart's efforts to present a humanized version of the divine throughout his later works. The poet's Christianized version of the Psalms, infused with the grace of Christ and personal calls for divine aid, reflects his revision of the traditional view of God, as expressed in Burke's treatise: "In the scripture, wherever God is represented as appearing or speaking, every thing terrible in nature is called up to heighten the awe and solemnity of the divine presence" (69). Moreover, Smart expands Burke's definition of beauty—"that quality or those qualities in bodies by which they cause love, or some passion similar to it"—beyond "the merely sensible qualities of things" (91) to the possible implications of such aesthetic value.

The assumed dichotomy between the sublime and the beautiful can be examined a little further here. In his *Philosophical Enquiry*, Burke expresses the difference in terms of scale: "sublime objects are vast in their dimensions, beautiful ones comparatively small" (124). To some extent, this definition is pertinent because, as Smart suggests, the perimeters of his poem cannot expand to present the vast theme of God adequately. Smart's transcription of this theme into artistic beauty that is comprehensible to human readers can itself be viewed as a solution for this shortcoming. It might be posited that human expression cannot reach the level of the sublime and that beautiful writing represents the zenith of poetic expression. At the same time, the possibility of transcription and even the mention of "precious" signs in *Jubilate Agno* suggests that the use of beauty to describe a special language cannot be conceived in terms of physical appearance alone. Here, John Milbank's comparison between the sublime and the beautiful might be drawn upon to reassess the Burkean distinction. Milbank identifies beauty as something that is perceived, an "aura of invisibility hovering around the visible." Conversely, the sublime is described as "an experience of the ineffable and overwhelming."[22] It is not possible to transmit such an experience fully through poetry, but Smart's perception of the divine as beautiful can be depicted more easily. Within a linguistic, poetic context, this can be taken further. Smart aligns the poetry of harmonious nature with Christ, the Logos and incarnation with which man can share reciprocal communication. Seen in this light, Christianity provides a special physical and historical tangibility in the form of the incarnation, a figuring of the divine that almost prompts artistic expression. The sublime does not offer the same tangibility. Richard Viladesau's description of "aesthetic beauty as a means of the mind's 'ascent' to God—or, from another point of view, as a medium of divine self-revelation" is thus vital to an understanding of Smart's manipulation of artistic forms to represent divine language.[23]

It is unsurprising, then, that beauty reaches beyond superficial appreciation in Smart's poem of multiple languages to become an aim of his verse: "For in my nature I quested for beauty, but God, God hath sent me to sea for pearls" (B30). The Biblical resonances of this line suggest the value of expressive beauty. The poet reverses the parable of the pearl of great price (Matthew 13:45–46), and Smart himself is presented as an unwilling seeker of pearls, cast out "to sea" in his search. The parable in Matthew's Gospel presents an allegory to demonstrate the great sacrifice that is required to enter the kingdom of Heaven. The merchant in the tale "sold all that he had" to gain the "pearl" of heaven; Smart suggests that he has sold all he has (of sanity, possessions, or poetic license?) in his quest to achieve beauty of expression and a true transcription of Christ's poetry. As Hawes notes, Smart's status as translating poet is one of privilege: "though seemingly degraded, [he] is in reality magnified by his divinely enforced quest for the pearl of great price."[24] If we return to the original subject of artistic creation, we find in Erik Routley's account a less ethereal explanation for the poet's sense of sacrifice:

> It is not perhaps quite fair to say that to its maker the picture presents itself as a series of blobs of paint, the music as a series of marks on paper, or the church as a heap of stones. But any artist who has mastered to any degree the very arduous business of translating his conception into communicable form will tell you that the process of *making* involves very little, if any, thought about beauty.[25]

In essence, Smart's struggle is no different from that of any artist trying to find purity of expression in words, notes, shapes, or colors. Notably, though, as a poet he aims for the presentation of all art forms through the medium of words. The consciousness that beauty, as the human version of sublime expression, must be achieved in his writing presents a challenge and necessitates sacrifice in order to achieve a suitable, pure, poetic register.

The forging of a connection between visual art and written language is not, of course, unusual, and the development of a simultaneous appreciation of poetry and painting can be seen from Dryden through to the eighteenth century. In the preface to his translation of Du Fresnoy's *De Arte Graphica* (1665), Dryden draws a connection between the two art forms as similar modes of expression, whereby the structure or syntax of writing might be linked to the arrangement or ratio of objects on a canvas. Dryden extends this allusion to poetic writing in particular: "Expression, and all that belongs to words, is that in a Poem, which Colouring is in a Picture."[26] The traditional linking of colors and words might explain Smart's own interest in creating a new spectrum that surpasses the Newtonian series of seven colors and which ranges from "white to pale," taking in thousands of color varieties in-between (B650–60). The attack on the Newtonian spectrum in Fragment B of *Jubilate Agno* is not only an onslaught on empiricism, but a comment on the nature of color, itself an element of Burke's description of the qualities of beauty.[27] In addition, Smart aligns colors with a certain kind of divine communication, suggesting that "the blessing of God upon all things descends in colour" (B662). An immediate natural application is suggested for this: "the blessing of God unto perfection in all bloom and fruit is by colouring" (B669). That is, Smart considers the coloring of flowers in creation as a sign of divine blessing that can be extended to the various colors of other natural elements. It can be seen from this that the poet perceives color as a divinely ordained element of creation. Smart's yoking together of colorful flowers and poetry in *Jubilate Agno*—"For flowers are peculiarly the poetry of Christ" (B506)—thus points towards verbal expression, and the idea that there might be correct colors for the verbal painting of poetic description. Poetic painting that achieves the correct hue, it might be conjectured, will be the recipient of godly blessing.

Through the manipulation of color, then, the artist might be able to represent a kind of beauty that can reflect the sublime. As Philip Shaw recognizes, sublimity has a tendency to defeat both senses and words, "yet through this very defeat, the mind gets a feeling for that which lies beyond thought and language."[28] In "On the Immensity of the Supreme Being," submitted for the Seatonian Prize in 1751, Smart portrays the instinctive humility of the mortal artist, who is overshadowed by sublimity:

In vain thy pencil Claudio, or Poussin,
Or thine, immortal Guido, wou'd essay
Such skill to imitate—it is the hand
Of God himself—for God himself is there.[29]

Because of this underlying feeling that even prominent painters must adopt a special mode for divine illustration, the colors listed in the *Jubilate* cannot be restricted to a spectrum of only seven colors: in brown alone, Smart suggests, there are "ten thousand acceptable shades" (B669). To restrict the artist's color range would lessen his ability to form an accurate impression of the divine artist and his work. As Cicely Davis notes:

> Until the latter half of the eighteenth century colour was considered a mere appendage to the linear design; and this fact could be paralleled in poetry, for words were likewise an extrinsic beauty.[30]

Smart routinely commandeers the "extrinsic" as an unseen, mysterious element that is essential to divine language. In the *Jubilate*, beauty is used as the human indicator that something close to divine expression may have been achieved in art. In its position as a quality that cannot be measured empirically, but only through examples, beauty might thus be regarded as analogous to God.

A further artistic form that is invoked in *Jubilate Agno* is music, as the poet uses song and instrumentation to create a new language of praise that reaches beyond the spoken word. Smart was by no means the only writer of this era to find an important link between poetry and harmony. Indeed, the burst of activity in hymn-writing and Psalm translation led by Isaac Watts and his contemporaries during the eighteenth century suggests the development of a new awareness of music as a potential channel for communicating with God. Watts's *Essay Toward the Improvement of Psalmody* (1707) is particularly significant here because of the importance that it accords to singing:

> To speak the glories of God in religious Song, or to breathe out the joys of our own spirits to God with the melody of our voice, is an exalted part of divine worship.[31]

Watts supports this claim via an exhaustive study of the instances of singing in the New Testament, which is designed to justify the wholehearted integration of newly Christianized psalms into liturgy. In *Jubilate Agno*, this "exalted part of divine worship" is not only concerned with the participation of singers in church but also includes the involvement of all the "tongues" of creation in the harmony of divine praise, which is suggested as the origin of laudatory speech: "For my seed shall worship the Lord JESUS as numerous and musical as the grasshoppers of Paradise" (B100). In Smart's view, the sound created by generations of men singing in praise of God achieves harmony akin to the sound made naturally by insects—and so music is identified as a natural element of praise and divine description. The curious power of a hymn, in which the congregation is found singing the same words simultaneously, thus arises in *Jubilate Agno* as part of the new form of language.

A concern with musical purity can also be discerned in Smart's fascination with instruments and instrumental sound. The promotion of certain instruments such as the harp and the trumpet in *Jubilate Agno* has a scriptural precedent. The trumpet appears throughout the Old Testament in ceremonial contexts, whereas the harp is inextricably linked with David and the Psalms. Importantly, both instruments also have significance in the heavenly music of the Book of Revelation. The harp is closely associated with the divine throughout Smart's poem, in which it becomes a symbol of pure, powerful, reactive sound:

> For GOD the father Almighty plays upon the HARP of stupendous magnitude and melody. . . .
> For innumerable Angels fly out at every touch and his tune is a work of creation. (B246–47)

The inexplicable actions of the deity are translated into a musical context as something that is comprehensible to Man, and the "stupendous magnitude and melody" appears to refer to extra notes beyond the usual tones of music. The new dimension of a musical language is tied up with creation that is described as a mysterious sleight of hand. Again, we can see how Smart manipulates the comprehension of artistic beauty and applies it beyond the physical properties recognized by Burke to a conception of the divine as powerfully beautiful.

In his survey of church music, Paul Westermeyer suggests that it is possible to gain greater insight through the musical setting of a work because "music is also the means to interpret a text."[32] Yet in *Jubilate Agno*, music itself becomes a sort of language that requires interpretation. Smart dissects the sounds of music in the search for meaning and form:

> For the trumpet rhimes are sound bound, soar more and the like.
> For the Shawm rhimes are lawn fawn moon boon and the like.
> For the harp rhimes are sing ring string and the like. (B585–87)

Clearly, the plethora of articulated sounds accumulated here does not make the musical expression any more readable because no actual explanation is provided. Nevertheless, the transcription of sound vocalizes the music into poetic form and an instrumental hymn of praise is created within Smart's unsung poem. The monosyllabic notes of the instruments' sounds illustrate the heavenly quality that the poet praises in the trumpet, "the most direct and acceptable of all instruments" (B244). Directness or purity of sound correlates to pure expression in the spoken word. In music, the risk of "cant" (language that is distant from God) is perhaps more dangerous in the context of aesthetic temptation and the possibility that music might also divert the praising focus away from the spirit of God towards the carnal musician. The Platonic concept of the struggle between word and flesh, instrumental in the polemic over the use of music in early Christian tradition, lurks in church music and in suspicions about those who, in the words of Alexander Pope, "to the *Church* repair, / Not for the *Doctrine*, but the *Musick* there."[33] Smart's solution for the correct introduction of music into a liturgical setting is found in the promotion of musical instruments that require the least human intervention. Both the harp and the trumpet are in some sense 'pure' instruments that involve no artifice in playing. The trumpets of the Psalms and instruments up to the 1830s were played without valves, so that the notes that were produced were truly "natural," being produced by variation of aperture and breath rather than by mechanical intervention. Likewise, the harp has a string tuned to each note and its "rhimes" are played from these perfect ratios. In this way, the music that Smart valued most highly was that which achieved "God's natural key" with the least intervention from man.

In *Jubilate Agno*, the divine is viewed as Creator and praised by his creatures. The poet celebrates each creative act of God with zeal, transcribing it into a counterpart language of artistic creation that his readers might be able to comprehend:

> Hallelujah from the heart of God, and from the hand of the artist inimitable, and from the echo of the heavenly harp in sweetness magnifical and mighty. (A41)

God figures in the poem as the creator of language, the creator of music and the "artist inimitable." Furthermore, God can be praised through imitation of the "echo" of his own heavenly speech, that is transcribed into human measures through the sweet notes of the harp. Smart's poetic construct of communication is important because it translates a sense of sublime ("magnifical") mystery that is otherwise inaccessible. For Smart, artistic beauty stands as the human counterpart to the divine and sublime; Creation is achieved in and through the alphabet, the logos of Christ, the notes of the harp, and the painted color of the flowers. Each of these chimes with the "liberal disciplines" approved by Augustine in *On Christian Teaching*, as they teach the reading of signs and "provide an excellent ladder for the soul's ascent" to God.[34]

This analysis of the 1759 fragment of *Jubilate Agno* paints a clearer picture of Christopher Smart's challenge to the contemporary view of divine sublimity as described in Burke's *Philosophical Enquiry*. In the poem, Smart manipulates signs in letters, colors, and musical notes in order to overcome a sense of inarticulacy in the face of the sublime deity. By referring to the possibility of an expressive language beyond the confines of traditional religious poetry, the poet moves away from the Burkean model of terror and magnitude towards an interpretation of the beauty of human creativity. By stretching Burke's idea of beauty to encompass concepts in addition to sensible features, Smart locates artistic beauty as the human counterpart to divine creation. Through the description of letters beyond language, innumerable colors, and pure music, Smart suggests that the unknowable language of God can be reflected in the beauty of art. In the poet's own words, "all the inventions of man, which are good, are the communications of Almighty God" (B401).

Notes

1. Edmund Burke, *A Philosophical Enquiry into the Origin of our Ideas of the Sublime and Beautiful*, ed. J. T. Boulton (London: Routledge, 1958), 67–68. Subsequent references are given parenthetically.

2. Christopher Smart, "On the Power of the Supreme Being," in *Miscellaneous Poems, English and Latin*, ed. Karina Williamson, vol. 4 of *The Poetical Works of Christopher Smart*, ed. Karina Williamson and Marcus Walsh (Oxford: Oxford University Press, 1987), 274 (line 8).

3. Donald Davie, *A Travelling Man: Eighteenth-Century Bearings* (Manchester: Carcanet, 2003), 127.

4. Jeanne Murray Walker, "*Jubilate Agno* as Psalm," *Studies in English Literature* 20 (1980), 449–59.

5. Tom Keymer, "Presenting Jeopardy: Language, Authority, and the Voice of Smart in *Jubilate Agno*," in *Presenting Poetry: Composition, Publication, Reception*, ed. Howard Erskine-Hill and Richard A. McCabe (Cambridge: Cambridge University Press, 1995), 112.

6. Robert Lowth, *Lectures on the Sacred Poetry of the Hebrews*, trans. G. Gregory, 2 vols. (London: Johnson, 1787), 1:307.

7. Geoffrey H. Hartman, "Christopher Smart's 'Magnificat': Toward a Theory of Representation," *ELH* 41 (1974): 429–54.

8. Smart, *Jubilate Agno*, ed. Karina Williamson, vol. 1 of *Poetical Works* (Oxford: Oxford University Press, 1980), B252. References indicate the fragment and line number, and will be given parenthetically.

9. Smart, "On the Eternity of the Supreme Being," in *Miscellaneous Poems*, 148 (lines 13–14).

10. Smart, "On the Immensity of the Supreme Being," in *Miscellaneous Poems*, 186 (lines 49–50).

11. Smart, "On the Eternity of the Supreme Being," in *Miscellaneous Poems*, 150 (lines 83–84).

12. Smart, "On the Eternity of the Supreme Being," in *Miscellaneous Poems*, 148 (line 7).

13. Augustine, *Confessions*, ed. and trans. Henry Chadwick (Oxford: Oxford University Press, 2001), 5.

14. Zephaniah, 3:9.

15. Clement Hawes, *Mania and Literary Style: The Rhetoric of Enthusiasm from the Ranters to Christopher Smart* (Cambridge: Cambridge University Press, 1996), 169.

16. Alun Morris David, "Christopher Smart and the Hebrew Bible" (PhD dissertation, University of Cambridge, 1994), 115.

17. Henry More, *Conjectura Cabbalistica; or, A Conjectural Essay of Interpreting the Mind of Moses according to a Threefold Cabbala* (London: Fletcher, 1653), 56.

18. Smart, "On the Eternity of the Supreme Being," in *Miscellaneous Poems*, 148 (line 6).

19. Hartman, "Christopher Smart's 'Magnificat,'" 450–51.

20. Daniel C. Matt, *The Essential Kabbalah: The Heart of Jewish Mysticism* (New York: HarperSanFranciso, 1996), 102.

21. Murray Cohen, *Sensible Words: Linguistic Practice in England, 1640–1785* (Baltimore: Johns Hopkins University Press, 1977), 6.

22. John Milbank, "Beauty and the Soul," in *Theological Perspectives on God and Beauty*, ed. J. Milbank, Graham Ward, and Edith Wyschogrod (Harrisburg: Trinity Press International, 2003), 3.

23. Richard Viladesau, *Theology and the Arts: Encountering God through Music, Art and Rhetoric* (New York: Paulist Press, 2000), 4.

24. Hawes, *Mania*, 145.

25. Erik Routley, *Church Music and the Christian Faith* (London: Collins, 1980), 33.

26. John Dryden, *De Arte Graphica*, in *"De Arte Graphica" and Shorter Works*, ed. Alan Roper, vol. 20 of *The California Edition of the Works of John Dryden*, ed. Vinton A. Dearing (Berkeley and Los Angeles: University of California Press, 1989), 71.

27. As Burke describes: "First, the colours of beautiful bodies must not be dusky or muddy, but clean and fair. Secondly, they must not be of the strongest kind. Those which seem most appropriated to beauty, are the milder of every sort; light greens; soft blues; weak whites; pink reds; and violets. Thirdly, if the colours be strong and vivid, they are always diversified, and the object is never of one strong colour; there are almost always such a number of them (as in variegated flowers) that the strength and glare of each is considerably abated" (117).

28. Philip Shaw, *The Sublime* (London: Routledge, 2006), 3.

29. Smart, "On the Immensity of the Supreme Being," in *Miscellaneous Poems*, 187 (lines 79–82).

30. Cicely Davis, "Ut Pictura Poesis," *Modern Language Review* 30 (1935): 162.

31. *The Works of the Late Reverend and Learned Isaac Watts*, 6 vols. (London: Longman, 1753), 4:273.

32. Paul Westermeyer, *Te Deum: The Church and Music; A Textbook, A Reference, An Essay* (Minneapolis: Fortress Press, 1998), 38.

33. Alexander Pope, *An Essay on Criticism*, in *Pastoral Poetry and "An Essay on Criticism,"* ed. E. Audra and Aubrey Williams, vol. 1 of *The Twickenham Edition of the Poems of Alexander Pope*, ed. John Butt (London: Methuen, 1961), 277 (lines 342–43).

34. Augustine, *On Christian Teaching*, ed. and trans. R. P. H. Green (Oxford: Oxford University Press, 1997), 65.

Part IV

ENLIGHTENMENT AND ITS DISCONTENTS

7

AT FIRST SIGHT, DENIS DIDEROT and Jean Le Rond d'Alembert's *Encyclopédie; ou, dictionnaire raisonné des sciences, des arts et des métiers* seems to be an ideal text through which to examine the ideas and significance of any one year in the mid-eighteenth century. It appeared, at least at first, at roughly yearly intervals; counted among its contributors some of the leading thinkers and writers of its day; and engaged, through its mission to present all aspects of human knowledge, with a range of current issues (whether political, social, or philosophical). The text also presented itself quite consciously as the product of its time. As Diderot explained in 1755, in his entry "ENCYCLOPÉDIE": "Nous avons vû que l'*Encyclopédie* ne pouvoit être que la tentative d'un siecle philosophe; que ce siecle étoit arrivé" ("We saw that the *Encyclopédie* could only be the work of a philosophical century, and that this century had arrived").[1] History has indeed born out Diderot's assessment of the *Encyclopédie*. The project became the most important publishing venture of the eighteenth century and spawned a number of counterfeits, translations, and adaptations; it transformed Diderot from a struggling hack into an acclaimed writer and *philosophe*; and, during the Revolution and long after, the 'encyclopédistes', like the 'philosophes', were often held accountable for the collapse of the Ancien Régime.[2]

However, the *Encyclopédie*'s situation in 1759 is more complex than might at first appear. 1759 should have seen the appearance of the eighth volume, but 1759 was also the year in which the *Encyclopédie* hit its greatest crisis, which entailed the condemnation of all of the volumes published so far and the official suspension of the project as a whole. Had the project ended at this point, there is little doubt that the second half of the eighteenth century would have developed, and thought, very differently. Without entering into the thorny subject of how far the *Encyclopédie*—and the critical mindset it sought to encourage—influenced the extraordinary events of the 1780s and 1790s, it is certainly true to say that, without the *Encyclopédie*'s final ten volumes, we would not have had d'Holbach's excoriating attack on the priesthood and its corruption ("PRETRES" ["PRIESTS"]), any of the group of articles on alternative political systems ("Monarchie absolue" ["Absolute monarchy"], "Monarchie limitée" ["Limited monarchy"], "REPUBLIQUE" ["REPUBLIC"]), or Diderot's affirmation of the primacy of reason ("RAISON")—let alone the eleven groundbreaking plate volumes which, in themselves, constituted an unprecedented illustrative encyclopedia of France's arts and trades.[3]

Despite the ultimate victory of the *Encyclopédie* project over its enemies, it remains the case that the break in publication creates difficulty in situating volume VIII (the focus of this essay) in any precise point in time. The volume seems to have been almost ready for the press in late 1758, and was scheduled to appear in 1759, but did not in fact reach the public until 1768, along with the other remaining nine text volumes. Equally, we cannot be sure how far the version of volume VIII which appeared in 1768 was the same as that which would have appeared had publication indeed gone ahead in 1759. Diderot's correspondence in 1759, for example, suggests that new articles continued to be written for volume VIII for several months after its initial scheduled publication date.[4] Linking individual articles to particular years is thus problematic, as articles appearing in volume VIII in 1768 may possibly have been written some considerable time before their scheduled publication date of 1759, or not until the early- to mid-1760s. It is almost impossible to view any one *Encyclopédie* volume, especially Volume VIII, as representative of a particular point or year in time, and the following analysis should be understood as working within the limitations that such conditions generate.

Yet it remains the case that 1759—and 1758—were crucial years for the *Encyclopédie*. Despite the qualifications that need to surround a synchronic reading of these years in the work's publishing history, therefore, an examination of the *Encyclopédie* at this time, and of the impact of events on its content and philosophy, is certainly worthwhile. Philip Blom, for example, has argued that the events of these years radically changed the very nature of the project. The crisis of 1759, and the ensuing abandonment of the *Encyclopédie* by a number of key figures, led to the shifting of much of the actual work to the chevalier de Jaucourt. Under de Jaucourt, articles were produced at an astounding rate, with little time for great refinement and sophistication wit; and although we still find in the final ten volumes articles written with great passion, erudition, and humor, many articles were clearly written under the pressure of time and the knowledge that the *Encyclopédie* simply had to be completed, if it were not to fail entirely.[5] Similarly, John Lough notes that the final ten volumes contain far fewer radical articles than the first seven volumes, although there were still plenty of articles which would have offended the *Encyclopédie*'s enemies.[6] While this is undoubtedly true, I would suggest that, although the events of 1759 may have made the Encyclopedists rather more wary than they had been previously, the project's philosophical focus remained essentially the same. Indeed, if anything, the break in the *Encyclopédie*'s publication in 1759, as a result of the project's crisis and the resultant problems in the relationships and personal circumstances of its principal contributors, brought the Encyclopedists to reflect more fully on one of the central questions of the project, and an issue that lay at the heart of the Enlightenment itself: namely, the nature of man and the human experience.

Eight years before it was plunged into crisis, the *Encyclopédie* project had begun with royal approval and public acclaim. Since 1751, volumes I–VII had appeared to a broadly yearly timetable, and the project had already survived one skirmish with the censors in the early 1750s. The doctoral thesis of the abbé de Prades, an *Encyclopédie* contributor, had alarmed the Jesuit faction at the Sorbonne with its subversive content; a link was made to the *Encyclopédie* and it was claimed that de Prades and the Encyclopedists were engaged in a plot to spread anti-Christian sentiments. The government issued an *arrêt de conseil* in 1752 suppressing the project's first two volumes, but no arrests were made and only nominal fines were levied: most importantly, the *privilège* (permission to publish) was not revoked.[7] However, several factors combined in the late 1750s to bring the project into direct conflict with its critics and with the political and religious authorities. The appearance of volume VII, in late 1757, coincided both with an increase in the number and virulence of printed attacks from the project's critics, and with the draconian new censorship law that followed Damiens's assassination attempt on the King in January of that year, which declared that "Tous ceux qui seront convaincus d'avoir composé, fait composer et imprimer des écrits tendant à attaquer la religion, à émouvoir les esprits, à donner atteinte à notre autorité et à troubler l'ordre et la tranquillité des nos etats, seront punis de mort" ("All those convicted of having written, caused to be written, or printed, works intending to attack religion, stir up spirits, challenge our authority or disturb the order and tranquillity of society, are punishable by death").[8] D'Alembert's article "GENEVE" ("GENEVA"), which appeared in volume VII, did nothing to calm matters. D'Alembert's highly positive assessments of Geneva's political organization and religious life were rightly judged by the *Encyclopédie*'s critics as designed to encourage the reader to make unflattering comparisons with France's own situation. Rousseau's *Lettre à M. d'Alembert sur les spectacles* (1758), which refuted d'Alembert's suggestion that the ban on theatres should be lifted, is merely the most famous of the many attacks on the article and, by extension, on the *Encyclopédie* itself.[9] Additionally, the publication of Claude-Adrien Helvétius's atheistic philosophical text, *De l'esprit*, in July 1758, brought all Enlightenment works under fire, and in particular the *Encyclopédie*. Although he had never contributed to the *Encyclopédie*, Helvétius was well known as a friend of several Encyclopedists, and Diderot himself was widely (although falsely) suspected of having written several passages of *De l'esprit*.

It was in 1759, however, that the catastrophe struck. In January, the *avocat général*, Omer Joly de Fleury, denounced the *Encyclopédie* before the Paris Parlement, and the work's publishers were forbidden to sell any more copies until it had been thoroughly examined by a group of experts appointed by the Court. Six weeks later, the royal government issued an *arrêt du conseil*, withdrawing the *Encyclopédie*'s *privilège*, and police agents were sent to Diderot's house to confiscate all papers relating to the project.[10] The enterprise seemed doomed. Yet when the agents arrived at Diderot's residence, no material was found: the manuscripts had already been moved to a place of safety, namely the office of the sympathetic director of the book trade, Guillaume-Chrétien de Lamoignan de Malesherbes. Indeed, despite the apparent threat to the enterprise, a core group of *Encyclopédie* contributors around Diderot maintained a defiant and hopeful mood regarding the project's future. After considerable negotiation between the contributors, the publishers, and related allies, *Encyclopédie* publication resumed in the form of the plate volumes, while the authorities turned a blind eye (according a *permission tacite*) to the ongoing clandestine preparation of a further ten text volumes (volumes VIII-XVII), which would appear together in 1768.

If the threat to the *Encyclopédie*'s completion was finally overcome, though, it was perhaps inevitable that these fractious events would tell heavily on relations between the Encyclopedists themselves. The outcry over d'Alembert's article "GENEVE," together with more general attacks on the *Encyclopédie* and growing friction between himself and Diderot, led d'Alembert in early 1758 to declare his intention to resign from the project altogether; and it was not until the spring of 1759 that he formally agreed to resign his editorship but to continue contributing mathematical and scientific articles. The correspondence of both Voltaire and Diderot during these years details the negotiations between

the Encyclopedists over this issue. Diderot's letters to his friend, Friedrich Melchior Grimm, and his mistress, Sophie Volland, for instance, contain outbursts
of irritation at d'Alembert's behavior, highlighting his "impétuosité puérile"
("puerile impetuousness") and rendering in considerable detail what Diderot
saw as d'Alembert's self-serving reasoning and intractability.[11] Voltaire, by contrast, approved of d'Alembert's resignation and urged Diderot to do the same.
While this has often been interpreted as an invitation to renounce the project
completely if necessary, it is also possible that Voltaire had in mind a more strategic move; namely, that the joint resignation of both editors would constitute
a united front against their critics, thus presenting a statement more powerful
than any fractured continuation of the project. "Enfin mon avis," explained
Voltaire to d'Alembert in April 1758, "est toujours que les enciclopédistes et
consors soient inséparables, qu'ils quittent tous ensemble, et qu'ils reprennent
tous ensemble, et qu'ils terrassent leurs indignes ennemis" ("Ultimately my
opinion is, as ever, that the Encyclopedists and their associates are inseparable,
that they give up together, that they restart together, and that they strike down
their disgraceful enemies").[12] Here, though, the advice of the Enlightenment's
patriarch went unheeded, and Diderot continued with the project, albeit in the
face of increasing desertion from previous contributors.

In addition to d'Alembert's desertion, Rousseau had broken with the *philosophes* some time earlier (although his contribution to the *Encyclopédie* was not
considerable); and even among those Encyclopedists who continued to contribute
to the project, relations were far from easy. While unstinting in his support, for
example, Paul Thiry d'Holbach—one of the *Encyclopédie*'s wealthiest and most
socially influential collaborators, and author of articles on both scientific and
religious subjects—proved to be somewhat uncongenial as both friend and host
during Diderot's visits to d'Holbach's country estate of Grandval in the course of
1759. Diderot's letters to Sophie and Grimm during the summer and autumn of
1759 portray Grandval as something of a free-thinking rural idyll, but nevertheless an idyll which risked being troubled by the mood swings and idiosyncrasies
of its host. Furthermore, while the chevalier de Jaucourt proved his dedication to
the project by taking on increasingly more work, there seems to have been a lack
of true friendship between himself and Diderot. Although the "Avertissement" to
volume VIII richly eulogised de Jaucourt's contribution to the project, Diderot's
private opinion of the chevalier was far less warm. In sum, although the project
continued, defiant and resolute, the "sentiment de bienveillance réciproque"
("feeling of reciprocal benevolence"), which Diderot had presented in his article

"ENCYCLOPÉDIE" as a central attribute of the *Encyclopédie* contributors, had become increasingly unstable by the late 1750s.[13]

In addition to the internal problems within the broad group of *Encyclopédie* contributors, Diderot had, in July and August 1759, to deal both with the emotional impact of his father's death and a visit to the family home at Langres to reconcile tensions between his brother, the abbé, and his sister, nicknamed Soeurette.[14] Despite this self-imposed role as go-between, the three weeks which Diderot spent at Langres in the summer of 1759 seem to have offered him time to reflect in a more personal, immediate manner on questions of human nature and morality which he was planning to address in writing. According to his letter to Grimm at this time, Diderot was working on plans for plays entitled *Le Train du monde, ou les moeurs honnêtes commes elles le sont*; *Madame de Linan ou l'Honnête femme*; and *L'Infortunée, ou les Suites d'une grande passion* (*The Way of the World, or Honest Morals As They Are*; *Madame de Linan, or The Honest Woman*; and *The Unfortunate Woman; or The Effects of a Great Passion*).[15]

The crisis of the late 1750s, then, serious as it was, was not only a threat to the actual continuation of the *Encyclopédie* project. Rather, the external pressure placed upon the project by its censors and critics was doubled by internal tensions among the contributors themselves. Such tensions threatened to jeopardize the core principles of the project—which Diderot, in his 1755 article, had defined as collaboration, reciprocal fellow-feeling, and an altruistic desire to contribute to the good of humanity.[16]

1759 may thus be seen as a considerably important year for the *Encyclopédie*, in terms of both the project itself and the relationships and personal circumstances of its principal collaborators. To what extent, then, can we discern the influence of this fraught period on the actual content of the *Encyclopédie*? As noted earlier, any attempt to link volumes and articles to particular years must remain tentative. Nevertheless, it is worthy of note that Volume VIII, in covering the letters H to J, contains a whole host of articles relating to issues of human behavior and (im) morality. Such articles include "HOMME" ("MAN"), "Humaine espèce" ("Human species"), "Humeur" ("Mood"), "JALOUSIE" ("JEALOUSY"), "IDIOT" ("IDIOT"), "IGNOBLE" ("IGNOBLE"), "ILLICITE" ("ILLICIT"), and "IMPARDONNABLE" ("UNPARDONABLE"). Given the alphabetical nature of the project, this is to some extent circumstantial. But it is not entirely so, as may be seen from the "Avertissement" which opens volume VIII. This brief introduction to the volume, written shortly before its publication in 1768, presents the achievements of the project against the background of the difficulties it had encountered. In doing so, its opening paragraph focuses not on the intellectual challenge of the encyclopedic enterprise, but on the moral worth of the project, the virtue of those involved in it, and the vices of the enemies against which the *Encyclopédie* contributors had had to fight:

> Lorsque nous commençâmes à nous occuper de cette Entreprise, la plus vaste peut-être qu'on ait jamais conçue en Littérature, nous ne nous attendions qu'aux difficultés qui naîtroient de l'étendue & de la variété de son objet; mais ce fut une illusion passagere, & nous ne tardâmes pas à voir la multitude des obstacles physiques que nous avions pressentis, s'accroître d'une infinité d'obstacles moraux auxquels nous n'étions nullement préparés. Le monde a beau vieillir, il ne change pas; il se peut que l'individu se perfectionne, mais la masse de l'espece ne devient ni meilleure ni pire; la somme des passions malfaisantes reste la même, & les ennemis de toute chose bonne & utile sont sans nombre aujourd'hui comme autrefois.[17]

> [When we began our involvement with this enterprise, the biggest perhaps that has ever been conceived of in literature, we expected only those difficulties arising from the scope and variety of its subject-matter; but this was a passing illusion, and we were not long in seeing the multitude of physical obstacles we had foreseen supplemented by an infinity of moral obstacles for which we were in no way prepared. The world may well age, but it does not change; it may be that the individual perfects himself, but the mass of the species becomes neither better nor worse; the sum of destructive passions remains the same, and the enemies of every good and useful thing are today, like always, without number.]

The moment of the project's crisis may thus be said to have highlighted to the Encyclopedists the importance of reflecting on the human faults which brought this crisis about. Importantly, this reminder itself brought the project more firmly back to a consideration of what was, after all, the central element in the *Encyclopédie*'s presentation of human knowledge: the human subject itself. As Diderot had argued in his entry "ENCYCLOPÉDIE":

> Une considération sur-tout qu'il ne faut point perdre de vûe, c'est que si l'on bannit l'homme ou l'être pensant & contemplateur de dessus la

surface de la terre; ce spectacle pathétique & sublime de la nature n'est plus qu'une scene triste & muette. L'univers se taît; le silence & la nuit s'en emparent. Tout se change en une vaste solitude où les phénomenes inobservés se passent d'une maniere obscure & sourde. C'est la présence de l'homme qui rend l'existence des êtres intéressante; & que peut-on se proposer de mieux dans l'histoire de ces êtres, que de se soûmettre à cette considération? Pourquoi n'introduirons-nous pas l'homme dans notre ouvrage, comme il est placé dans l'univers? Pourquoi n'en ferons-nous pas un centre commun? Est-il dans l'espace infini quelque point d'où nous puissions avec plus d'avantage faire partir les lignes immenses que nous nous proposons d'étendre à tous les autres points? Quelle vive & douce réaction n'en résulterait-il pas des êtres vers l'homme, de l'homme vers les êtres?[18]

[One consideration above all that must not be forgotten, is that if man or the thinking and contemplating being were banished from the face of the earth, the sublime and pathetic spectacle of nature becomes nothing more than a sad and mute scene. The universe is silenced; silence and night take hold. Everything changes into one vast solitude where unobserved phenomena occur in obscurity and silence. It is the presence of man which makes the existence of other beings interesting; what can we better propose for the history of these beings, than to bear this consideration in mind? Why not place man in our project as he is placed in the universe? Why not make him the common focus? Is there, in the infinity of space, another point from which we could to better advantage extend the immense lines which we propose to develop to every other point? What lively and soft reaction would not result from this link from other beings to man, from man to other beings?]

This emphasis on the human subject at the center of all knowledge runs throughout the *Encyclopédie*, for instance in d'Alembert's account of the origins of knowledge in man's senses and its development through mankind's needs, and in the Encyclopedic tree of knowledge, the *Système figuré des connoissances humaines*, rooted in the three human faculties of memory, reason, and imagination, and with its three central branches of history, philosophy, and the creative arts.[19] And it is equally in evidence in volume VIII, the volume arguably the most affected by the 1759 crisis.

The temptation to see a particular historical aptness in the convergence of the central *Encyclopédie* volume (the eighth of seventeen text volumes) with its moment of greatest crisis and a set of articles dealing with the *Encyclopédie*'s central focus is, then, strong. Indeed, it is not untenable to suggest that the possibilities offered by the historical circumstances surrounding Volume VIII were noted by the Encyclopedists themselves. *Encyclopédie* contributors and editors were, after all, adept at playing with the alphabetical ordering of the work for their own ends. The article "AGNUS SCYTHICUS" in the *Encyclopédie*'s first volume, for instance, which moves from a discussion of a mythical plant to an elaboration of the methods to be used in independently judging the truth of even the most authoritative-sounding 'facts', is conveniently placed to act as a guide for the reader as he or she progresses through the rest of the project. Similarly, the *Encyclopédie*'s final article, de Jaucourt's "ZZUÉNÉ," quickly dismisses the original subject of the article, "ville située sur la rive orientale du Nil, dans la haute Egypte, au voisinage de l'Ethiopie" ("town situated on the east bank of the Nile, in upper Egypt, near the border with Ethiopia"), and passes on to a valedictory celebration of the project's achievements:

> Pour étendre l'empire des Sciences & des Arts, dit Bacon, il seroit à souhaiter qu'il y eût une correspondance entre d'habiles gens de chaque classe; & leur assemblage jetteroit un jour lumineux sur le globe des Sciences & des Arts. O l'admirable conspiration! Un tems viendra, que des philosophes animés d'un si beau projet, oseront prendre cet essor! Alors il s'élevera de la basse région des sophistes & des jaloux, un essaim nébuleux, qui voyant ces aigles planer dans les airs, & ne pouvant ni suivre ni arrêter leur vol rapide, s'efforcera par de vains croassemens, de décrier leur entreprise & leur triomphe.[20]

> [To spread the empire of the Sciences and the Arts, said Bacon, it is to be wished that there were a correspondence between knowledgeable men in each group; and their cooperation would shed glorious light on the globe of the Sciences and the Arts. O admirable conspiracy! The day will come, when philosophers animated with this great aim will dare to take their flight! And from the lower regions a nebulous swarm of sophists and jealous men will arise, who, on seeing these eagles glide through the air, and being unable either to follow or to halt their swift flight, will attempt to denigrate their enterprise and their triumph with futile cawing.]

It is entirely possible, then, to read significance into the placement of particular discussions within the project as a whole. In the opening volume of the *Encyclopédie*, readers were presented with an article instructing them on how to assess any form of 'knowledge' with which they might be presented; and, at the end of the project, we are invited to share in the victory of the Encyclopedists over their enemies. So while articles entitled "HOMME," "JALOUSIE," "HEUREUX," or "IRRELIGIEUX" are only to be expected in an alphabetical volume running from "H" to "ITZEHOA," I would suggest that the (admittedly coincidental) timing of this volume gave the Encyclopedists a perfect opportunity to engage in the reflections on human nature, its vices and its virtues, which made the *Encyclopédie* such an important yet risky Enlightenment enterprise.

Looking more closely at Volume VIII, what we find are a group of articles that offer a snapshot of key *Encyclopédie* debates around human nature, behavior, and relationships. The activity of the mind is a key element here: Voltaire's article on the imagination, for example, runs to several pages, examining in detail both the origins and the workings of the imagination and discussing a number of different types of imagination—active, passive, and inventive (560–63). But central, of course, is the question of epistemology. Just as d'Alembert espoused Lockean epistemology in the "Discours Préliminaire" to the *Encyclopédie*, so here we find Diderot's article, "INNÉ," stating that "il n'y a d'*inné* que la faculté de sentir & de penser; tout le reste est acquis. Supprimez l'oeil, & vous supprimez en même tems toutes les idées qui appartiennent à la vûe" (574: "nothing is *innate* but the ability to feel and think; everything else is acquired. Remove the eye, and you remove at the same time all ideas relating to sight"). What might seem a relatively unremarkable article by Diderot nevertheless contains seeds of a more radical philosophy, which has important implications for his understanding of human behavior. His statement in the middle of "INNÉ," that "toutes ces idées & tous ces sens supprimés, il ne reste aucune notion abstraite; car c'est par le sensible que nous sommes conduits à l'abstrait" ("suppress all these ideas and all these senses, no abstract notion will remain; because it is through the sensible that we are led to the abstract"), following as it does his comments on the suppression of sight, is just a short step away from the theories espoused in his controversial earlier text, the *Lettre sur les aveugles* (1749), which had earned him three months in Vincennes prison. If all of our knowledge and abstract ideas are developed from the knowledge we gain through our senses, argued Diderot in the *Lettre*, then so is our morality (a blind man will have a different hierarchy of virtues and vices) and even our religious beliefs. "Si vous voulez que je croie en Dieu," Diderot has the blind mathematician,

Saunderson, argue to the priest at his death bed, "il faut que vous me le fassiez toucher" ("If you want me to believe in God, you must let me touch him").[21]

That Diderot only hints at this extension of his argument in "INNÉ" is perhaps an indication of how much more wary he had become in the intervening decade. Nevertheless, materialist theories of life and human nature are still in evidence in the *Encyclopédie*'s eighth volume. "IMPÉRISSABLE" ("IMPERISHABLE"), again by Diderot, presents the theory of the eternity of matter, and Diderot employs another visual metaphor in "HAZARD" ("CHANCE") to explain the determinism which is a key element of his materialism. Using the example of a painter who 'accidentally' achieves the representation of the foam on the mouth of a horse by throwing a sponge at the canvas in a fit of irritation, Diderot explains that there is no such thing as accident, or chance, as even though the painter himself did not intend the sponge to create that effect, this was no chance occurrence but rather a result of the combination of the direction in which he threw the sponge, the distance it travelled, the force employed, the shape of the sponge, and of gravity acting upon it. "L'on trouveroit en calculant bien qu'il étoit absolumment impossible, sans changer les lois de la nature, que l'effet n'arrivât point," states Diderot, concluding: "Nous en dirions autant de l'univers, si toutes les propriétés de la matiere nous étoient bien connues" (74–75: "Upon careful calculation one would find that it was absolutely impossible, without changing the laws of nature, for the effect not to happen. We would say as much of the universe, if all the properties of matter were fully known to us"). Once again, an informed reader would have appreciated that "universe" and "matter" encompassed all known phenomena, including intellectual and 'spiritual' processes; and once again, Diderot's wariness is shown by his leaving deliberately ambiguous the actual role of the painter, and of God, in the act of 'creation'.

This materialist determinism finds its way, too, into more explicit discussions of human behavior and motivations, and in particular the question of how far one's moral character is a matter of choice and intention or of heredity and environment. For Diderot, as he outlines in the article "HABITUDE," behavior is not a matter of being deliberately 'virtuous' or 'vicious' but, rather, an effect of influences that are often beyond our control:

> Si l'on considere jusqu'où les enfans ressemblent quelquefois à leurs parents, on ne doutera guere qu'il n'y ait des penchans héréditaires. Ces penchans nous portent-ils à des choses honnêtes & louables, on est heureusement né; à des choses deshonnêtes & honteuses, on est malheureusement né. (17)

[If one considers the extent to which children sometimes resemble their parents, one will not doubt that there are hereditary tendencies. If these tendencies steer us towards honest and praiseworthy things, one is fortunately born; towards dishonest and shameful things, one is unfortunately born.]

Even if not all of the Encyclopedists went as far as Diderot did towards a deterministic understanding of human behavior, it becomes clear on reading the articles on human behavior in this volume that a new, secular morality was beginning to emerge. Examples here are Diderot's articles, "HAINE" ("HATRED"), "HESITATION" ("HESITATION"), "Humeur" ("Mood"), "IMPARTIAL" ("IMPARTIAL"), and "INTEGRE, INTEGRITÉ" ("HONEST, HONESTY"); Voltaire's "HEUREUX, HEUREUSE, HEUREUSEMENT" ("HAPPY, HAPPILY"); de Jaucourt's "JALOUSIE" ("JEALOUSY"); and the unsigned articles "HAUTAIN" ("HAUGHTY") and "Hauteur" ("Haughtiness"). Such articles deal with aspects of human behavior from a worldly, rather than from a religious, perspective, and the criticism of a religious approach to morality implicit in this bias is more explicitly evident in other, related, articles. Notably, what is at stake here is the disjunction between human impulse and religious doctrine: moral values are universal, founded as they are in human nature, argues Diderot in "IRRELIGIEUX" ("IRRELIGIOUS"), whereas religious values are particular and therefore limited (909). Diderot's article on "JOUISSANCE" ("ENJOYMENT") seems almost a deliberate attempt to shock traditional religious morality: after a brief and generalist definition of the term, the article moves swiftly to an exploration of the pleasure of orgasm. Diderot defends his subject against an imagined prudish critic by giving Nature a voice: "Crois-tu que ta mere eût exposé sa vie pour te la donner, si je n'avois pas attaché un charme inexprimable aux embrassemens de son époux? Tais-toi, malheureux, et songe que c'est le plaisir qui t'a tiré du néant" (889: "Do you believe that your mother would have risked her life to give life to you, had I not lent the caresses of her husband such an inexpressible charm? Hush then, unfortunate, and understand that it is pleasure which brought you out of nothingness"). Such light-hearted articles aside, there is a serious point to be made: trying to make human nature conform to arbitrary and inflexible laws is not only unfeasible but, more importantly, harmful both to individuals and to society. In his article "INDISSOLUBLE," thinking perhaps of his own unhappy marriage, Diderot warns of the dangers of unbending moral and legal strictures: "Les legislateurs qui ont préparé aux hommes des liens *indissolubles*, n'ont guere connu son inconstance naturelle. Combien ils ont fait de criminels et malheureux?" (684: "The legislators who designed *indissoluble* bonds for men can hardly have understood their natural inconstancy. How many criminals and unhappy men have they created?"). Human nature may be shaped by external factors (and thus malleable), but it is also inconstant and drawn to pleasure: the only way to make men better is to understand them as they are.

Finally, to return to the historical moment of volume VIII and to the Encyclopedists themselves, one further element that is worthy of note in the articles in this volume is the extent to which the Encyclopedists can be seen to reflect upon their own situation, as the self-reflective act of writing about Man leads to the self-reflexive act of writing about writers and writing. One of the most notable *Encyclopédie* attacks on its critics is found in the article "JESUITES" ("JESUITS"), written after the expulsion of the Jesuits from France in 1764. The article takes the form of a gleefully 'sympathetic' examination of where exactly the Jesuits went wrong; namely, that they had outstretched their talents and sought too much secular power (512–16). Other, more subtle hints to the *Encyclopédie*'s situation, and to the relationships between the Encyclopedists themselves, are also to be found in the volume. Diderot's suggestions about how to remedy arguments caused by ill-humor, for example, are not only pertinent to his own familial situation in 1759 but also, perhaps, a small and indirect dig at d'Alembert's own ill-humor, as he advises the person of ill-humor to

> Courir chez un malheureux pour le soulager ou pour le consoler, se livrer à une occupation utile, faire une action qui doive plaire à l'ami qu'on estime, s'avouer à soi-même la faute qu'on a faite. (351)

> [Run to relieve or console the unhappy, devote oneself to a useful occupation, do something which would please an esteemed friend, admit to oneself the mistake one has made.]

Articles that comment in a general way on struggles against adversity may likewise be read as an expression of the Encyclopedists' own determination to continue in the face of opposition. The article "IGNOMINIE" ("IGNOMINY"), for example, may serve as a warning to the *Encyclopédie*'s enemies, reflecting as it does on the difference between the ignominy brought about by one's own actions and that created by unjust condemnation, which leads rather to the shaming of the calumniators (549). Equally, Diderot's article "INSURMONTABLE" registers a challenge to those who would wish to see the *Encyclopédie* crushed by insurmountable opposition:

> Les projets qui paroissent les plus faciles au premier coup, présentent ensuite des difficultés *insurmontables*. Lorsque nous jugeons qu'une chose est *insurmontable*, c'est par le rapport des moyens aux obstacles. Ainsi ce jugement suppose deux choses bien connues, la force des moyens & la grandeur des obstacles. (804)

> [The projects which seem the easiest at first sight, later present *insurmountable* difficulties. When we judge that a thing is *insurmountable*, this is due to the relationship of resources to obstacles. So this judgment relies on two things to be known, the strength of the resources and the size of the obstacles.]

Despite his efforts to persuade Diderot to resign from the project, though, it is Voltaire who proves the most outspoken defender of the *Encyclopédie* within its own pages. His articles for Volume VIII are peppered with observations on the art of compiling a dictionary, some of which are not entirely complimentary. His concluding comments to the article "HABILE" ("SKILFUL"), for instance, reflect his personal discontentment at not being given important enough subjects on which to write:

> On craint d'enfler ce Dictionnaire d'inutiles déclamations; ceux qui président à ce grand & important Ouvrage doivent traiter au long les articles des Arts & des Sciences qui instruisent le public; & ceux auxquels ils confient de petits articles de littérature doivent avoir le mérite d'être courts. (6)

> [One fears inflating this Dictionary with useless declamations; those who preside over this large and important work must give length to the articles on the Arts and Sciences which instruct the public; and those to whom they entrust short articles on literature should have the merit of being brief.]

Yet Voltaire's support for the philosophical aims of the project was never in doubt, and his parting shot in the article "HEUREUX" ("HAPPY") is unmistakably an attack on those who had tried—and failed—to defeat the *Encyclopédie*:

On a voulu priver le public de ce Dictionnaire utile, *heureusement* on n'y a pas réussi. Des ames de boue, des fanatiques absurdes, préviennent tous les jours les puissans, les ignorans, contre les Philosophes; si *malheureusement* on les écoutoit, nous retomberions dans la barbarie dont les seuls Philosophes nous ont tirés. (195–96)

[Certain people wanted to deprive the public of this useful Dictionary, *fortunately* they have not succeeded. Minds of mud, absurd fanatics, every day warn the powerful and the ignorant against the Philosophes, if *unfortunately* they were heard, we would fall back into the very barbarity from which the Philosophes alone have saved us.]

Voltaire's outspoken critique of the opponents of the *Encyclopédie*, who are cast here as flawed thinkers and irrational enthusiasts, can serve both as a pithy testament to the crisis of 1759, and as a celebration of the central Enlightenment project that survived it.

Notes

1. Denis Diderot, "ENCYCLOPÉDIE," in *Encyclopédie; ou, dictionnaire raisonné des sciences, des arts, et des métiers*, ed. Denis Diderot and Jean Le Rond d'Alembert, 28 vols. (Paris: Briasson, David, Le Breton, and Durand, 1751–1772), 5:644. All English translations are my own.

2. On the afterlife of the *Encyclopédie* see Robert Darnton, *The Business of Enlightenment: A Publishing History of the "Encyclopédie," 1775–1800* (Cambridge, MA: The Belknap Press, 1979). For an almost completely fictitious account of the *Encyclopédie* 'conspiracy' against the Ancien Régime, see Stéphanie Félicité du Crest, comtesse de Genlis, *Les Diners du baron d'Holbach, dans lesquels se trouvent rassemblés, sous leurs noms, une partie des gens de la Cour et des littérateurs les plus remarquables du 18e siècle* (Paris: J. C. Trouvé, 1822).

3. Article titles in capitals denote main articles; article titles in lower-case denote sub-articles. Thus, "Monarchie absolue" and "Monarchie limitée" are sub-articles of the main article "MONARCHIE." Sub-articles were often written by a different author to that of the main article.

4. Diderot to Anne-Robert-Jacques Turgot, [21 January 1759], and to Friedrich Melchior Grimm, [April/May 1759], in *Correspondance*, ed. Georges Roth and Jean Varloot, 16 vols. (Paris: Editions de Minuit, 1955–1970), 2:110–12, 118–31.

5. See Philip Blom, *Encyclopédie: The Triumph of Reason in an Unreasonable Age* (London: Fourth Estate, 2004), chaps. 13–15.

6. John Lough, *The "Encyclopédie"* (London: Longman, 1971), 163.

7. For a detailed account of the *Encyclopédie*'s publication history, see Lough, *"Encyclopédie."*

8. Cited in Claudine Lavigne, "Les Stratégies de Voltaire face à la censure," in *Censure, autocensure et art d'écrire: de l'antiquité à nos jours*, ed. Jacques Domenech (Paris: Editions Complexes, 2005), 165.

9. See, for example, Lough, *"Encyclopédie,"* 221–23, 267–68; Gerhard Stenger, *L'Affaire des cacouacs: trois pamphlets contre les philosophes des Lumieres* (Saint-Etienne: Publications de l'Université de Saint-Etienne, 2004); Abraham Chaumeix, *Préjugés légitimes contre l'Encyclopédie*, 8 vols. (Paris: Herissant, 1758–1759); and Jean-Jacques Rousseau, *Lettre à M. d'Alembert sur les spectacles*, in *Oeuvres complètes*, ed. Bernard Gagnebin and Marcel Raymond, 5 vols. (Paris: Gallimard, 1959–1995), 5:9–52.

10. In addition, on 5 March 1789, both the *Encyclopédie* and *De l'esprit* were placed on the Index of prohibited books. See Catherine Maire, "L'Entrée des Lumières à l'Index: le tournant de la double censure de l'*Encyclopédie* en 1759," *Recherches sur Diderot et sur l'Encyclopédie* 42 (2007): http://rde.revues.org/index2363.html.

11. Diderot to Grimm, [April/May 1759], and to Sophie Volland, [14 October 1759], in *Correspondance*, 2:118–31, 272–79.

12. Voltaire to d'Alembert, 10 April [1758], in *Correspondence and Related Documents*, ed. Theodore Besterman, vols. 85–135 of *The Complete Works of Voltaire* (Oxford: Voltaire Foundation, 1968–1977), D7708.

13. Diderot, "ENCYCLOPÉDIE," in *Encyclopédie*, 5:636.

14. Diderot's descriptions of his brother and sister are revelatory not only of their characters but also of Diderot's own vision of human nature and relationships: his brother is "un bon chrétien qui me prouve à tout moment qu'il vaudrait mieux être un bon homme et que ce qu'ils appellent la perfection évangélique n'est que l'art funeste d'étouffer la nature" ("a good Christian who continually proves that it is better to be a good man, and that what they call Christian perfection is nothing but the dark art of smothering nature"), while his sister is "vive, agissante, gaie, dédidée, prompte à s'offenser, lente à revenir, sans souci nu sur le présent, ni sur l'avenir, ne s'en laissant imposer ni par les choses ni par les personnes; libre dans ses actions, plus libre encore dans ses propos; c'est une espèce de Diogène femelle" ("lively, active, gay, desiccated, quick to take offense, slow to forgive, who worries neither about the present nor the future, yielding to nothing and no-one; free in her actions, freer still in her speech; a kind of female Diogenes"): Diderot to Sophie Volland, 16 August 1759 and 31 July 1759, in *Correspondance*, 2:217–27, 188–91.

15. Diderot to Grimm, 20/21 July 1759, in *Correspondance*, 2:175–79.

16. Diderot describes the *Encyclopédie* as "ouvrage qui ne s'exécutera que par une société de gens de lettres et d'artistes, épars, occupés chacun de sa partie, et liés seulement par l'intérêt général du genre humain, et par un sentiment de bienveillance réciproque" ("a work which could only be undertaken by a society of men of letters and artists, scattered, each occupied with his own subject, and bound solely by the general good of humanity and by a feeling of reciprocal benevolence"): Diderot, "ENCYCLOPÉDIE," in *Encyclopédie*, 5:636.

17. Diderot, "Avertissement," in *Encyclopédie*, 8:i. Further references to volume VIII of the *Encyclopédie* will be given parenthetically.

18. Diderot, "ENCYCLOPÉDIE," in *Encyclopédie*, 5:641.

19. Diderot, "Explication détaillée du système des connoissances humaines," in *Encyclopédie*, 1:xlvii–li.

20. De Jaucourt, "ZZUÉNÉ ou ZZEUENE," in *Encyclopédie*, 17:751.

21. Diderot, *Lettre sur les aveugles*, ed. Marian Hobson and Simon Harvey (Paris: Flammarion, 2000), 59.

8

F AMOUSLY DIALOGIC IN THEME and structure, Samuel Johnson's *Rasselas* consists largely of conversations. Among other topics, the subject of causal relations crops up with surprising frequency in its characters' "materials for talk."[1] They debate the "relations and qualities of causes and effects" and question how far it is possible to know the "connexion of causes and events" (88, 122). Knowledge is dependent on such relations for, as Imlac asserts, "To know any thing . . . we must know its effects" (112). As the tale's resident rationalist, Imlac cleaves to the dictum that "the cause must have been before the effect" (112), but his model of logical priority must contend with the law of unintended consequences. Nekayah asks him what "is to be expected from our persuit of happiness, when . . . happiness itself is the cause of misery" (129), and even the usually implacable Imlac is forced to concede that causes can be "so various and uncertain, so often entangled with each other, so diversified by various relations" that to fix on determinate causal relationships would be to "live and die enquiring and deliberating" (67). Imlac's further admission that "[e]very man is placed in his present condition by causes which acted without his foresight" (67) underlines how the tale's survey of the vicissitudes of fortune is informed by philosophical questions of contingency and necessity.

Johnson's humanism and pessimism incline his narrator to frame such questions in terms of the mind's inadequacy to perceive them objectively. In its implied refusal to believe that "the deficiencies of the present day will be supplied by the morrow" (7), the tale's opening sententia makes a point not just about the vanity of human wishes but also about human cognition and its inherent bias towards relationships of logical consummation. *Rasselas* confronts this bias with the recognition that human beings use narratives of cause and consequence to help them to structure the external world, often misleadingly. In its broad philosophical sweep from the opening caution against credulous hope and expectation to its "conclusion, in which nothing is concluded" (175), the narration acknowledges literary fiction as a special case of a general human predisposition to overdetermine, oversimplify, and overinvest in causal logic. By way of corrective, *Rasselas* performs what Fred Parker calls a "sceptical identification of a mismatch between the fluid complexities of experience and the rational categories of the mind."[2] While such skepticism anticipates the philosophical program of postmodernism, it is firmly rooted in a contemporary debate about the nature of causation which was provoked by David Hume's controversial analysis of the topic. The present essay will trace in *Rasselas* some echoes and resonances of this debate. I will offer the Johnsonian condition of 'idleness', a key concern of his writing at this time, as an important analogue for Humean causelessness. Idleness can be understood, firstly, as an artistic realization of the day-to-day consequences of living in a universe lacking apparent connections between cause and effect and, secondly, as a psychological state afflicting those who enquire too deeply into such connections. By juxtaposing Hume on causation with Johnson on inaction, I wish to extend the established points of connection between the two writers. My aim is to show how *Rasselas*, like Johnson's other writing around 1759, engages with a question common to the philosophical project of both—namely, what one philosopher in *Rasselas* calls the "relations and qualities of causes and effects" (88).

Thanks to Hume, such relations were a matter for topical debate in the 1750s. Hume's best-known skeptical enquiry questions whether causality, which is usually assumed to be a relation between external objects, has any existence other than as a perception in the mind. Although past experience provides what seems intuitively like a certain answer, there is no way to know empirically, in Hume's most famous example, what will happen to one billiard ball after it is struck by another. Hume generalizes this principle beyond the billiard room to the sum of human knowledge about physical phenomena. "We cannot give a satisfactory reason, why we believe, after a thousand experiments, that a stone will fall, or fire burn," Hume writes in the *Enquiry concerning Human Understanding* (1748; first published under this title in 1758); "If we reason *a priori*, anything may appear able to produce anything."[3] Such statements are now generally interpreted to concern the limits of knowledge and the nature of human understanding: Hume's point is not that there is no causality, but rather that it cannot be empirically known or asserted incontrovertibly in the same way as the *a priori* truths of logic or mathematics. Modern philosophical accounts of Hume generally emphasize this distinction, along with the point that Hume's primary aim was to describe how humans apprehend causal relations rather than flatly to refute them.[4] Hume's contemporaries, by contrast, interpreted his account of causation as a deliberate and egregious denial of any necessary connection between cause and effect.[5] Richard Popkin details the growing controversy that this view provoked, from its beginning in the 1740s through the "serious arguments" of the following decade, and the eventual growth of a "national industry" in Hume-denial. As Popkin asserts, even though Hume's atheism was their ultimate target, contemporaries recognized that "the heart of Hume's case was his analysis of causality," and set out firstly to refute this analysis.[6] Hume's friend and distant cousin, Lord Kames, although not otherwise known for the orthodoxy of his views, was driven by his relative's apparent ultra-skepticism to affirm his own belief in "a fixed and settled train of causes and effects." "Nothing that happens," wrote Kames, "is conceived as happening of itself, but as an *effect* produced by some other thing"—a protest that is echoed in *Rasselas* when Imlac stresses that "the cause must have been before the effect" (112).[7] By bringing such intuitions into dispute, Hume's reasoning threatened to produce an anomic universe, which reduced temporal succession and necessary connection to a random string of unconnected events. It was a vision, wrote John Leland, of a world in which "[a]ll events are loose, separate, and unconnected, and only follow one another, without connection; and therefore there can be no continued chain of necessary causes at all." Leland's own response was to assert that Hume's way of arguing "proceeds upon a wrong foundation, and . . . is contrary to truth and reason"—an unsurprising response to an interpretation which reads Hume as insisting, in Galen Strawson's words, "that there is definitely no 'because' in nature."[8]

The topicality of counter-assertions like those of Leland lends an additional, subtextual nuance to Rasselas's being confined by the "order of succession" (8) or to Pekuah's desire that she would "gladly be fixed in some unvariable state" (175). It may also suggest a reason why debates about causation feature prominently in *Rasselas* even though its author was notoriously dismissive of abstract philosophical speculation. Even today, Johnson's interest in the 'philosophical' is often restricted to the popular use of that term to mean 'stoical', an attitude summarized in his own contention that writing should teach people "better to enjoy life, or better to endure it."[9] Yet *Rasselas* shows that such practical manifestoes are more easily announced than implemented, because considering them in any detail will necessarily raise abstruse metaphysical questions. When Rasselas encounters a philosopher of the Stoic persuasion at the assembly of the wise men in Cairo, he is reduced to uncomprehending silence by the philosopher's speech:

> To live according to nature, is to act always with due regard to the fitness arising from the relations and qualities of causes and effects: to concur with the great unchangeable scheme of universal felicity; to co-operate with the general disposition and tendency of the present system of things. (88)

In addition to this passage's well-documented caricature of mid-eighteenth-century optimism, a further target of its satiric attack is unthinking complacency about causal relations, which the philosopher implies in his gloss of nature as synonymous with the "general disposition and tendency of the present system of things."[10] Johnson's critique of the Stoic goal of living according to nature is less antagonistic to the goal itself than to the philosopher's specious assumption of consensus about what nature is and how human behavior fits into its "general disposition." The problem, as Johnson's entry for the word in the *Dictionary* drily notes, is that nature is "difficultly defined."[11] Part of the difficulty is that any definition must necessarily touch on what Nicholas Hudson calls "that primary law of nature, cause and effect."[12] As the Cairo philosopher acknowledges, to know this "universal and unalterable law" would be to escape the vagaries of the human condition as outlined in the opening sentence of the text, and so escape "the delusions of hope, or importunities of desire" (86). In *Rasselas*, though, this philosopher is just one among many sages who merely restate the problem without offering a workable solution.

Underlying the tale's focus on practical ethics, the problem of causation brings a metaphysical aspect to its self-advertized interest in moral actions and their consequences, "the choice of life" (175). The importance and abstract nature of such philosophical topics in his work can be overshadowed by Johnson's withering scorn for impractical or implausible arguments, for example his deriding such "bigot[s] of philosophy" as "the follower of Berkeley, who, when he sits writing in his table, declares that he has neither table, paper, nor fingers."[13] Modern criticism has, however, gone beyond the well-worn example of Berkeley's idealism to trace the practical impact of philosophical topics in Johnson's writing and in the context of a mid-eighteenth-century intellectual culture that saw philosophy and literature as part of the same enterprise.[14] One result of this reappraisal has been a willingness to recast Johnson as a skeptical thinker and to compare him on this score to Hume, a figure once thought to represent his antithesis. Work in this field, especially when touching on the question of Johnson's religious belief, initially tended to portray him as an agonized (and self-deceiving) conservative who concealed behind some impressive stonewalling a "suppressed recognition that he could not refute Hume."[15] A critical turn to secular philosophical issues has produced a different perspective, as exemplified by Adam Potkay and Leo Damrosch's books on Hume and Johnson. Although Johnson and Hume lived in an age of epistemological crisis, Damrosch argues, they were "close enough to a tradition of stable ontology—a 'real' reality that was supposed to be independent of human minds and grounded in the order of the universe—to try to salvage the coherence and reassurance of the older view."[16] Potkay's *The Passion for Happiness*, as its cheerful title suggests, downplays the suggestion that either Johnson or Hume was responding to a crisis, affirming instead that the two writers "share a great deal of common ground, not as part of some existential quandary, but rather as moral philosophers."[17]

Both accounts overstate Hume's intellectual conservatism, dismissing apparently radical elements in his thought as the result of its misappropriation by modern relativist viewpoints. But both also make a useful point about the nature of Johnson's relationship with Hume. While the Johnson of Boswell's biography offers plenty of blustering ripostes to Hume and other "sceptical innovators," Potkay contends, this is a "creative representation" beyond which intriguing points of comparison can be revealed.[18] These, Damrosch and Potkay both argue, are best understood neither in terms of conscious influence nor by scouring Johnson's work for traces of a Humean textual subconscious. Instead, both critics offer a view of their subjects as singing on similar themes from slightly different hymn sheets. Hume and Johnson, according to Potkay, represent "contrapuntal, related but independent voices"; or, in Damrosch's equally musical motif, "choric voices in dialogue with each other."[19] Voices in dialogue, as I suggested at the beginning of this essay, characterize both the structure and the content of *Rasselas*. An important background note in this conversation, even though it is not the most obvious of its themes to modern readers, is the contemporary debate on causation, as inflamed by Hume.

James Watt contends, in his contribution to this volume, that Johnson's tale stages a quest for "properly comprehensive forms of knowledge," during which not only the naïve Rasselas but also the learned Imlac is "made to confront the limits of his knowledge." Testing epistemological boundaries inevitably raised what was at once knowledge's most obvious and most problematic object at the time: the relationship between cause and effect. Uncertainty about the limits of knowledge takes on a practical urgency in *Rasselas*, and partly explains why nothing in the text is concluded and why no one actually makes the "choice of life." As Parker comments, when "knowledge is uncertain . . . or seen as an expression of the mind's subjectivity" it is difficult to know how to live (or indeed to know how to know how to live), and this is one reason why the eponymous hero, in Parker's words, "did not succeed, and could never have succeeded, in his search for information that would permit him to make a 'rational choice of life.'"[20] An especially pressing choice at this time would have been between the traditional view of causation as an objective fact, and Hume's account of it as a psychological mechanism.

Rasselas refracts this choice through the mental life of its characters as well as through their conversations. It does not explicitly address Hume's account of causation, but it does assert the role of individual perception in constructing narratives of cause and effect. Through various characters' mental states, the narration repeatedly suggests that causal connections forged in the mind can also be scrambled there, as when Rasselas complains that "I fear pain when I do not feel it" and is told that his grievance has "no real cause" (14–15). The trajectory of the narrative as a whole stages the hero's effort to join causes meaningfully to effects, starting from a point where "he knew not yet with distinctness, either ends or means" (17). By the tale's inconclusive conclusion Rasselas has progressed, albeit minimally, from delusive fantasies to comforting daydreams of "a little kingdom, in which he might administer justice" (175). His choice of vocation is not accidental: the turn to law and government represents a move toward the institutions that, according to Bruno Latour, bear historical responsibility for the enculturation of causal relationships. Latour cites Michel Serres's observation that the language of causation comes into being "according to the debates of an assembly or after a decision issued by a jury," from whence it goes on to structure the culturally determined but apparently "natural" law of cause and effect. Legal language, argues Latour, transfers to the phenomenal world to provide the basis for the modern scientific idea of causation. This idea could not have come into existence "outside our trials and our courtrooms." "Without accusation," he argues, "we have no causes to plead, and we cannot assign causes to phenomena." Rasselas's concluding fantasy thus signifies a return to the security of the legal discourse that "stages the very identity of cause."[21]

The tale's most sustained enquiry into the reality of causes comes in chapter LXI's encounter with the astronomer, who claims a causal connection between his will and meteorological effects in the external world:

> I have possessed for five years the regulation of weather, and the distri-
> bution of the seasons: the sun has listened to my dictates, and passed
> from tropick to tropick by my direction; the clouds, at my call, have
> poured their waters, and the Nile has overflowed at my command: I
> have restrained the rage of the dog-star, and mitigated the fervours of
> the crab. (144–45)

As diagnosed by Imlac, the astronomer's delusion invokes the theory of the
imagination presented in Hume's *Enquiry concerning Human Understanding*. Two
specific features of the astronomer's condition recall the *Enquiry*'s psychological
model of causation. He projects onto the external world a causal connection that is
felt in the mind, and his control of the weather presents an outlandish alternative
to commonsense notions of causality.

Hume offers a scenario similar to that of the astronomer in support of his
contention that it "is only experience which teaches us the nature and bounds of
cause and effect, and enables us to infer the existence of one from another." In
terms that the astronomer recalls, Hume asserts that "The falling of a pebble may,
for aught we know, extinguish the sun; or the wish of a man control the planets
in their orbits" (*Enquiry*, 164). This example is not concerned to offer a serious
alternative to most people's notions of the laws of nature, but rather to expose the
work of storytelling involved in subjecting the inanimate world to 'laws', metaphors derived from the discourses of judicial and political authority. People use
their experience of the world to select and construct plausible narratives based on
these metaphors, including that of causality. The idea that effects could be inferred
from causes without reference to such an experiential framework is as viable as the
notion, offered as self-evidently absurd, that planetary motion might be subject to
the control of some hidden intelligence. This serves heuristically to reveal widely-
held beliefs about causation as consensual fictions, which differ from delusional
ones not categorically but only in degree and quality.

Rasselas invests the mind's capacity for fiction-making with similar power
but makes more of its potential for both comedy and pathos. When Nekayah and
Pekuah laugh at the astronomer, for example, Imlac offers a sympathetic interpretation which stresses the dangers of too much time spent in solitary thought:

> When we are alone we are not always busy; the labour of excogitation
> is too violent to last long; ardour of enquiry will sometimes give way to
> idleness or satiety. . . . In time some particular train of ideas fixes the
> attention, all other intellectual gratifications are rejected, the mind, in

weariness or in leisure, recurs constantly to the favourite conception, and feasts upon the luscious falsehood whenever she is offended with the bitterness of truth. Then fictions begin to operate as realities, false opinions fasten upon the mind, and life passes in dreams of rapture or anguish. (151–52)

Imlac's etiology of delusion closely resembles Hume's account of the workings of the imagination. One crucial difference, though, is that, for Hume, Imlac's picture of fictions operating as realities could adequately describe normative as well as aberrant states. When, in section V of the *Enquiry*, Hume turns to discuss the imagination's "unlimited power" to combine ideas, he offers a working model of mental processes very similar to Imlac's diagnosis of how "some particular train of ideas" might make "false opinions fasten upon the mind." As Hume says of the imagination:

> It can feign a train of events, with all the appearance of reality, ascribe them to a particular time and place, conceive them as existent, and paint them out to itself with every circumstance, that belongs to any historical fact, which it believes with the greatest certainty. Wherein, therefore, consists the difference between such a fiction and belief? (*Enquiry*, 47)

Hume's answer is that this difference must be learnt and felt: the ability to distinguish beliefs from fictions "lies in some sentiment or feeling." Such a feeling compels the imagination, "whenever any object is presented to the memory or senses," to conceive by the force of custom "that object which is usually conjoined to it." Hume uses the word "object" here to mean any object of perception, including events. Custom is therefore the force that joins cause to its effect. "If I see a billiard-ball moving towards another, on a smooth table, I can easily conceive it to stop upon contact," Hume argues (*Enquiry*, 48). Our customary experience of the world, however, compels us to feel that the first ball will instead cause the second one to move. This feeling is so strong that it generally goes unrecognized as such and tends to be mistaken by ordinary people for an objective force in the external world. As John P. Wright puts it, the "vulgar mistake an associational connection for a genuinely perceived rational connection."[22] Causation is thus as much a product of sentiment as morality is: "when the same object is always followed by the same event; we then begin to entertain the notion of cause and connexion," Hume says. "We then *feel* a new sentiment or impression, to wit a customary connection in the thought or imagination between one object and its usual attendant"

(*Enquiry*, 78; emphasis added). Normative causal relations, in Hume's view, are guaranteed by the same criteria that the astronomer cites: constant repetition over long periods habituates the mind to entertain, to expect, and to *feel* a connection between effects and causes. When Imlac asks him for proof of the effects that he claims, the astronomer's reply shows how Hume's model has the potential to validate extreme solipsism: "it is sufficient that I *feel* this power that I have long possessed and every day exerted it" (147; emphasis added).

Although it resembles that of Hume, Johnson's portrayal of the relationship between subjective experience and the external world does not go to the same extremes of relativism. The astronomer's belief is a regrettable delusion rather than a necessary illusion, and whereas Hume's descriptive account willingly embraces "a fiction that works," as Damrosch puts it, Johnson's moralizing vision contrasts such fictions unfavorably to the realities for which they are mistaken.[23] It would therefore be hyperbolic, as Peter Loptson contends, to argue from surface similarities to Hume to a "fundamental philosophical unity" between him and Johnson on the subject of causation.[24] Nonetheless, there are teasing similarities between Hume's philosophical exempla and Johnson's psychological case studies. Part of the reason for this is that Hume's philosophical agenda is in many ways a psychological one, focused on the stories people unconsciously construct to make sense of the world. As Helen Beebee argues, Hume is primarily interested not in metaphysical questions but in providing "an account of the mental mechanism that generates beliefs about matters of fact."[25] This overlaps quite closely with the project of *Rasselas*, the work of a "superb literary psychologist," to quote Loptson, who was finely attuned to "the whispers of fancy, and . . . the phantoms of hope" (7).[26] From this opening sentence on, *Rasselas* stridently insists that nearly everybody is wrong not only in their most cherished beliefs but also in their most reflexive and basic intuitions. While Johnson's project shares this much with Hume, though, they diverge when it comes to the question of how to get past this realization.

As Fred Parker states, Hume exposes belief in causation and the external world as "a fiction to which we are habituated at so deep a level, that only the most intense and abstruse effort of philosophical thought can, for a moment, expose it as such."[27] While this exposure, and the effort involved in reaching it, could in theory prove psychologically damaging, Hume's well-known response is to neutralize their effect through sociable indifference. This is achieved in a famous passage at the end of the first book of *A Treatise of Human Nature* (1739). Hume surveys the implications of his arguments through what seems like an unusually confessional persona, admitting that their "*intense* view of manifold contradictions and imperfections in human reason" have "so wrought upon me, and heated my brain, that I am ready to reject all beliefs and reasoning." But Hume's step away from this crisis is taken as easily as that from one gaming table to another, as he sets aside the cosmic billiard balls to enter a reassuring world of convivial regularities: "I dine, I play a game of back-gammon, I converse, and am merry with my friends; and when after three or four hour's amusement, I wou'd return to these speculations, they appear so cold, and strain'd, and ridiculous, that I cannot find in my heart to enter into them any farther."[28] Hume's *Enquiry concerning Human Understanding* also adopts this sanguine perspective, but bypasses the skeptical crisis required to reach it. In place of the earlier text's skeptical aporia, the *Enquiry* offers a "*mitigated* skepticism" (*Enquiry*, 161; emphasis in original). The "great subverter of *Pyrrhonism* or the excessive principles of scepticism," Hume now writes, "is action, and employment, and the occupations of common life" (*Enquiry*, 158–59).

Like common sense, however, common life can sometimes be in short supply. Inaction, underemployment, and idleness are arguably occupations as common, if not more common, than the dynamic opposites offered in Hume's idealized picture. Hume's analysis of causation assumes as the subject of its thought experiments a kind of ideal gentleman: psychologically robust, clubbable, and apt to prefer backgammon to billiards. This is an appealing basis from which to reason about the nature of human understanding, but it is not a universally applicable one. In Michael Williams's pithy summary, "the Humean condition is not the human condition," and certainly not the human condition as Johnson tended to conceive it.[29] Whereas *Rasselas* proceeds from the assumption that "no human mind is in its right state" (150), Hume's analysis of causation presupposes a mind not merely healthy but rather at the peak of fitness, primed to switch with practiced ease between dizzyingly counterintuitive speculation and leisurely conviviality. The astronomer is one of a number of imperfect minds offered by Johnson that fail to meet the psychological standards of Hume's ideal experimental subject. *The Idler*, which appeared in the *Universal Chronicle* between April 1758 and April 1760, extends this theme to introduce a cast of characters who replay Hume's revolutionary critique of the psychology of causation as both tragedy and farce.

Like *Rasselas*, *The Idler* mixes humor and pathos in depicting what it calls "a species of misery or of disease, for which our language is commonly supposed to be without a name, but which I think is emphatically enough denominated 'Listlessness.'" The Idler's correspondent, Dick Linger, defines this merely as "a want of something to do."[30] But listlessness and idleness might also be interpreted as symptoms of the ethical paralysis induced by extreme philosophical doubt. Various commentators have identified this state, which occurs both at the end of *Rasselas* and at the conclusion of the first book of Hume's *Treatise*, with *ataraxia*, the condition of serene indifference, identified as the endpoint of the skeptical enquiry in Sextus Empiricus's *Outlines of Pyrrhonism*.[31] But whereas for Pyrrho (and arguably for Hume in the *Treatise*) this condition represents serene indifference, the successful outcome of a therapeutic process, its equivalent in Johnson's fiction is at once a sickness unto death and a way of life. For Johnson, as Gwin J. Kolb observes, "to talk about one's troubles is to reveal a degree of pleasure in them," and the Idler's talk of idleness, much like the endless conversations about choice in *Rasselas*, presents it as a condition to be enjoyed *and* endured because it may not be cured.[32]

This is in marked contrast to Hume, who shrugs off philosophically induced idleness in the *Treatise* and bypasses it in the *Enquiry*. But such nonchalance could only be learned by experience. Writing in 1734 about his early life, Hume spoke of being seized five years previously by a "Laziness of Temper" during which "all my Ardor seem'd in a moment to be extinguisht."[33] Johnson also famously suffered from listlessness in his youth, and in *The Idler* he begins in age to anatomize it with mocking solemnity. To live in idleness is to inhabit a mode in which temporal succession is minimal and, in extreme cases, absent. As Johnson maintains in a number published in February 1759, shortly after the completion of *Rasselas*: "If the parts of time were not variously coloured, we should never discern their departure or succession, but should live thoughtless of the past, and careless of the future, without will, and perhaps without power to compute the periods of life."[34] Although achieved by different means, this state closely resembles the "heroic Humean" universe from which will and intention are entirely absent and meaningful succession is replaced by accidental regularity.[35]

Johnson's version of this universe presents a wry contrast to Hume's theory of mind. Whereas necessary connection remains for Hume a psychological process so habitually entrenched as to go generally unnoticed, Idlers succeed in joining causes to effects only with feeble ineptitude—either through half-baked intentions, or mistakenly through error. Invoking the legal language that is the ultimate source of our notions of cause and effect, Mr Idler affirms that there is "no mark more certain of a genuine Idler, than uneasiness without molestation, and complaint without a grievance."[36] This condition also afflicts Rasselas, who complains: "I fear pain when I do not feel it; I sometimes shrink at evils recollected, and sometimes start at evils anticipated" (14). Like the astronomer, whose condition Imlac ascribes to "idleness or satiety," Rasselas comes to assent to the fictions of his own mind, when he chases after a robber only to realize that the whole scene has been "feigned to himself" (18). Eventually, Rasselas, having "regretted his regret," decides to alter his course by "resolving to lose no more time in idle resolves" (20). The narrator's use of polyptoton, where the same word is repeated with a different inflection, echoes Dick Linger's use of the same rhetorical figure in his final resolution: "I am now beginning in earnest to begin a reformation."[37] In both cases, the structure of the sentence conveys a double displacement that makes the declared intention unlikely to reach fulfillment.

Together, the various afflictions of Rasselas and assorted Idlers present psychological equivalents to the physical wrecks encountered in the Bath coffeehouse by Matthew Bramble, in Tobias Smollett's *The Expedition of Humphry Clinker* (1771). They are casualties of the mid-eighteenth century's other great conflict: the war on causality. *Idler* 24 presents such cases in varied array. Whereas the astronomer makes spurious causal connections, there are others who, unlike him, make no connections at all—even in the mind, where (according to Hume) all causal relations are forged. There are even, the Idler says, human minds in which nothing connects with nothing; minds where (to return to John Leland's nightmare vision of the Humean universe) everything is "loose, separate, and unconnected":

> It is reasonable to believe, that thought, like every thing else, has its causes and effects; that it must proceed from something known, done or suffered; and must produce some action or event. Yet how great is the number of those in whose minds no source of thought has ever been opened, in whose life no consequence of thought is ever discovered; who have learned nothing upon which they can reflect; who have neither seen nor felt anything which could leave its traces on the memory; who neither foresee nor desire any change of their condition, and have therefore neither fear, hope, nor design, and yet are supposed to be thinking beings.[38]

Here, the Idler seems to subvert his own reasonable supposition that "every thing . . . has its causes and effects." His parade of 'philosophical zombies' is initially quite frightening, but Johnson's punchline, when it comes, is to reveal them as a crew of quintessential Idlers: "maiden aunts with a small fortune; . . . younger brothers that live upon annuities; . . . traders retired from business; . . . soldiers absent from their regiments, . . . widows that have no children."[39] Even though this is one of Johnson's better jokes, it shares, along with much of his writing around 1759, a seriousness arising from its acute insights into the condition of idleness.

Not only is the "psychology of boredom," as Catherine Parke maintains, "central to an understanding of Johnson's distinctive approach as a critic and moralist," his notion of idleness by this time goes beyond common laziness to describe ethical paralysis, moral torpor, and physical inertia not as sins but as a tragicomic inevitability.[40] As Fred Parker notes, this represents a significant change from Johnson's earlier presentation of idleness. Whereas, in *Rambler* 85 (1751), "to be idle is to be vicious," by the time Johnson was writing *Rasselas* "personal idleness seems the natural response to . . . the idleness of existence as revealed by sceptical thought."[41] *Rasselas* presents this revelation comically, and without the melodrama of Hume's *Treatise*. But in marked contrast to the confident progress of Hume's thought beyond skeptical aporia, Johnson's Abyssinian idlers merely struggle from ignorant lassitude to informed stasis, where they are denied even the comfort of complete mental inactivity afforded the supposedly thinking beings of *Idler* 24.

Rasselas's characters follow a steeply declining learning curve, where the desire to effect practical change eventually subsides into subdued or stunned contemplation of the difficulty of doing so. This aspect of the text's philosophical program is announced and enforced with the remorseless logic of slapstick in chapter VI's "dissertation on the art of flying" (22). The description of how Rasselas's mechanist friend, setting out to test his flying wings, "leapt from his stand and in an instant dropped into the lake" (28) comically enacts a textbook example of causation, the motion of falling bodies. Robert Boyle's *Free Enquiry into the Vulgarly Received Notions of Nature* (1686) constitutes one of the textbooks in question. Johnson quotes extensively from Boyle's text in the revised entry on 'nature' in the fourth edition of the *Dictionary*. When "the stone falls or the flame rises," Boyle says, "we may say, that *the motion up or down is spontaneous*, or *produced by its proper cause*."[42] Boyle's phrase "proper cause" is suggestive, given that propriety connotes the languages of commerce and decorum as well as science. The notion that an inanimate object falls to earth in accordance with what is right and proper illustrates how the pseudo-legal discourse of causation grafts narratives of ownership and rectitude onto the phenomenal world. It personifies abstractions and makes people into an impersonal force—as we still do when we speak of the 'properties' of inanimate objects, or when describing someone's goods as their 'effects'. In *Rasselas*, Johnson literalizes the implied moralizing of such language. The mechanist's fall is occasioned not only by gravity but by pride, specifically his presumption that, because "only ignorance and idleness need crawl upon the ground" (24), he can transcend the condition of idleness.

The astronomer's confidence stands in contrast to the hesitancy of Rasselas, who opines that "no man will be able to breathe in these regions of speculation and tranquility" (26). Although intended in their respective concrete senses to denote "examination by the eye" and the upper air's lack of motion, Rasselas's reservations about "speculation and tranquility" have clear metaphorical undertones when applied to the text's philosophical themes, especially if we recall that "speculations" are what drive Hume from his desk to the backgammon table.[43] *Rasselas* strenuously tests the skeptical doctrine that sustained intellectual speculation might lead to mental tranquility, and finds it wanting. When the mechanist's flight is brought to an abrupt halt but his mind continues to race with "terrour and vexation" (28), readers are presented with an ironic contrast between the achievement of physical stasis and the persistence of mental restlessness. He has become an Idler—held fast both by physical inertia and frenetic but fruitless mental activity. Enforced from the beginning, this unique form of idleness comes by the end of the text to represent the only achievable option in the choice of life. *Idler* 101 compresses this aspect of *Rasselas*'s moral vision into a few paragraphs with the tale of Omar; who, despite being possessed by "a restless desire of seeing different countries," has "always resided in the same city" and is bound by "unalterable resolutions of contemplative retirement . . . to dye within the walls of Bagdat."[44] A similar fate befalls *Rasselas*'s main characters. Whether they choose like Imlac and the astronomer to be "carried along by the stream," like Pekuah to be "fixed in some unvariable state," or like Nekayah and Rasselas to busy themselves in constructing kingdoms and colleges of the imagination, the travelers achieve a form of bustling inactivity far removed from Hume's preferred specific against excessive contemplation of causes and effects: "action, and employment, and the occupations of common life."

This contrast highlights the separate but overlapping relationship between *Rasselas* and Hume's account of causation. While Hume's project certainly contributes to *Rasselas*'s "epistemological conditions of production" (to quote Watt's essay in this volume), Hume and *Rasselas* remain, as the title of this essay signals, in synchronic apposition rather than intimate connection. Johnson's fiction and Hume's philosophy fix independently on topical themes—in Potkay's words, "perhaps *the* characteristic themes of their historical moment: trust in observation and commonsense."[45] Although it suggests to a surprising extent that such trust is misplaced, *Rasselas* takes shape from the imaginative possibilities (and the psychological damage) that result from enquiring into causes. *Rasselas* is thus an exposition, at once humorous and serious, of the problem of causation as it presented itself in 1759. Hume's philosophy provided both the most accessible and the most radical available treatments of this problem, and Johnson's presentation of it often follows the contours of Hume's thought. But although Johnson's psychological case studies give life to Hume's philosophical exempla, it would be foolish to give the impression that Johnson had Hume's *Treatise* and *Enquiries* at his elbow as he labored through "the evenings of one week" in January 1759 to produce *Rasselas*.[46] It would be more accurate to say, by way of conclusion, that although these two authors find common cause in rejecting 'commonsense' narratives of the world, they ultimately do so to very different effect.

Notes

1. Samuel Johnson, *The History of Rasselas, Prince of Abyssinia*, in *Rasselas and Other Tales*, ed. Gwin J. Kolb, vol. 16 of *The Yale Edition of the Works of Samuel Johnson* (New Haven: Yale University Press, 1990), 175. Subsequent references will be given parenthetically.

2. Fred Parker, "The Skepticism of *Rasselas*," in *The Cambridge Companion to Samuel Johnson*, ed. Greg Clingham (Cambridge: Cambridge University Press, 1997), 130.

3. David Hume, *An Enquiry concerning Human Understanding*, in *Enquiries concerning Human Understanding and concerning the Principles of Morals*, ed. L. A. Selby-Bigge, 3rd ed., rev. and ed. P. H. Nidditch (Oxford: Clarendon Press, 1996), 162, 164. Subsequent references will be given parenthetically (preceded by "*Enquiry*").

4. This is a necessarily broad overview of a variety of modern perspectives on Hume, which differ in many aspects but which all reject the traditional or 'naïve regularity' interpretation of his views on causation. A good survey of these perspectives can be found in Kenneth A. Richman's introduction to *The New Hume Debate*, ed. Rupert Read and Richman (London: Routledge, 2000), while a more combative account can be found in Helen Beebee, *Hume on Causation* (London: Routledge, 2006).

5. Kenneth P. Winkler, "The New Hume," in *New Hume Debate*, 68–71.

6. Richard Popkin, *The High Road to Pyrrhonism*, ed. Richard A. Watson and James E. Force (San Diego: Austin Hill, 1980), 62, 70, 197.

7. Henry Home, Lord Kames, *Essays on the Principles of Morality and Natural Religion*, 2nd ed. (London: C. Hitch, L. Hawes, R. and J. Dodsley, and others, 1758), 162, 156.

8. John Leland, *A View of the Principal Deistical Writers of the Last and Present Century* (London: B. Dod, 1755), 22, 9; Galen Strawson, *The Secret Connexion: Causation, Realism, and David Hume* (Oxford: Clarendon Press, 1989), 86–87.

9. Johnson, review of Soame Jenyns, *A Free Enquiry into the Nature and Origin of Evil*, in *Samuel Johnson: The Major Works*, ed. Donald Greene (Oxford: Oxford University Press, 1984; rev. ed. 2000), 536. First published in the *Literary Magazine* 2 (1757).

10. Nicholas Hudson identifies Bolingbroke and Shaftesbury as Johnson's principal targets in this chapter: *Samuel Johnson and Eighteenth-Century Thought* (Oxford: Clarendon Press, 1988), 101. Kolb's edition of *Rasselas* notes that the phrase "a life led according to nature" is "a translation of the Stoic catchword invented by Zeno of Citium": *Rasselas and other Tales*, 83n.

11. Johnson, *A Dictionary of the English Language*, 4th ed., 2 vols. (Dublin: Thomas Ewing, 1775), s.v. "nature."

12. Hudson, *Samuel Johnson and Eighteenth-Century Thought*, 9.

13. Johnson, *Idler* no. 10 (17 June 1758), in *The Idler and The Adventurer*, ed. W. J. Bate, John M. Bullitt, and L. F. Powell, vol. 2 of *Works* (New Haven: Yale University Press, 1963), 33.

14. Three major works on Hume and Johnson which pursue this point are Leo Damrosch, *Fictions of Reality in the Age of Hume and Johnson* (Madison, WI: University of Wisconsin Press, 1989); Adam Potkay, *The Passion for Happiness: Samuel Johnson and David Hume* (Ithaca: Cornell University Press, 2000); and Fred Parker, *Scepticism and Literature: An Essay on Pope, Hume, Sterne, and Johnson* (Oxford: Oxford University Press, 2003), 163.

15. Steven Lynn, *Samuel Johnson after Deconstruction: Rhetoric and "The Rambler"* (Carbondale, IL: Southern Illinois University Press, 1992), 95.

16. Damrosch, *Fictions of Reality*, 4.

17. Potkay, *Passion for Happiness*, 5.

18. Potkay, *Passion for Happiness*, 1.

19. Potkay, *Passion for Happiness*, 2; Damrosch, *Fictions of Reality*, 5.

20. Parker, *Scepticism and Literature*, 23.

21. Bruno Latour, *We Have Never Been Modern*, trans. Catherine Porter (London: Prentice Hall, 1993), 83–84.

22. John P. Wright, "Hume's Causal Realism: Recovering a Traditional Interpretation," in *New Hume Debate*, 94.

23. Damrosch, *Fictions of Reality*, 37.

24. Peter Loptson, "Hellenism, Freedom, and Morality in Hume and Johnson," *Hume Studies* 37 (2001): 171.

25. Beebee, *Hume on Causation*, 39.

26. Loptson, "Hellenism," 171.

27. Parker, *Scepticism and Literature*, 163.

28. Hume, *A Treatise of Human Nature*, in *A Treatise of Human Nature: A Critical Edition*, ed. David Fate Norton and Mary J. Norton, 2 vols. (Oxford: Clarendon Press, 2007), 1:175.

29. Michael Williams, "Hume's Skepticism," in *The Oxford Handbook of Skepticism*, ed. John Greco (Oxford: Oxford University Press, 2008), 105.

30. Johnson, *Idler* no. 21 (2 September 1758), in *The Idler and The Adventurer*, 66.

31. On Hume and Pyrrhonism see Markus Lammenranta, "The Pyrrhonian Problematic," in *Oxford Handbook of Skepticism*, 29, and Popkin, *High Road to Pyrrhonism*, 103–49. On Pyrrhonism in *Rasselas* see Parker, *Scepticism and Literature*, 246, and Potkay, "The Spirit of Ending in Johnson and Hume," *Eighteenth-Century Life* 16 (1992): 162.

32. Kolb, ed., *Rasselas and Other Tales*, 14n.

33. Hume, "A Kind of History of My Life," in *The Cambridge Companion to Hume*, ed. David Fate Norton (Cambridge: Cambridge University Press, 1993), 346.

34. Johnson, *Idler* no. 43 (10 February 1759), in *The Idler and The Adventurer*, 136.

35. Alexander Rosenberg defines "heroic Humeanism" as "the doctrine that there is no difference between law-like or nomological generalization and a universal truth drawn from exceptionless accidental regularities": "Hume and the Philosophy of Science," in *Cambridge Companion to Hume*, 75. See also Alexander Rosenberg and Tom L. Beauchamp, *Hume and the Problem of Causation* (Oxford: Oxford University Press, 1981), 31.

36. Johnson, *Idler* no. 9 (10 June 1758), in *The Idler and The Adventurer*, 31.

37. Johnson, *Idler* no. 21 (2 September 1758), in *The Idler and The Adventurer*, 66.

38. Johnson, *Idler* no. 24 (30 September 1758), in *The Idler and The Adventurer*, 75.

39. 'Philosophical zombies' are hypothetical beings used by philosophers to make arguments about consciousness. As Robert Kirk explains, they are "very different from those seen in horror films, which seem to derive from voodoo belief": *Zombies and Consciousness* (Oxford: Clarendon Press, 2005), 24. Rather, they resemble the unthinking beings of *Idler* no. 24 in being physical duplicates of humans who live and behave like humans, differing from them only in that they lack phenomenal consciousness.

40. Catherine N. Parke, *Samuel Johnson and Biographical Thinking* (Columbia, MI: University of Missouri Press, 1991), 80.

41. Parker, *Scepticism and Literature*, 245.

42. Quoted in Johnson, *Dictionary*, "nature."

43. Kolb, ed., *Rasselas and Other Tales*, 26n.

44. Johnson, *Idler* no. 101 (22 March 1760), in *The Idler and The Adventurer*, 311.

45. Potkay, *Passion for Happiness*, 59.

46. *Boswell's Life of Johnson*, ed. George Birkbeck Hill, rev. L. F. Powell, 6 vols. (Oxford: Clarendon Press, 1934–1950), 1:341.

Part V

ORIGINALITY AND APPROPRIATION

9

ECCENTRICITY, ORIGINALITY, AND THE NOVEL:

TRISTRAM SHANDY, VOLUMES 1 AND 2

MOYRA HASLETT

L AURENCE STERNE'S *Tristram Shandy* is the most famously eccentric novel of the eighteenth century, but contemporary ideas of eccentricity have usually only been assumed. While early readers certainly responded to its first installment as a work which was odd, singular, or whimsical, for example, they rarely used the term 'eccentric'. Partly, this was because the word itself was only beginning to shed its predominant sense of geometrical or astronomical deviation in favor of the more figurative definitions of idiosyncratic style, behavior, or personality with which we are now familiar. If we remember its primary definition as a form of deviation, however, we can more easily trace the ways in which ideas and debates about eccentricity and originality were interlinked at this time. As the mid-eighteenth century saw 'eccentric' become a term to describe a peculiar characteristic or person, so too did 'original' become a term to describe an eccentric personality. The blurring between adjective and noun in what might be defined as 'eccentric', 'original', even 'novel', then, is a suggestive one, as distinctions between literary characters and textual characteristics collapsed in the particular form of the novel.

This essay explores ideas of eccentricity in fictional character and novelistic style, particularly in relation to the first two volumes of *Tristram Shandy*. It begins by returning to those geometrical definitions of the eccentric which were current in 1759, such that the northern setting, and initial publication, of the novel can be seen as themselves crucial elements of the book's eccentricity. More obviously, Sterne's array of Shandy gentlemen—Walter, Toby, and Tristram—represents his novel's preoccupation with eccentric character. This, more familiar, sense of the eccentric is read here in the context of the debates about literary originality that were taking place in 1759—the final year of a decade in which, as Richard Terry has argued, "debates about . . . culpable imitation, are conducted with unusual fervour and pertinacity."[1] In Edward Young's *Conjectures on Original Composition*, being true to one's individual character—even, perhaps, 'being' (rather than having) a character—will result in originality. Under the rubric of stylistic originality, distinctions between character and characteristics collapse (or, at least, interweave), particularly when the character is seen to be an eccentric one. And yet, Sterne's own idiosyncratic, singular style is now recognized to have been heavily indebted to a range of other texts—to the extent that, in *Tristram Shandy*, originality and derivativeness are not, necessarily, contradictory qualities. To explore this paradox further, the final part of the essay offers a brief survey of notable 'eccentricities' in fiction in the years preceding the first publication of *Tristram Shandy*. Among these earlier fictions is one published three years earlier—Thomas Amory's *The Life of John Buncle, Esq* (1756)—whose own idiosyncrasies provide an important context for *Tristram Shandy*. As serial publication of *Tristram Shandy* continued across the 1760s, Sterne's novel increasingly enfolded contemporary responses and new references into its fabric, as Thomas Keymer has shown in *Sterne, the Moderns, and the Novel* (2002). By contrast, this essay focuses on volumes one and two of the work in order to consider what might have made it seem extravagantly 'eccentric' in its first design. By reading the 1759 installment of *Tristram Shandy* against a backdrop of current ideas about eccentricity and originality, and immediate precursor texts that also manifested these qualities, this essay will suggest ways in which the persistent critical conundrum of *Tristram Shandy*—the question of how it can appear to be both 'typical' and 'singular'—might be approached anew.

That literary originality might be figured as a form of eccentric travelling is suggested in a number of texts published in 1759. For Edward Young, for example, "All Eminence and Distinction lies out of the beaten road; Excursion, and Deviation, are necessary to find it; and the more remote your Path from the Highway, the more reputable"; while, for Oliver Goldsmith, "the great mind will be bravely eccentric, and scorn the beaten road."[2] In these discussions, deviation from "the beaten road" is cast as not just a "reputable," but also as an 'eccentric' authorial maneuver. Notably, mid-eighteenth-century dictionary definitions of eccentricity rely almost entirely on meanings drawn from geometry or astronomy, in which such deviations are represented as spatial—as excursions in a literal sense. William Rider's *A New Universal English Dictionary* (1759), for example, defines eccentric as "departing, or deviating from a center."[3] Facetiously defining "the world" as being contained within the hamlets and parishes of rural Yorkshire, Sterne's *Tristram Shandy* initially positions itself as 'excentric' in this sense.[4] In introducing Tristram's midwife, Sterne locates her precisely within circles of gossip and fame, circles which recall the 'concentric' and 'excentric' circles of contemporary definition:

> [This midwife] had acquired, in her way, no small degree of reputation in the world;—by which word *world*, need I in this place inform your worship, that I would be understood to mean no more of it, than a small circle described upon the circle of the great world, of four *English* miles diameter, or thereabouts, of which the cottage where the good old woman lived, is supposed to be the centre.[5]

Sterne reminds his readers of this same, delimited "world" on a number of further occasions in his first volume: when he writes of Yorick's death in terms of leaving both "his parish,—and the whole world at the same time" (1.10.24); when we witness Walter Shandy's rage at London's gravitational pull, by which "men and money" flow out of the English provinces (1.18.52–55); and when Trim promises Toby that their miniature fortification "should be worth all the world's riding twenty miles to go and see it" (2.5.111). Although *Tristram Shandy* would shortly be published in a London edition (in April 1760), the novel's initial publication in York in December 1759 was also an important part of the defiantly local implications of these first volumes.[6]

This awareness of the 'excentric' nature of the novel's provincial setting is also evident in its situating of that world within greater definitions of "the world," as in the novel's gestures towards circles that lie beyond a radius of four or five miles:

> I think I told you that this good woman [the midwife] was a person of no small note and consequence throughout our whole village and township;---that her fame had spread itself to the very out-edge and circumference of that circle of importance, of which kind every soul living, whether he has a shirt or no,----has one surrounding him;--which said circle, by the way, whenever 'tis said that such a one is of great weight and importance in the *world*,——I desire may be enlarged or contracted in your worship's fancy, in a compound-ratio of the station, profession, knowledge, abilities, height and depth (measuring both ways) of the personage brought before you. (1.13.39)

While the midwife's "world" is envisaged once again as a local, provincial one, Tristram hints that his own narrative will be read by an enlarged circle of "all the *world*," although he allows the suggestion of a definite, mathematically precise circumference to be lost in a conspiratorial, ultimately unfinished whisper (1.13.40). In late 1759, with a metropolitan audience already envisaged in the design to send 500 copies of the York imprint to London for sale by the Dodsleys, and advanced plans to publish a London edition, that ostentatious whisper—"all this is spoke in confidence"—is an appropriate gesture of only apparently cautious ambition. Both Sterne's and Tristram's designs upon the wider world are later echoed by Walter Shandy, whose desire to publicize to "the world" his theory concerning the name "Tristram" leads to the writing of his dissertation on the subject (1.19.63). If, as Tristram counsels us, we do not forget the meaning of that larger circle, "all the *world*," we can recognize that Walter Shandy certainly desires to be read beyond the four miles which is the index of the midwife's reputation, and that Tristram's own hope that "the world [shall] run mad after" his autobiography matches the ambition of his father (1.9.16). The consciousness of the wider world—beyond rural Yorkshire, the larger circles, the "beaten road," or (as in Tristram's reference to those who ride unusual hobby-horses) "the King's high-way" (1.7.12)—thus makes the insistent localism of *Tristram Shandy*'s actual setting all the more pronounced, flagging up the contrast between the little "world" of rural Yorkshire and the great "world" of metropolitan London, and the 'excentricity' of locating a fictional character in the former.

Alongside the novel's conscious positioning of itself as 'excentric' to metropolitan London in publication and setting, its first two volumes also present famously eccentric characters in the portrayals of Walter Shandy, Uncle Toby, and Tristram Shandy himself. All three are introduced as examples of singularity, oddness, whimsicality, idiosyncrasy, and originality: terms which Sterne, in common with other writers of the 1750s, uses interchangeably. More unusually, Tristram reflects specifically upon the Shandy trait of 'eccentricity':

> I have . . . oft times wondered, that my father, tho' I believe he had his reasons for it, upon his observing some tokens of excentricity in my course when I was a boy,—should never once endeavour to account for them in this way; for all the SHANDY FAMILY were of an original character throughout. (1.21.73)

When Goldsmith writes of how the great writer should be "bravely eccentric" in "scorn[ing] the beaten road," he almost certainly uses the term in the literal, geometric sense of 'excentricity'. Because the context of the argument concerns aesthetic originality, though, his use may not entirely preclude the sense in which the representation of an individual or a literary style might itself be defined as 'eccentric'. Sterne's own use of the term, in the passage above, is more decisively that of its modern, figurative sense—a use which is significant in being relatively rare in the mid-eighteenth century. Although the *OED* gives a citation from 1685 as its first example of "eccentric" as meaning "Of persons and personal attributes: Deviating from usual methods, odd, whimsical," it gives no further occurrences between the next citation of 1695 and 1771, and provides no earlier example of "eccentric" as a noun than 1832. Johnson's *Dictionary* (1755) is the only mid-century dictionary to offer, after three geometrical definitions, the sense of the eccentric as "[i]rregular; anomalous; deviating from stated and constant methods." While the definition itself begins to gesture towards more familiar senses of eccentricity as that which is, more figuratively, 'odd', the citations do not lend themselves easily to this modern sense. The evidence of mid-century dictionaries, then, confirms that figurative, literary, uses of the word were relatively uncommon.

Sterne's choice of "excentricity" to describe the peculiar foibles of male Shandys is certainly confirmed by the portraits themselves. Walter Shandy, for instance, holds strong opinions on a variety of subjects: from the power of personal names to determine individual fate to the necessity of a flourishing provincial culture; from the importance of patriarchal modes of government (at home and at large) to the advantage of male midwives; from the location of the soul to the relative merits of different methods of birth (the ideal being a breech delivery or, even better, a caesarean section). These views are presented as singular, certainly as "odd" and "whimsical." And, when Tristram describes his father's odd theories as being "far out of the high-way of thinking," he explicitly picks up on the metaphor of 'excentric' travelling (2.19.170). Toby's character is equally singular, with his hobby-horsical fixation on turn-of-the-century military campaigns, and obsession with the art of fortification. Indeed, Toby is first introduced to us by way of a philosophical reflection upon how the English climate has been thought to generate "odd and whimsical characters" (1.21.71), so that his own personal eccentricity can be faux-patriotically described by Tristram as being "of that particular species, which does honour to our atmosphere" (1.21.72–73).

In a discussion of the idea of "excessive" character, Deidre Lynch has argued that the mid-eighteenth century witnessed "the heyday of the English eccentric," and both Lynch and Shearer West have discussed the popularity of odd or un-usual characters in eighteenth-century England, focusing particularly on popular prints.[7] Although their own examples are drawn from 1770 onwards (notably the Darly prints of eccentric Macaronis, and the hunt for "Oddities" in the letters pages of *The Town and Country Magazine*), we can see much earlier anticipations of this fascination with queer fellows and odd types in such popular literary figures as Sir Roger de Coverley in *The Spectator* (1711–1714), Parson Adams in Henry Fielding's *Joseph Andrews* (1742), and Commodore Trunnion in Tobias Smollett's *Peregrine Pickle* (1751). The opening volumes of *Tristram Shandy* consciously return to earlier debates about English eccentricity when Tristram ponders whether the Shandys' singularities might be due to the English climate or to patrilineal heredity. England's widely varying weather results in widely varying character types, and Dryden and Addison are invoked to show how commonplace this view is thought to be (1.21.71). In *Spectator* 371 (6 May 1712), Addison had indeed argued that "our Nation is more famous for that sort of Men who are called *Whims* and *Humorists*, than any other Country in the World."[8] More recently, Goldsmith, in *An Enquiry into the Present State of Polite Learning in Europe* (1759), had written of how, "Though our descriptions and characters are drawn from nature, yet they may appear exaggerated, or faintly copied, to those, who [are] unacquainted with the peculiarities of our island."[9] Shearer West and Paul Langford have both argued that English singularity was viewed, during this period, as the natural outcome of English political liberty. This somewhat insular view can be detected in several patriotic flourishes in Young's *Conjectures on Original Composition*:

> Something new may be expected from *Britons* particularly; who seem
> not to be more sever'd from the rest of mankind by the surrounding sea,
> than by the current in their veins; and of whom little more appears to
> be required, in order to give us *Originals*, than a consistency of character,
> and making their compositions of a piece with their lives. (75–76)

What foreign genius, Young asks, would not envy Britain's originals: Bacon, Newton, Shakespeare, and Milton? For Tristram Shandy, similarly, nature is "most whimsical and capricious" in this "unsettled island" (1.11.27). Although Tristram ultimately decides that Shandy singularity is more a family trait than an English characteristic, the novel's obvious fondness for its eccentric characters might be situated in a developing tradition of pride in the English eccentric as a national type. Henry Bunbury's prints of *Tristram Shandy*, with their gallery of comic characters, would visually represent this popular affection for the English eccentric in the early 1770s, but these prints themselves mimic what Sterne's text—and Hogarth's frontispiece to its first London edition—had already suggested over a decade earlier.[10]

That the beginning of a renewed interest in the English eccentric might more properly be dated to the 1750s—even, more audaciously, to 1759 specifically—is possible if we read Young's *Conjectures* together with the first installment of *Tristram Shandy*.[11] Although Young celebrates 'originality' rather than 'eccentricity' as such, the absence of a specific definition of literary originality in the *Conjectures*, and the implied theme of eccentric personality which runs throughout the essay, suggest that singular characters might be thought to write in original ways. The association between personality and style is made directly in the quotation cited above ("little more appears to be required, in order to give us *Originals*, than . . . making their compositions of a piece with their lives"), as it is more obliquely in Young's use of the metaphor of 'excentric' excursion cited earlier. As he continues in this latter passage, "the more remote your Path from the Highway, the more reputable . . . the true Genius [crosses] all publick roads into fresh untrodden ground" (23). Young's argument that originality is intrinsic to human personality links the idea of singular character to idiosyncrasy of style. In his terms, Nature "brings us into the world all *originals:* No two faces, no two minds, are just alike; but all bear Nature's evident mark of Separation on them. Born *Originals*, how comes it to pass that we die *Copies?*" (42). Originality, Young implies, would be inevitable if we were to remain true to our unique personalities. At the present time, however, the anxiety created by illustrious predecessors (who "engross, prejudice and intimidate" [17]), the lure of easy imitation (42–43), and man's unawareness of his own genius (45–55), all impede the creation of original work.[12] As Adam Rounce has suggested in his essay in this volume, Young's proposal of originality was also an attempt to keep at a distance from authorship the taint of commercial and pragmatic realities; realities that were embodied in the countless novels published during the 1750s, and denounced by the literary reviewers as having—in a representative dismissal—"no character at all."[13]

The particular, distinct character of *Tristram Shandy* resided not only in its portraits of queer fellows and odd types but, also, in its eccentric narrative and print features. *Tristram* is, after all, an autobiography which begins at the moment of its subject's conception and fails to reach the point of his birth during the first two volumes, and a book in which the Dedication makes an ostentatiously belated appearance in the eighth chapter. From the outset, moreover, Tristram's irrepressible digressions often, mischievously, leave the reader flagging behind, perhaps most irreverently so when the female reader is chastised: "—How could you, Madam, be so inattentive in reading the last chapter?" (1.20.64). The bold idiosyncrasy of the novel's voice is paralleled by its unusual typography, examples of which in the first installment include the black page (1.12.37–38) and Yorick's tombstone epitaph (1.12.35), the asterisks and pointing hands (2.17.141), the strange fonts (such as the bold gothic script of 1.15), the occasional footnote (1.20.65), the expressive setting of "Shut the door" (1.4.6), and the widely varying dash lengths and multiple hyphens. These last were particularly eccentric in the York edition of 1759, in which runs of two to five hyphens appear, only to be replaced with standard dash lengths in the London edition. In his discussion of the typesetting of the first volumes, Melvyn New concludes that "the [York] compositor was attempting to duplicate what he saw in the manuscript, a labor the London compositors were perhaps unwilling to undertake to indulge Sterne's whimsicality."[14] Sterne's command earlier in the year that the publisher of *A Political Romance* should not alter "so much as . . . one Comma or Tittle," his claim that every page of the York edition of *Tristram Shandy* would be personally corrected by him, and his later request that the lengths of the dashes be altered in volumes 5 and 6, all suggest that these features were vitally important to Sterne's sense of the book as idiosyncratically his own.[15]

The 'slap-dash' effect of the dashes conveys the expressive immediacy and intimacy of the narrator's conversation with his readers, but it also suggests the chaotic inner consciousness of Tristram, whose zany threads of thought lead off in all directions and breezily mix serious intellectualism with colloquial informality. Style—of voice, of writing, of print—becomes an obvious indicator of personality, such that the eccentricities of *Tristram Shandy*'s typography, narrative style, and characterization constantly reinforce the eccentric personalities of Tristram, Walter, Toby, and Yorick. We can see this blurring between style and character in the shift from text to author in Young's comment that "We read *Imitation* with somewhat of his languor, who listens to a twice-told tale: Our spirits rouze at an *Original*; that is a perfect stranger, and all throng to learn what news from a foreign land" (12). Increasingly, readers would respond to the idiosyncrasy of *Tristram Shandy* as a badge of its author's own, foundational, eccentricity. That Sterne was happy to think of himself in these terms is evident in an early comment that he made about *Tristram Shandy*: that "the air and originality" of his book "must resemble the author."[16]

That *Tristram Shandy* was an 'original' text was clearly understood from the outset. Among the first reviews of the opening volumes were several short notices which remarked particularly on the novel's idiosyncrasy. The reviewer for the *London Magazine* exclaimed "Oh rare Tristram Shandy! . . . what shall we call thee?—Rabelais, Cervantes, What?"; while the *Royal Literary Magazine* observed that the novel "affects (and not unsuccessfully) to please, by a contempt of all the rules observed in other writings."[17] The novelty of *Tristram Shandy* was also inferred in the opening lines of William Kenrick's article in the *Monthly Review*: "Of Lives and *Adventures* the public have had enough, and, perhaps, more than enough, long ago. A consideration that probably induced the droll Mr. Tristram Shandy to entitle the performance before us, his Life and *Opinions*."[18] Several early imitations of *Tristram Shandy* also noted the novelty of the work. As the author of *Yorick's Meditations upon Various Interesting and Important Subjects* (1760) put it, for example, "every chapter of Tristram's Life and Opinions teems with something new and extraordinary."[19] Such responses highlighted a feature of the work which was clearly advertised in Sterne's narrative itself—as when Tristram proclaims that "I shall confine myself neither to [Horace's] rules, nor to any man's rules that ever lived" (1.4.5), or that "the machinery of my work is of a species by itself" (1.22.80–81). Tristram's constant reminders that he has no predetermined plan also lend the text an air of improvisation. Indeed, by contrast to those who merely copy, Tristram declares himself to be of "so nice and singular a humour" that he would rather tear the last page out of his first volume than have his reader predict what he will write next (1.25.89). These kinds of assertion were crucial to the conception of the emerging novel long before 1759—most famously in Fielding's statement in *Tom Jones* (1749) that "as I am, in reality, the Founder of a new Province of Writing, so I am at liberty to make what Laws I please therein."[20] In *Tristram Shandy*, though, Sterne's claims for the idiosyncrasy of his work are particularly insistent.

Despite its obvious eccentricity, however, the earliest responses to *Tristram Shandy* also included several accusations of the text's derivativeness. The reviewer in the *Critical Review*, for example, implied that uncle Toby, corporal Trim, and Dr Slop were imitations of similarly eccentric characters in a "modern truly Cervantic performance": Smollett's *Peregrine Pickle*.[21] One reader in Utrecht, the Rev. Robert Brown, thought Sterne indebted to Montaigne.[22] And, having repeatedly accused *Tristram Shandy* of copying earlier conventions, *The Clockmakers Outcry against the Author of the Life and Opinions of Tristram Shandy* (1760) ends with a decisive, if unsubstantiated, accusation of plagiarism by way of a final postscript:

> We learn this moment that the affecting *Episod* of YORICK's Death in VOL I is intirely borrowed. Wherefore we suspend our approbation of that article, as well as of some other striking ones; and can thence easily account for the inequality of matter and style—Between jest and earnest, we think it incumbent on the author, for the sake of himself and patrons, to invalidate this report, if in his power. Should it be proved![23]

Later approaches to Sterne's novel would uncover specific source texts and, eventually, accuse him of plagiarism on a larger scale. The development of John Ferriar's criticism of Sterne, from the relatively neutral identification of Robert Burton's *The Anatomy of Melancholy* (1621) as a key source for *Tristram Shandy* in his essay "Comments on Sterne" (1793), to the more moralistic tenor of his *Illustrations of Sterne* (1798), exemplifies this shift.[24] By contrast, references to Sterne's derivativeness among the initial responses to *Tristram Shandy* do not identify specific borrowings. Although *The Clockmakers Outcry* hints that a specific source might be found, it breaks off at the point of a hypothesis, rather than with an identification. The allusion to *Peregrine Pickle* in the *Critical Review* is also suggested only tentatively: the reviewer deliberately withholds the title of the "modern truly Cervantic performance" because of its author's "delicacy" (that author, Smollett, being also the editor of the review journal). If early readers, or reviewers, were conscious of *Tristram Shandy*'s copious quotations from and allusions to other texts, they did not remark upon these.[25] When the *Monthly Review* argued that Johnson's *Rasselas* could not be thought original, as its (initially anonymous) author appeared to suggest, it not only openly judged the work a "threadbare" imitation of Persian and Turkish tales, but subtly reinforced this argument by identifying a silent quotation in a footnote to the review.[26] Although such source-hunting was relatively rare in reviews in 1759, its occasional appearance suggests that literary debts could be highlighted in negative reviews. Edward Young was forthright in his condemnation of those authors who copied books rather than Nature; of imitators who read and write rather than think and compose, as original authors do (54). Young's theory, however, could not accommodate those authors, like Laurence Sterne, whose originality did not exclude extensive quotations from other books. For, in presenting the history of what "passes in a man's own mind" (2.2.98), Sterne presented his audience with a portrayal of a reader, as much as of an author.

Recent work, building upon the immense scholarship of the annotations to the Florida edition of *Tristram Shandy*, has highlighted how extensive Sterne's textual borrowings are. Beyond the 208 authors cited by name in *Tristram Shandy*, there are huge numbers of unacknowledged sources, and the figure is still rising.[27] Imitations, quotations, and echoes of other texts are so thoroughly part of the fabric of the novel that, as Jonathan Lamb has argued, textual borrowing figures as much as a trope as it exists as a practice, and imitation and allusion become the very means of self-expression.[28] Sterne's echoes and quotations of other texts are not acts of literary theft, but the means by which his fictional narrator, Tristram, can appear to be singularly himself. In Lamb's essay on "Sterne's System of Imitation," an account of Sterne's "original imitation," there is no beyond or outside of imitation. Even Tristram's progressive-digressive style and his foregrounding of the disparity between life and art, features which Tristram himself proclaims to be distinctly new, were already anticipated by Thucydides, Montaigne, and Cervantes. Threaded through Lamb's discussion is the figure of the "original," the "odd," the "peculiar" self.[29] For, if imitation is inevitable, then the eccentric personality speaks through or within other texts as surely as—or rather, to an even greater extent than—the apparently 'conventional' self.

Lamb's essay on Sterne's imitation presented itself at the outset as an attempt to "strike a balance" between two dominant, but competing, modes of situating *Tristram Shandy*: within a tradition of Renaissance humanist wit, or as a proleptically modern fiction which anticipates the experimental narrative play of Joyce or Woolf. Since 1981, when the essay was first published, this distinction has shifted so that *Tristram Shandy* is now read either in relation to satiric, learned wit or in relation to the contemporary novel of the 1750s. Thomas Keymer's monograph, *Sterne, the Moderns, and the Novel* (2002), was the first full-length study of how we might think of the topicality of *Tristram Shandy*; of how its self-conscious experimentalism was typical of, rather than anomalous within, fiction of the 1750s. During the last decade, further work—by Janine Barchas, Patricia Meyer Spacks, and Robert Folkenflik—has continued to explore what *Tristram Shandy* shares with other novels of the mid-eighteenth century.[30]

Fiction of the 1750s is certainly peopled with eccentric characters pursuing idiosyncratic hobby-horses: Smollett's Commodore Trunnion, who lives and breathes the nautical life on land in *Peregrine Pickle* (1751), for example, or Thomas Amory's proselytizing Unitarian, John Buncle, who pole-vaults down mountainsides to encounter learned ladies and male philosophers in *The Life of John Buncle, Esq* (1756). The decade also witnesses a whole host of "it-narrators," including a lapdog, a waistcoat, a post-chaise, a pair of lady's slippers, and Queen Elizabeth's pocket-pistol.[31] When Charlotte Charke declares that "I confess myself an Odd Mortal" in 1755, and John Buncle that "may it be written on my stone,—*Here lies an odd man*" in 1756, both narrators suggest that it is their oddness which claims the right of readers' attention.[32] To a lesser extent, there are also 'excentric' settings and wanderings to be found in fiction of this period: among the furthest reaches of the globe or the most remote locations of Britain (the South Seas of *The Voyages, Travels and Wonderful Discoveries of Capt John Holmesby* [1757], for example, or the outer Hebrides of Amory's *Memoirs of Several Ladies of Great-Britain* [1755]); and among fantastical lands peopled by strange winged humans, phantasmal islands, or into the very geology of the earth (Robert Paltock's *The Life and Adventures of Peter Wilkins* [1751]; *A Voyage to O'Brazeel* [1752]; and *A Voyage to the World in the Centre of the Earth* [1755]). Eccentric narrative styles—or new kinds of textual play—are certainly commonplace in fiction of the 1750s. One of the most startlingly original novels of the decade is Sarah Fielding and Jane Collier's *The Cry* (1754), in which a Chorus of fashionable types continually interrupts Portia's attempts to tell her story with carping attacks and, frequently, open hostility; chapters are replaced with dramatic "scenes"; and new English words are invented, not only because of their appropriateness, but because of their novelty.[33] In Amory's *The Life of John Buncle, Esq*, Buncle's digressions are marshaled into footnotes which often threaten to overwhelm his narrative, and the narrative itself struggles to contain the extraordinarily heterogeneous topics—shells, theology, microscopes, poetry, mathematics, *et cetera*—which intrigue and consume Buncle himself.

The most frequently cited novel among these examples is *The Life of John Buncle, Esq* (1756), a text which has long been noted as a possible 'eccentric' precursor, or at least parallel, for Sterne's more famous eccentric novel. In an essay on teaching *Tristram Shandy*, for example, Maximillian Novak has suggested that Sterne's hybrid narrative modes might be read through the context of fiction's aspiration to comprehensiveness in the 1750s, as best exemplified by *John Buncle*:

> How, then, is one to explain the sudden emergence of what must seem to be a work extraordinarily different from everything that came before? Were there world enough and time, it might be possible to have students read selections from a novel of the 1750s such as Thomas Amory's *History of John Buncle* [sic] (1756) to demonstrate how the form of the novel had expanded to accommodate a jumble of disparate material drawn from theology, science, and contemporary events under an autobiographical format.[34]

The modern edition of *John Buncle* reveals that, in addition to its encyclopedic range and other previously noted features (such as its play upon oral and print cultures, its literary inventiveness and overt allusions to Locke, and its probing of paradoxical experiences of time and space), the novel also anticipates *Tristram Shandy* in the extent of its literary borrowing, which is sometimes overt, sometimes covert, and often impossible to categorize in this way. Annotations to this edition indicate that Amory's novel quotes from at least 154 different sources, although this feature of the work was unremarked in reviews and responses during the eighteenth century. Indeed, contemporary responses focused on the idiosyncrasy of the text. In the *Monthly Review*, Ralph Griffiths praised its "bold and eccentric manner," stressed its extravagance and uncommonness throughout his extensive review, and concluded that its author "is truly original in all things, inimitable in some, and despicable in none; for his very faults seem to be only the deviations of a great genius, a *little warped*."[35] Writing in the *Critical Review*, Thomas Francklin was far less positive, poking fun at its idiosyncratic style in a collage of quotations from *Buncle* itself:

> Mr *John Buncle* . . . the *lepid ruralist*, is *without all peradventure*, the most *doleful* jumble of *miscellany thoughts, replications*, and *hairing, staring diabolism* that was ever *posited* in the *sensory* of a man's *head*; and . . . writing is a province which, in spite of his *noachical language*, he was never *chalked out for*.[36]

Yet the phrase "lepid ruralist" is a quotation (from John Dalton), as is "noachical language" (which comes from Thomas Sharp)—and as such, their idiosyncrasy is not entirely new. As with the yet more inventive Sterne, not only does a highly original style prove to be entirely commensurate with widespread plundering of other texts, but a consciously 'inimitable' style only encourages parodic imitation.[37] The recovery of the "thorough-stitch'd" (3.38.274) nature of *Buncle* adds a new dimension to critical debates about how to read and to situate *Tristram Shandy*, for Amory's novel, published three years before the first installment of *Tristram*, suggests that extensive learning, textual indebtedness, and playful handling of sources can be 'novelistic', and that Sterne's 'Renaissance' wit needs to be rethought in terms of the full range of eccentric possibilities evident in fiction of the 1750s.

John Buncle and *Tristram Shandy*, we might then say, are highly original and indeed eccentric novels not so much despite, but even because of, the extent of their literary borrowing. This is at least partly because of the nature of Tristram Shandy and John Buncle themselves—apparently ordinary, yet evidently eccentric narrators, whose narration of the events and experiences of their lives is subordinated to "opinions," garrulously articulated despite (or rather *through*) copious digressions. In their spiraling, accumulating narratives, neither Buncle nor Tristram can keep pace with the aspiration to write their lives and opinions. Both keep getting 'side-tracked', to return to the metaphor of geometrical 'excentricity'. In her comparison of *John Buncle* and *Tristram Shandy*, Katie Trumpener notes that

Buncle's discursive construction of space—continually losing his way in the upper Pennines, geography is rendered both "tangible and elusive"—is mirrored in
Tristram's experiments with time.[38] Neither Buncle nor Tristram desire to travel,
or read, "straight forwards" (1.20.65), but the distinction between their relative
obsessions with space and time might suggest a mode of differentiating between
the eccentric and the original. As the eccentric deviates geometrically from a
center, the original implies, though it does not always fulfill, the temporal idea of
priority. Such a distinction might begin to tell us why the 'eccentric' *Buncle* had
so few imitators, whereas the 'original', or 'novel', *Tristram Shandy* ushered in a
"*Shandy*-Age" of parodies and sequels.[39]

   Probably the most famous contemporary response to *Tristram Shandy* is
Samuel Johnson's statement that "Nothing odd will do long. *Tristram Shandy* did
not last."[40] Now, with the benefit of over two centuries of hindsight, we can see
that Sterne's *The Life and Opinions of Tristram Shandy, Gentleman* (1759–1767) has
continued to be celebrated and loved because of its very eccentricity. Thomas Amory
might be said to have suffered a contrary trajectory: one in which Buncle's proud,
even cultivated, 'oddness' was read first as a form of whimsicality, and later as a form
of madness.[41] One of the few exceptions to this trajectory was the assessment of
George Saintsbury; who, in the early twentieth century, called for a "history of the
eccentric novel," with *The Life of John Buncle, Esq* as its inaugural text.[42] Although
such a history is yet to be written, in recent work on fiction published in the mid-
century, on how self-conscious experimentalism was relentlessly copied, and how
the brash modernity of the novel was continually renewed, it might be said to have
begun. This essay hopes to have contributed to this project, by exploring what 'eccentricity' might have meant at the moment of *Tristram Shandy*'s first publication,
and by showing how the mid-eighteenth century bore witness to the "expansiveness
of novelistic self-imagining," in which the eccentric, the whimsical, the singular, and
the odd could—paradoxically—also be considered as paradigmatic.[43]

Notes

1. Richard Terry, *The Plagiarism Allegation in English Literature from Butler to Sterne* (Basingstoke: Palgrave Macmillan, 2010), 142.

2. Edward Young, *Conjectures on Original Composition: In a Letter to the Author of "Sir Charles Gran-dison"* (London: A. Millar and R. and J. Dodsley, 1759), 22–23; Oliver Goldsmith, *The Bee* no. 4 (27 October 1759), in *The Collected Works of Oliver Goldsmith*, ed. Arthur Friedman, 5 vols. (Oxford: Clarendon Press, 1966), 1:430. Subsequent references to Young's *Conjectures* will be given parenthetically.

3. William Rider, *A New Universal English Dictionary* (London: W. Griffin, 1759), unpaginated.

4. Hereafter, I will use the older spelling, 'excentric', to denote geometrical deviation, and the more modern spelling, 'eccentric', to denote oddness in personality.

5. Laurence Sterne, *The Life and Opinions of Tristram Shandy, Gentleman: The Text*, ed. Melvyn New and Joan New, vols. 1–2 of *The Florida Edition of the Works of Laurence Sterne* (Gainesville: University Presses of Florida, 1978), 1.7.10. Subsequent references to *Tristram Shandy* are given parenthetically in the text, citing volume, chapter, and page number in the Florida edition.

6. For the argument that the London edition of April 1760 was in fact the third edition (coming after a second, authorized, Dublin edition), see Kenneth Monkman, "*Tristram* in Dublin," *Transactions of the Cambridge Bibliographical Society* 7 (1979): 343–68. Although Sterne wrote to Robert Dodsley in October 1759 that "All Locality is taken out of the Book," the provincial setting and publication remain as important 'out of the way' characteristics of the first volumes: *The Letters, Part 1: 1739–1764*, ed. Melvyn New and Peter de Voogd, vol. 7 of *Works* (Gainesville: University Press of Florida, 2009), 97.

7. Deidre Lynch, "Overloaded Portraits: The Excesses of Character and Countenance," in *Body and Text in the Eighteenth Century*, ed. Veronica Kelly and Dorothea E. von Mücke (Stanford: Stanford University Press, 1994), 142; Shearer West, "The Darly Macaroni Prints and the Politics of 'Private Man,'" *Eighteenth-Century Life* 25 (2001): 170–82.

8. *The Spectator*, ed. Donald F. Bond, 5 vols. (Oxford: Clarendon Press, 1965), 3:396.

9. Goldsmith, *An Enquiry into the Present State of Polite Learning in Europe*, in *Collected Works*, 1:293.

10. Paul Langford's study of English eccentricity similarly dates its profile to the later decades of the century, with only a few earlier exceptions: *Englishness Identified: Manners and Character, 1650–1850* (Oxford: Oxford University Press, 2000), 267–312. For an account of the Bunbury prints see Peter de Voogd, "Henry William Bunbury, Illustrator of *Tristram Shandy*," *Shandean* 3 (1991): 138–44.

11. For a related argument that Sterne covertly alludes to the *Conjectures* in the passage on English eccentricity referred to above (*Tristram Shandy*, 1.21), see Tim Parnell, "'The whole made more saleable': Young's *Conjectures on Original Composition* and the Reworking of 'The Life & Opinions of Tristram Shandy,'" *Shandean* 20 (2009): 28–36.

12. Elizabeth L. Mann quotes John Armstrong (in "Of Imitation" [1758]) as the first to articulate a connection between individual personality and original style: "The Problem of Originality in English Literary Criticism, 1750–1800," *Philological Quarterly* 18 (1939): 114–15. Young, however, develops this point into a much more extensive discussion.

13. *Monthly Review* 20 (March 1759), 275–76: review of [Eleonore Guichard], *The Bracelet, or the fortunate Discovery*.

14. Melvyn New, Appendix to *The Life and Opinions of Tristram Shandy*, vol. 2, p. 822.

15. Sterne, *Letters*, 99n10, 97; New, Appendix to *The Life and Opinions of Tristram Shandy*, vol. 2, pp. 835–37.

16. Sterne, *Letters*, 91.

17. *London Magazine* 29 (February 1760), 111; *Royal Literary Magazine* 1 (February 1760), 56.

18. *Monthly Review*, Appendix to vol. 21 (July–December 1759), 561 (January 1760).

19. *Yorick's Meditations upon Various Interesting and Important Subjects* (Dublin: James Hunter, 1760), 6.

20. Henry Fielding, *The History of Tom Jones, A Foundling*, ed. Fredson Bowers, 2 vols. (Oxford: Clarendon Press, 1974), 1:77 (II.i).

21. *Critical Review* 9 (January 1760), 73–74.

22. Sterne, *Letters*, 168.

23. *The Clockmakers Outcry against the Author of the Life and Opinions of Tristram Shandy* (London: J. Burd, 1760), 44. This pamphlet response was published in May 1760. For further accusations of imitation, see pp. 22, 24, 25, 30–31, and 36. For the argument that this work was by Sterne himself, see Anne Bandry, "Imitations of *Tristram Shandy*," in *Critical Essays on Laurence Sterne*, ed. Melvyn New (New York: G. K. Hall, 1998), 43–44.

24. John Ferriar, "Comments on Sterne," in *Memoirs of the Literary and Philosophical Society of Manchester* 4 (1793), 45–86, and *Illustrations of Sterne: With other Essays and Verses* (London: Cadell and Davies, 1798).

25. The full extent of these literary debts is indicated by the notes to the Florida edition: *The Life and Opinions of Tristram Shandy, Gentleman: The Notes*, by Melvyn New with Richard A. Davies and W. G. Day, vol. 3 of *Works* (Gainesville: University Presses of Florida, 1984).

26. *Monthly Review* 20 (May 1759), 433n.

27. Nicholas Barker, "The Library Catalogue of Laurence Sterne," *Shandean* 1 (1989): 8–24.

28. Jonathan Lamb, *Sterne's Fiction and the Double Principle* (Cambridge: Cambridge University Press, 1989), 3, and "Sterne's System of Imitation," *Modern Language Review* 76 (1981): 794–810.

29. Lamb, "Sterne's System," 796, 799, 800.

30. Thomas Keymer, *Sterne, the Moderns, and the Novel* (Oxford: Oxford University Press, 2002); Janine Barchas, *Graphic Design, Print Culture and the Eighteenth-Century Novel* (Cambridge: Cambridge University Press, 2003); Patricia Meyer Spacks, *Novel Beginnings: Experiments in Eighteenth-Century Fiction* (New Haven: Yale University Press, 2006); Robert Folkenflik, "*Tristram Shandy* and Eighteenth-Century Narrative," in *The Cambridge Companion to Laurence Sterne*, ed. Thomas Keymer (Cambridge: Cambridge University Press, 2009), 49–63.

31. Francis Coventry, *The History of Pompey the Little; or, The Life and Adventures of a Lap-Dog* (London: M. Cooper, 1751); *Memoirs and Interesting Adventures of an Embroidered Waistcoat* (London: J. Brooke, 1751); *The Travels of Mons. Le Post-chaise. Written by Himself* (London: J. Swan, 1753); *The History and Adventures of a Lady's Slippers and Shoes* (London: M. Cooper, 1754); *The Adventures and Metamorphose of Queen Elizabeth's Pocket-Pistol* (Dublin: T. Birn, 1756).

32. Charlotte Charke, *A Narrative of the Life of Mrs Charlotte Charke*, ed. Robert Rehder (London: Pickering and Chatto, 1999), 46 (and see also p. 140); Thomas Amory, *The Life of John Buncle, Esq*, ed. Moyra Haslett (Dublin: Four Courts Press, 2011), 47. Even the rational, sensible heroine of *The Cry* (1754) defends the pleasures of talking "nonsense" and of being "whimsical": Sarah Fielding and Jane Collier, *The Cry: A New Dramatic Fable*, 3 vols. (London: R. and J. Dodsley, 1754), 2:55–56, 3:159.

33. Fielding and Collier, *The Cry*, 1:92–99 ("turba"), 2:17–28 ("dextra").

34. M. E. Novak, "Satirical Form and Realistic Fiction in *Tristram Shandy*," in *Approaches to Teaching Sterne's "Tristram Shandy,"* ed. Melvyn New (New York: MLA, 1989), 141–42.

35. *Monthly Review* 15 (December 1756), 585, 604.

36. *Critical Review* 2 (October 1756), 227.

37. See Betty Schellenberg, "'The Measured Lines of the Copyist': Sequels, Reviews, and the Discourse of Authorship in England, 1749–1800," in *On Second Thought: Updating the Eighteenth-Century Text*, ed. Debra Taylor Bourdeau and Elizabeth Kraft (Cranbury, NJ: Associated University Presses, 2007), 25–42.

38. Katie Trumpener, *Bardic Nationalism: The Romantic Novel and the British Empire* (Princeton, NJ: Princeton University Press, 1997), 167–68.

39. For Samuel Richardson's reference to a "*Shandy*-Age," see his edition of Daniel Defoe, *A Tour thro' the Whole Island of Great Britain*, 4 vols. (London: D. Browne, T. Osborne, C. Hitch, and others, 1761–1762), 3:249.

40. *Boswell's Life of Johnson*, ed. George Birkbeck Hill, rev. L. F. Powell, 6 vols. (Oxford: Clarendon Press, 1934–1950), 2:449 (20 March 1776). Although Thomas Keymer has argued that Johnson's comment refers to the novel's serial publication, not to its reception, I have accepted the more conventional reading here as part of the book's later reception: *Sterne, the Moderns, and the Novel*, 101.

41. Haslett, introduction to *John Buncle*, 35–36.

42. George Saintsbury, *The English Novel* (London: Dent, 1913), 140, and *The Peace of the Augustans: A Survey of Eighteenth-Century Literature as a Place of Rest and Refreshment* (London: G. Bell and Sons, 1916), 152.

43. The phrase "expansiveness of novelistic self-imagining" is taken from Spacks, *Novel Beginnings*, 18. Lamb's discussion of the contradiction of a "derived singularity" in the Shandy family is also pertinent here: *Sterne's Fiction and the Double Principle*, 46.

SHAKESPEARE'S "PROPRIETY" AND
THE MID-EIGHTEENTH-CENTURY NOVEL:
SARAH FIELDING'S *THE HISTORY OF
THE COUNTESS OF DELLWYN*

KATE RUMBOLD

10

T HE PLOT OF *The History of the Countess of Dellwyn* (1759) differs radically from those of Sarah Fielding's other works of prose fiction. Best known for her sentimental novel, *The Adventures of David Simple* (1744), which follows David's earnest quest to find a true friend (and sees him finding three), Fielding also produced a children's novel, *The Governess* (1749)—in which a "Little Female Academy" of girls learns, over the course of one particularly instructive week, to live and work in harmony—and, in collaboration with Jane Collier, a "dramatic fable," *The Cry* (1754), in which the good-hearted heroine, Portia, defends herself against a jury of untruth. In her final novel, *The History of Ophelia* (1761), Fielding would go on to portray a young woman whose native goodness is undimmed by her removal from Welsh seclusion to glittering London society, and who is ultimately rewarded with marriage to her kindly protector, Lord Dorchester.[1] By contrast, the opening pages of *The History of the Countess of Dellwyn* see the young, vain Miss Charlotte Lucum marrying the decrepit Lord Dellwyn for personal advancement—a far cry from Fielding's other, more virtuous protagonists. After this inauspicious opening, in which the doddery groom drops the wedding ring three times, the remainder of the novel sees their miserable relationship guiltily unravel. Like Fielding's earlier works, *The Countess of Dellwyn* is didactic in tone, but its warning is starker: that "the natural Tendency of Virtue" is "towards the Attainment of Happiness; and, on the contrary, that Misery is the unavoidable Consequence of vicious Life."[2] The Countess's story is not resolved into marriage, but degenerates instead into adultery, divorce, and wretched social exile.

The numerous literary and philosophical quotations incorporated into the novel help to advance this didactic point. Fielding's narrator ranges widely across literary periods and genres in her borrowings; drawing, for example, on writings by Virgil, Horace, Montaigne, Ben Jonson, Abraham Cowley, René le Bossu, Samuel Butler, John Milton, Jean de la Bruyère, Joseph Addison, Jonathan Swift, and Alexander Pope.[3] These authors are invoked not only to discuss the Countess's wayward actions and reactions (for example, chapter VI of volume I is titled "An Exemplification of the Truth of Montaigne's Observation, that we laugh and cry for the same Thing"); they also help the narrator to consider, in a prefatory discussion, the value of fiction and the responsibility of the author:

> *Bossu* declares it to be the Opinion of both *Aristotle* and *Horace*, That Poets teach moral Philosophy. . . . Then *Bossu* assigns the cause why the Poets thus excel simple Philosophers, and says, that it arises from the Nature of the Poetry, which in every kind is wholly an Imitation. (1:xv–xvi)

The preface suggests that the moral force of the poet lies in creating fictional characters who are a truthful and accurate "Imitation" of human nature. Such creations will have a powerful effect on readers precisely because they are drawn from real life (if not, as Fielding warns her more gossipy readers, from identifiable "Individuals" [1:iv]).

Shakespeare's presence in *The Countess of Dellwyn* far outstrips that of any other author. Within this didactic setting, his fifty overt appearances might seem to suggest that his words represent a reliable moral presence in the novel; a source of legitimacy for Fielding's improving agenda. But Shakespeare was not, at this juncture, a ready-made authority figure. In 1759, "Shakespeare," while widely admired, was still under construction, en route from the "provincial playwright" much adapted and improved at the start of the century to the "national poet" celebrated nearer its end.[4] In the middle decades of the century, he remained associated with the dubious, as well as with the positive, connotations of the stage, and still required the assistance of editors to elevate his words above "the barbarity of his age."[5] Adaptations may have begun to dwindle by the 1750s as the perceived sacredness of Shakespeare's words increased, but a playgoer could still encounter enduringly popular 'improved' versions of his work, such as Colley Cibber's *Richard III* and Nahum Tate's *King Lear* (whose famously happy ending, uniting Cordelia and Edgar, provided the poetic justice that Shakespeare's play apparently did not).

In *The Countess of Dellwyn*, the word "propriety" hovers around references to Shakespeare. Rather than providing a simple signal of his respectability, though, the word refers to the supreme accuracy with which he constructed his dramatic characters. Among the authors invoked in the preface who, with more insight than philosophers, accurately imitate Nature, Shakespeare is admired in superlative terms:

> The great Master, and the deepest Penetrator into the inmost Recesses of human Nature, in the Instructions which he with such great Propriety and Judgment introduces from the Mouth of *Hamlet* to the Players, may, if the Writer pleases, be most Part of it adopted also by him for his own Advantage. (1:vii)

To call Shakespeare a "Master . . . of human Nature" was, by 1759, commonplace. In *The Cry*, Portia had referred to "that grand master of human nature (I need not say I mean *Shakespear*)."[6] Early eighteenth-century editors of Shakespeare's plays valued, even above his language, his understanding of the workings of Nature—a quality that equated him with Isaac Newton in the popular imagination.[7] Here, Fielding's preface upholds Shakespeare as excellent for his accurate imitation of Nature, and admires him for the "great Propriety and Judgment" with which he makes his characters speak in ways that seem entirely natural in their circumstances. His plays also appear to proffer guidance for modern writers: Fielding goes on to quote Hamlet's advice to actors to "o'er-step not the Modesty of Nature" and "to hold, as it were, the Mirror to Nature," as if these are rules for the successful construction of character.

But the word "propriety," as this essay will show, also connects Shakespeare with a contemporary discourse of sympathetic judgment that would be fully articulated in 1759 in Adam Smith's *The Theory of Moral Sentiments*. This model of sympathy required the observer to assess the fittingness of the afflicted person's behavior to their circumstances; it called for discernment, as well as warmth of feeling, in the sympathizer. It is quickly apparent how closely this kind of sympathetic judgment is related to the accuracy, or propriety, of fictional characterization, as Fielding sees it:

> As the Writer must be thoroughly acquainted with the Bent of the Dispositions of the Miser, the Lover, the Friend, and the Parent, before he can make any of them act with Propriety on this or any other Occasion, so must the Reader also have some Degree of Knowledge of them before he can judge truly whether they are represented right or wrong, or distinguish what is natural from the wild Fancies of the Poet's Brain. (1:xiii)

Propriety of character is, then, judged with the same tools by which one might, in 1759, judge the propriety of sympathy. Sympathetic judgment is at once an authorial skill and a quality that closely matches the sensitive but exacting scrutiny, the ability to assess and discern, that Fielding wishes to cultivate in her readers.

This essay will argue that the impartial yet sympathetic judgment that Fielding demanded of her reader played an important part in elevating Shakespeare during the second half of the eighteenth century. As well as praising Shakespeare's accuracy in her preface, Fielding invokes his words when describing her characters in the novel itself. She invites the reader to judge the fittingness of her characters' behavior—usually overreactions motivated by vanity and greed—in comparison with the behavior of Shakespeare's characters, which is famously well suited to their circumstances. By sheer repetition, this contrasting of their relative formal propriety takes on a distinctly moral hue: by frequently suggesting that their bad behavior falls short of Shakespeare's characters in its *formal* fittingness, Fielding's novel can start to give the impression that Shakespeare's fictional creations represent a *moral* benchmark. More than this, the accurate characterization that makes Shakespeare a "master of human nature" will help to embody Shakespeare himself in the novel as a moral author figure. His quoted insights, targeted at a guilty protagonist, now give the impression of finger-wagging knowingness: he seems to see inside the Countess's mind, and torment her for her bad decisions. Fielding's novel thus exemplifies—and, because of the disagreeable nature of her characters, even exaggerates—the way in which the mid-eighteenth-century novel did not simply borrow or convey, but actively helped to construct, a moral authority for Shakespeare.

At the same time, the Countess's thwarted encounters with Shakespeare are often funny. The black comedy that can result from Sarah Fielding's tough-minded, satirical use of Shakespeare challenges critical assumptions about the way that she, and other female novelists, related to the dramatist (variously, relying on his masculine authority or sharing his feminine sensibility).[8] It also reveals a less earnest side to an author long categorized as the devoted mentee of Samuel Richardson and Henry Fielding. Whether by giving her most virtuous characters Shakespearean names (Portia, Ferdinand, and Cordelia in *The Cry*; Ophelia in her eponymously titled history), or keeping her worst characters at arm's length from his words in a way that actively invites the reader's judgment, Sarah Fielding epitomizes the way that mid-century novelists at once construct an impression of authority for Shakespeare, and exploit it for their own ends.

When Fielding quotes from Shakespeare in *The Countess of Dellwyn*, she might seem to be invoking, as his role in eighteenth-century fiction has been briefly summarized, "a moral touchstone by which to try heroines."[9] Early in the novel, we hear how Charlotte Lucum's father, keen to secure her lucrative marriage to the wealthy Lord Dellwyn, coerces her into frequent socializing. Her reluctant forays into polite society become first tolerable, and then all-consuming:

> She was introduced among a Set of Acquaintance, to whose Splendor
> in Dress she could by no means arrive, and consequently she often
>   *'Pined in thought,'*
> Like *Viola,* in *Shakespeare's Twelfth Night;*
> But it could not be said, with Propriety, that, like *Viola,*
>   *She sat, like* Patience, *on a Monument,*
>   *Smiling at* Grief.
> For, however possible it may be to support disappointed Love with
> Patience, it is one of the characteristical Marks of disappointed Vanity,
> to throw the Mind into Perturbation and Impatience. (1:41)

If the words "Like *Viola,*" that follow the first quotation from *Twelfth Night,* briefly extend to Charlotte the possibility of identifying with Shakespeare's heroine, the narrator's blunt follow-up—"But it could not be said, with Propriety, that, like *Viola,* / She sat, like* Patience, *on a Monument,* / Smiling at* Grief"—shuts down the possibility of any continued association between the two women. Viola's "disappointed Love" and Charlotte's "disappointed Vanity," the former's "Patience" and the latter's "Perturbation and Impatience," are presented as black-and-white opposites, in an almost mock-heroic disjuncture. The fact that the women could not be compared "with Propriety" might suggest, to the modern reader at least, that this distinction—between a virtuous Viola and a shallow Charlotte—is at heart a moral one.

In 1759, however, the now-familiar connection of "propriety" with proper, moral behavior—namely, "Conformity to accepted standards of behaviour or morals, esp. with regard to good manners or polite usage; seemliness, decorousness, decency; (observance of) convention"—was not yet dominant.[10] Four years before Fielding's novel was published, "propriety" had been defined firstly in relation to "Peculiarity of possession; exclusive right," and secondly to "Accuracy or justness," in Samuel Johnson's *Dictionary.*[11] While the moral connotation is not entirely absent, then, we must not underestimate the formal sense of fittingness that the word denotes in 1759: that is, as the *OED* also puts it, "Appropriateness to circumstances or conditions; suitability, aptness, fitness; conformity with what is required by a rule, principle, etc.; rightness, correctness, accuracy."[12]

Within weeks of the publication of *The Countess of Dellwyn*, Adam Smith would exploit the 'fittingness' definition of propriety in his model of rational sympathy. In Part One of *The Theory of Moral Sentiments*, "Of the Propriety of Action," in a chapter entitled "Of the manner in which we judge of the propriety or impropriety of the affections of other men, by their concord or dissonance with our own," Smith proposes that:

> In the suitableness or unsuitableness, in the proportion or disproportion which the affection seems to bear to the cause or object which excites it, consists the propriety or impropriety, the decency or ungracefulness of the consequent action.[13]

The propriety of emotional behavior or "affection" can be gauged by its "suitableness," or fittingness, to the "cause or object which excites it." This propriety is determined by an act of judgment on the part of the observer, who assesses how they might respond to a similar "cause or object":

> When the original passions of the person principally concerned are in perfect concord with the sympathetic emotions of the speaker, they necessarily appear to this last just and proper, and suitable to their objects; and, on the contrary, when, upon bringing the case home to himself, he finds that they do not coincide with how he feels, they necessarily appear to him unjust and improper, and unsuitable to the causes which excite them. (16)

In Smith's model of sympathy, the emotions of the "person principally concerned" are measured against their circumstances and, if deemed "suitable to their objects"—that is, appropriate to the circumstances, as far as the observer (or, here, "speaker") perceives them—will earn the observer's sympathy.[14]

"Propriety," then, demands judgment. This rational version of sympathetic identification is distinct from David Hume's earlier, more whole-hearted model of sympathy through fellow-feeling. Smithian sympathy seems at once instinctive and actively intellectual: passions and emotions effortlessly "appear" and "seem" to the observer in the quotations above, yet Smith also speaks of "bringing the case home" for assessment. The observer must measure the behavior of the person not only against their own feelings, but against their perception of the person's circumstances. Critics have remarked on the dispassionate nature of this model of sympathy. John Mullan, for instance, observes that it demands a "willed uninvolvement" ("sympathy . . . does not arise so much from the view of the passions, as from that of the situation which excites it"), while Terry Eagleton has noted the "paradoxical quality" of a kind of sympathy that involves "entering into another's experience while retaining enough rational capacity of one's own to assess what one finds there," keeping a "cognitive distance" that is at odds with spontaneous imaginary ethics.[15] For Smith, in 1759, sympathizing with another person thus comprises not only a generous sharing of fellow-feeling but, also, an act of rational judgment.

Returning to *The Countess of Dellwyn* with this concept of "propriety" in mind, it is clear that to say that Charlotte and Viola could not be compared "with Propriety" is not, in 1759, to hold the former up to an ethical standard—to an ever-fixéd mark of morality. Instead, it is to invite the reader to judge the fittingness of the characters' sentiments. Judged as an individual, like anyone with whom one might or might not sympathize, Viola's muted response to her "Grief," like "Patience, *on a Monument*," shows precisely the kind of restraint that would, in Smith's eyes, attract sympathy. Charlotte has no such self-control. To Smith, her reactions would appear "extravagant and out of proportion," and thus, as impartial spectators, we "necessarily disapprove of them" (18).[16] Judged as fictional constructions, Viola is upheld as an exemplary match of a character's behavior to her circumstances, while Charlotte's overreaction to her situation seems deliberately to flout the "propriety of character" (though, in fact, her *emotions* and her response, Fielding tells us, are well matched; she shows the "characteristical Marks of disappointed Vanity"). But she appears all the more out of kilter when held up against Viola for assessment: the careful opposition of "disappointed Love" and "disappointed Vanity" enacts the yawning gulf between Charlotte's histrionic emotions and (to borrow Smith's term) their "objects."

This is a tougher, more judgmental version of sympathy than is usually found in modern criticism of Sarah Fielding and of the novel genre. More typically cited is the opening page of Smith's *Theory*:

> As we have no immediate experience of what other men feel, we can form no idea of the manner in which they are affected, but by conceiving what we ourselves should feel in the like situation.

This memorable notion is often accompanied by an idea taken from the same paragraph in Smith:

> By the imagination we place ourselves in his situation, we conceive ourselves enduring all the same torments, we enter as it were into his body, and become in some measure the same person with him, and thence form some idea of his sensations, and even feel something which, though weaker in degree, is not altogether unlike them. (9)

This compelling, even sociable, image of imaginative fellow-feeling is the part of Smith's work that most resembles the model of sympathy earlier proposed by Hume. This passage from Smith has been applied to Fielding's first and best-known novel, *David Simple*, the story of a sensitive hero who loses himself all too readily in the fortunes and feelings of those around him. *David Simple* has been described as a "novel of sensibility in embryo," and the rational, critical elements of that novel, most fully embodied in the intellectual figure of David's friend, Cynthia, have been ascribed to a masculine, satirical tradition separate from the more feminine sympathy displayed by David and his other friends.[17] These more judgmental aspects of Smith's model of sympathy are evidently less appealing to modern critics. For John Mullan, for instance, Smith's notion of impartial spectatorship demands an impossible degree of self-control, as well as an abstract knowledge of "objects" against which to measure people's behavior. Accordingly, Smith's *Theory* is relatively marginalized, compared with Hume, in Mullan's often-cited account of fiction's "language of feeling," which continues to dominate current understanding of the function of sympathy in the eighteenth-century novel.

For Sarah Fielding, however, the detached, "impartial" spectatorship that Smith outlined was a perfectly reasonable expectation of her reader. Championing good reading is a common strategy of the mid-eighteenth-century novel—a maneuver designed to distinguish it from other, more dubious and potentially distracting forms of prose fiction, notably romance—and it is particularly pronounced in Sarah Fielding's work. Her fiction is laced with lessons on how to read well, and warnings about the dangers of unthinking identification with literary characters. Her novel for children, *The Governess*, sees Mrs Teachum urging her pupils not to lose themselves imaginatively among fictional giants and fairies, but to read with the careful attention that would enable them to "reap . . . benefit from a story"—even, she allows, from plays.[18] *The Cry* contrasts Portia, a warm and thoughtful admirer of Shakespeare, to the reformed Cylinda, who regrets having stormed and strutted emotionally with Shakespeare's characters in her youth, rather than extracting, and applying, their wisdom. As Cylinda reflects, she once considered putting aspics to her veins "like Cleopatra," was "ready to say as Macbeth does of physic, that it cannot cure the diseases of the mind," and "Like Hamlet . . . could have said, / *I will fight with* her *on this score, / Until my eye-lids will no longer wag, /*—For, *I love* Eustace." Unable to discern the most important and applicable parts of Shakespeare's writings, she clutched instead at grand emotional statements, wildly disproportionate to her situation. Knowing this, she ruefully concludes that her life has been "(without metaphor) a tale told by an idiot, and my imagination a strutting player, full of sound and fury signifying nothing." As readers, she and Portia are polar opposites: Cylinda played "juglers [sic] tricks with my mind, instead of planting there any seed which could produce me real advantage or pleasure," and she is thus, she laments, a "contrasting picture" to Portia's wise discernment.[19]

The principles of good reading (and the practice of bad reading) are nowhere more prominent, though, than in *The Countess of Dellwyn*. From the opening pages, the "judicious Reader" is exhorted to look beyond the "incidents" of the story to the "Moral." They are not to read the book in the way that "Children see Tragedies" or the "Multitude in holiday-time see Shakespeare's Henry the Eighth, mesmerised only by noise and show" (1:xxxiii). Underscoring the lesson learned by Cylinda in *The Cry*, the narrator of *The Countess of Dellwyn* makes a further distinction, also with reference to Shakespeare, between "reading with the Attention which is necessary to digest, and extract Utility from Writings" and "skimming over the Surface of Authors, with the view only of filling up a Chasm of Time, which is not so fortunate as to be engaged to some more entertaining Amusement" (2:166). In this novel, more overtly than in her others, Fielding trained her reader to scrutinize fiction with the kind of rational attention with which Smith's "impartial spectator" was to decide whether a situation warranted his sympathy.

This process of judgment has a positive effect on 'Shakespeare'. As we have seen, Fielding holds up her characters against Shakespeare's to contrast the overreaction of the former to the well-fitted sentiments of the latter. The repeated act of comparison helps to create the impression that his characters are an accurate standard—the "objects" against which to compare others in like situations. Indeed, the Shakespearean phrase, "like patience on a monument," frequently to be found quoted in mid-century fiction, was already becoming a detached trope that was judged accurately to represent the pining lover. An anxious Tom Jones, in Henry Fielding's novel of 1749, and a hopelessly adoring Clementina in Richardson's *Sir Charles Grandison* (1753–1754), are both described (or, in Clementina's case, describe themselves) in these words.[20] By the time the heroine of Frances Burney's *Evelina* (1778) is pestered with the words at a ridotto by a fashionable young man, it is evident that, in its accuracy, this has become a hackneyed trope to describe any lady who lacks a dance partner.[21] It is as if Shakespeare, praised in the eighteenth century for his ability to match his characters' speeches with their circumstances, becomes a repository of emotional expressions that seem "suitable to their objects," and against which others' behavior can be measured.

In *The Countess of Dellwyn*, Fielding provides frequent opportunities for such measurement in the deliberate oppositions or disjunctures which she sets up between the emotional situations of Shakespeare's characters and her own. Charlotte, for instance, is taken under the wing of Lady Fanny Fashion, whose frequent purchases drive Charlotte to jealous distraction. The dazzling new earrings and necklace which Lady Fanny sports for their visit to Court have Charlotte retiring early to her apartment professing a headache, but

> no rest that night was to be found: Not *Macbeth*, but
> *Di'monds, hath murdered Sleep:*
> Diamonds, as adequate to the purpose as any ruffian whatsoever. (1:46)

To her distress, Charlotte can still see these diamonds when she closes her eyes and tries to sleep. This preposterous image of life-threatening jewellery is a deliberate play by Fielding on the impropriety, or lack of fittingness, of Charlotte's reaction to their trivial cause, compared with the murderous circumstances, and the more appropriate torment, of *Macbeth*. When she starts, "as if she had seen all the Ghosts in *Richard the Third*, and her Mind, at that time, might be likened to a Theatre, on which the Tragedy of a glittering Cross, and a pair of Diamonds, was acting, with much more Propriety than the envious Critic called Othello The Tragedy of the Handkerchief" (1:46–47), Fielding ironically hints that Charlotte's histrionics even outdo Shakespeare (with not one but "all the Ghosts," and "much more Propriety"). Just as when the narrator suggests that "Lady *Dellwyn* had full as much Reason to call Lady *Fanny* her evil Genius, as ever *Mark Anthony* had to give that Denomination to *Caesar*" (2:15–16), Fielding's reader, as "impartial spectator," is prompted to laugh at, rather than sympathize with, Charlotte's disproportionate response to Lady Fanny's (admittedly splendid) display of jewellery.

Yet because the feelings on Charlotte's side—vanity and pride—are not only excessive but also disagreeable, their frequent opposition to the emotions described in Shakespeare's plays can start to give the impression that Shakespeare's characters are not simply fitting in their behaviors but, furthermore, on the side of the good. The construction "Not Macbeth" is repeated throughout the novel, keeping Charlotte at a syntactical, as well as situational, distance from Shakespeare. When she later laments her fall to adulterous disgrace, the narrator quotes:

> *I do repent me, as it is an Evil*
> *And take the Shame with Joy;*

are the expressive Words *Shakespeare* put into the Mouth of the penitent
Juliet. But Lady *Dellwyn*'s Vanity was too predominant to suffer her to
feel any thing but Rage and Despair. (2:206)

The bald conjunction, "But," becomes shorthand for the emotional gulf between the Countess's speechless "Rage and Despair" and the "expressive Words
Shakespeare put into the Mouth of" Juliet in *Measure for Measure*; between her
proud behavior and her disgraced situation; and between these two very different fictional women. Earlier in the volume, the narrator ended a digression on
Hotspur, Cordelia, and "Harry the Fifth" with an abrupt new sentence, "But
to return to Lady Dellwyn . . ." (2:31)—at once returning to the plot and
briskly distinguishing the Countess from these Shakespearean forebears. These
literary figures are celebrated as well-drawn characters: Shakespeare astutely
"put in the Mouth of" each of them observations that fitted their circumstances. But by being deliberately, repeatedly contrasted to the ill-tempered
Countess, they gain a new sense not just of accuracy but of moral superiority:
Juliet's "penitent" disposition sounds exemplary when juxtaposed against Charlotte's "Vanity."

   This emerging impression of the moral, as well as formal, propriety of
Shakespeare's characters is reinforced by a wider contrast to the Countess's mot-
ley associates. These unpleasant characters are also kept at a clear distance from
Shakespeare. Competing with the married Countess for the affections of Lord
Clermont, for example, Lady Fanny, with a "Drawing-up of her Upper-lip" and a
"supercilious contraction of her Eyebrow,"

> reversed the picture of the Ghost in *Hamlet*, of whom *Horatio* says, that
> he had
>   *A Countenance more in Sorrow than in Anger;*
> for her Looks rather shewed her filled with Indignation than Grief.
> (2:33)

The negative "reversed" and "rather" establish a direct opposition between Old
Hamlet's "*Sorrow*" and Fanny's shallow "Indignation." Indeed, the words "*Sorrow*," "*Anger*," "Indignation," and "Grief" form a neat chiasmus of quotation and
response that contrasts her haughty emotions to both her depraved circumstances
and the depth of feeling depicted in Shakespeare. More bluntly still, we are told
that "Lord Dellwyn was not like Othello" (2:114) when he insists, "without any
Emotion," on the improbability of his wife's betrayal.

The propriety of Shakespeare's observations is, however, a source of anxiety to Captain Drumond; who, scheming to engineer Dellwyn's jealousy, fears discovery and "wished such strong Pictures as *Shakespeare* drew of deep Villainy had never been written." Drumond lives in fear of being exposed by the acuteness of Shakespeare's characterization. As the narrator notes, however, he had

> no Occasion for being under any Apprehension on this Account. The noble Peer had never condescended to read any thing so trifling as *Shakespeare*'s Plays; and, if he had perused them, there was no manner of Danger that he should know the Characters again in real Life. (2:116)

Luckily for Drumond, the "noble Peer" (that is, the Countess's husband, Lord Dellwyn) is a poor reader, unwilling and unable to extract valuable wisdom from Shakespeare and other "trifling" fictional productions, and to apply this wisdom to the "real Life" that these plays so closely approximate. Yet Drumond's fear is revealing. In the pages of this novel, the "master of human nature," Shakespeare himself, is embodied not just as the creator of convincing, even (read selectively) worthy characters, but as an author with a searching moral insight of his own.

Unlike her husband, and the company she keeps, and like Fielding's other, more virtuous protagonists, the Countess herself is an accomplished, sensitive reader. She initially rejected marriage in favor of "Books, and a calm, rural retirement" (2:58). Reading philosophy to her father as a child, we are told, engendered in her "an utter Contempt of all Falsehood" (2:38). As a result, the truths that she avoids in adulthood—such as the knowledge that her own actions have obliged her to spend her life with the creaking Lord Dellwyn—are physically painful to her: they become so "glaring" that she can "no longer shut her Eyes close enough" to block them out (1:100). The accuracy of Shakespeare's observations makes him a particularly troubling source of uncomfortable truth:

> The more she considered, the more Reason she perceived for Self-Condemnation: she had no longer any Relish for her once favourite Amusement of Reading; and mostly disliked those Authors who have penetrated deeply into the intricate Paths of Vanity in the human Mind. (1:103)

The phrase "penetrated deeply into the intricate Paths of Vanity" recalls the prefatory description of Shakespeare as the "deepest Penetrator into the inmost Recesses of human Nature." Confirming the allusion to Shakespeare, the phrase is followed here by the observation that "to peruse, with Pleasure, true Pictures of Nature, requires either a hard or a clear Conscience; which *Shakespeare* has manifested to be his Opinion." For those with a guilty conscience, Shakespeare's accuracy, his ability to draw "true Pictures of Nature," makes him challenging, even painful to read.

Yet "Shakespeare" is not just presented passively as an uncomfortable reading experience. In the pages of this novel, he begins to sound like a knowing figure who actively looks into people's thoughts. Not only does he understand the general workings of "human nature," but he seems to have examined in particular the "intricate paths of Vanity," and "deep Villainy," in ways that threaten to expose the Countess and Captain Drumond respectively. The "propriety" or "accuracy" of Shakespeare's characterization leads, via the celebration of his knowledge of human nature, to his embodiment as an author with penetrating—and, in the case of the Countess, even reproving—insight. Thus, while other female authors had admired the way that he "Pierces the Souls of his Readers" and shows "discernment and penetration into characters," Fielding's novel literalizes the penetrative connotations of this by-now well-worn critical metaphor.[22] By applying this general observation to an individual, guilty protagonist, Fielding makes it sound morally searching, even invasive, so that Shakespeare becomes embodied as Charlotte's tormenting bugbear.

Fictional characters like Samuel Richardson's Clarissa had begun to model a direct relationship with "Shakespeare," quoting his characters' phrases as if they were Shakespeare's own advice: "as Shakespeare says," or even, as in the third edition of the novel, "as our beloved Shakespeare says."[23] In Fielding's own work, Cynthia, Camilla, Portia, and Ophelia all draw on Shakespeare for intellectual insight and emotional support. But the guilty Countess has no such comfort, since the Shakespeare quotations that continually cluster around her remain just beyond her control; she herself never quotes—or even, for that matter, speaks—in this entirely third-person narration. When she reflects that she "was doomed for Life to endure the Company, and even the Fondness, of a Man utterly disagreeable to her," we hear that she "wanted words to express herself, and was ready to exclaim with Hamlet, Oh! Horrible, horrible, most horrible!" (1:101–2). While she might be "ready" to borrow Hamlet's words, she does not actually do so. Likewise, when the Countess and her companions' "Minds were too much disturbed by Anxiety" so that they "could not calmly say with [Brutus] . . ." (2:260–61), the phrase "could not" means that the narrator retains control of the subsequent quotation. The Countess is, then, denied the propriety—in this case, the ownership—of fitting Shakespeare to her own situation. In her guilt, she is plagued by him instead.

Michael Dobson has demonstrated how, in the eighteenth century, Shakespeare was gradually "embodied" as a gentlemanly, even bourgeois, author—whether in marble form, in the respectably bookish statue built in his honor in Westminster Abbey, or in human form in the body of celebrity actor David Garrick, who spent much of his career claiming special proximity to the playwright.[24] Elsewhere, Margreta de Grazia has shown how the quotation mark went from signaling a "commonplace," where anyone might freely graze and borrow, to the "private property" of an individual author. Placed around Shakespeare's words, these marks would make lines from his plays appear to be his "own utterances; his self-expression."[25] These two processes are fascinatingly entwined in the mid-eighteenth-century novel. The much-vaunted accuracy of Shakespeare's observations leads, within *The Countess of Dellwyn*, to his embodiment as an all-knowing, all-seeing 'Author'. Just as novelistic characters were starting to draw not so much on his characters as upon Shakespeare's "own utterances" for advice and guidance, so, conversely, was the anti-heroine feeling the force of the insights she would rather deny, but could not shut out. "Shakespeare" is embodied in this novel as an authority and as an active tormentor; the Countess's guilty misdemeanors continually underscoring, by contrast, his apparent connection with the moral high ground.

The uncomfortable knowingness that Shakespeare acquires in *The Countess of Dellwyn* illustrates well the broader process by which he was accruing, via quotation, a new authority during the eighteenth century. As we have seen, Shakespeare was not a secure moral benchmark in 1759, but was valued, instead, for the propriety or justness with which he matched his characters' words to their circumstances. But the qualities required accurately to draw characters—"great skill, deep penetration, an accurate observation, and almost perfect knowledge of men," in Adam Smith's words—would become the source of his burgeoning moral authority.[26] When these emotional predicaments were cited in relation to novelistic characters, the emotional accuracy of Shakespeare's words was tested by comparison, and confirmed by the sympathetic judgment of the novels' readers. The novel played an extraordinary role in giving Shakespeare's words authority in the eighteenth century because, unlike even the fragments collected, from 1752, in dedicated anthologies, it allowed the reader to see the truth of these fragments being *experienced*, whether by Clarissa Harlowe or Robert Lovelace, Walter Shandy or Parson Yorick, Tom Jones or Partridge.[27] As Fielding says in her preface to *The Countess of Dellwyn*,

Imitation gives instruction by the Force of Examples, and Examples are so much the more powerful to persuade, as they prove the Possibility of following them. (1:xvi)

In the words of William Dodd's little-known novel, *The Sisters* (1754), about the actions of its two protagonists, the selective application of lines to particular "Examples" of fictional individuals "proved the truth of Shakespeare's observation."[28] Furthermore, by repeatedly holding up new novelistic situations against them, the novel helped to turn Shakespeare's accurate characterizations into emotional benchmarks against which to measure their suitability; a set of precepts for individual behavior.

To suggest that pieces of Shakespeare, through experience, became precepts, is to reorder an existing critical narrative of the eighteenth century, in which the tenets of public, epic precept apparently give way to private, novelistic experience, after a period of tension in the mid-eighteenth-century novel.[29] The idea that precepts are not inherited, but cumulatively created by reader approbation, would resonate with Smith. As he observes in his *Theory*,

> our continual observations upon the conduct of others, insensibly lead us to form to ourselves certain general rules concerning what is fit and proper either to be done or to be avoided. (303)

These "general rules" are, he suggests, gradually constructed. As Eagleton says of Smith's theory, they are not "*a priori* principles," but "inductions from our customary conduct."[30] The "objects" against which characters' behavior can be measured are not fixed standards, but accrue authority through repeated, collective acts of judgment. Not all of Shakespeare's work is a model of propriety, as Smith himself avers: the playwright's entry in the index to Smith's *Rhetoric and Belles Lettres* reads like a roll-call of offences against literary decorum.[31] In particular, Shakespeare's "inconceivable variety of characters" makes it "almost impossible to keep up the decorum and propriety of the pieces."[32] Novels, however, in their selective borrowings, minimized the effects of Shakespeare's excessive "variety of characters," and vested choice pieces of Shakespeare with authority, focusing the more general insight into human nature for which he was admired on to particular, well-observed lines, and turning them into valued "objects."

As in *The Countess of Dellwyn*, these quotations begin to function as synecdoche for an embodied, knowing author, "Shakespeare," with a moral agency of his own. Indeed, Shakespeare is elevated beyond a particular morality, to be praised and valued instead as a repository of "general and predominant truth."[33] In the later eighteenth century and into the nineteenth, Shakespeare would be increasingly excerpted, not so much as a source of "beauties" as a stock of advice: from Elizabeth Griffith's *The Morality of Shakespeare's Drama Illustrated* (1775) to even more helpful-sounding anthologies such as *Aphorisms from Shakespeare* (1812), *Apothegms from Shakespeare* (1850), *Sayings from Shakespeare* (1864), and *Shakespeare's Household Words* (1862, 1875), all of which are founded on the impression of direct communion with his wisdom, via the words of his plays. As this essay has shown, we can trace the origins of this phenomenon to the mid-eighteenth-century novel. By uniting admiration for his ethical and aesthetic qualities and fusing experience and precept, the novel, we might say, first made Shakespeare moral.

Sarah Fielding is constructed as an 'Author' in this period along similar lines to Shakespeare. She is praised in comparable terms to the playwright for the propriety of her characterization and, as she says of Shakespeare himself, her "deep Knowledge of Human Nature" (1:vi). In his preface to the second edition of *The Adventures of David Simple*, Henry Fielding admired the way that the sentiments of his sister's novels were carefully adapted to different characters, and even observed that *"there are some Touches, which I will venture to say might have done honour to the Pencil of the Immortal Shakespear himself."*[34] Just as recent work on Fielding as a professional female writer has helped to free her from the status of passive mentee of Henry Fielding and Samuel Richardson, her commitment to tough, evaluative reading shows her to be anything but slavishly dependent on Shakespeare's prior authority.[35] Fielding's strongest female characters are well versed in Shakespeare: they neither cling to his words, nor willfully identify with his characters, but instead read him well, and extract from him what is most valuable. The same goes for Fielding herself. If Shakespeare is a "moral touchstone" in her work, it is only because she makes him so.

Placing Fielding in the wider literary context of 1759 provides a more accurate framework for understanding how her fiction works. It reveals her proximity to a contemporary debate about rational sympathy that she transforms into a model of good readership, in order to further her didactic ends. It also offers a tantalizing glimpse of a less-than-earnest Fielding. Viewing *The Countess of Dellwyn* through the lens of *Tristram Shandy* permits a more comic, playful reading of its endlessly thwarted protagonist, plagued by pesky quotations from Shakespeare. Few would say of *Tristram Shandy*, as they have of *The Countess of Dellwyn*, that it was filled with quotations to make it more "mainstream," or to pad it out into a more profitable, two-volume novel.[36] The wry comedy of *The Countess of Dellwyn*—from "Diamonds *hath murdered sleep*" to the repeated refrain, after discussions of more appealingly sympathetic characters, that effectively says 'anyway, back to the Countess . . .'—is one element that an editor of Fielding's penultimate, and still unedited, novel might recuperate for a modern audience. Highlighting this satirical novel's resonances with Smith, sympathy, and even Sterne, and moving beyond the more familiar context of Samuel Richardson, Henry Fielding, and eighteenth-century women writers (be it the parallels between Fielding's professional career and Charlotte Lennox's, her fraught relationship with the Bluestockings, or her anticipation of Burney and Austen's ironic narrative stance), would enable us to hasten the progress of Fielding's critical journey from obedient "sister of Henry Fielding" to boldly experimental "Sarah in her own right."[37] The wider rewards to be gained in the process include a more nuanced understanding of the relationship between sympathy and the novel, and of the complex balance of feeling and judgment, both moral and literary, that it entails.

Notes

1. Fielding's diverse oeuvre also included two continuations of *David Simple*, in the form of a collection of letters (*Familiar Letters* [1747]) and a final instalment (*David Simple: Volume the Last* [1753]), literary criticism of Samuel Richardson's work (*Remarks on Clarissa* [1749]), a debate between two historical women (*The Lives of Cleopatra and Octavia* [1757]), and a translation of Xenophon's *Memoirs of Socrates* (1762).

2. Sarah Fielding, *The History of the Countess of Dellwyn*, 2 vols. (London: A. Millar, 1759), 1:iv. Subsequent references are given parenthetically.

3. Wayne Booth declares *The Countess of Dellwyn* "a pretentious parade of a little pointless learning": *The Rhetoric of Fiction* (Chicago: University of Chicago Press, 1961), 219. Fielding attracted similar criticism during her own lifetime. Shortly after the publication of *The Cry*, Lady Bradshaigh wrote to Samuel Richardson approving the work but faulting its "excessive" use of "verses, lines, scraps of plays, farces, songs etc.," and the constantly attendant phrase "'As *such* a one says, in *such* a play.'" Bradshaigh assumed that this style resulted from the female author's nervousness: "if the author ment [sic], to guard against an accusation of plagiarism, she might as well have added before every word, *as some body says*": Lady Bradshaigh to Samuel Richardson, 16 March 1754, in "Lady Bradshaigh to Samuel Richardson, 2–22 March 1754," Forster Collection reel 15, F.48.E.5.28, National Art Library, London. This passage has been crossed through in the manuscript.

4. Michael Dobson, *The Making of the National Poet: Shakespeare, Adaptation, and Authorship, 1660–1769* (Oxford: Clarendon Press, 1992).

5. Samuel Johnson, "Preface to Shakespeare," in *Johnson on Shakespeare*, ed. Arthur Sherbo, vols. 7–8 of *The Yale Edition of the Works of Samuel Johnson* (New Haven: Yale University Press, 1968), 7:71.

6. Sarah Fielding and Jane Collier, *The Cry: A New Dramatic Fable*, 3 vols. (London: R. and J. Dodsley, 1754), 1:112.

7. See Gefen Bar-On Santor, "Looking for 'Newtonian' Laws in Shakespeare: The Mystifying Case of the Character of Hamlet," in *Shakespeare and the Eighteenth Century*, ed. Peter Sabor and Paul Yachnin (Aldershot: Ashgate, 2008), 151–64.

8. Susan Sniader Lanser suggests that, in citing Virgil and Shakespeare, Fielding's characters are "validated through comparisons, often comparisons in which Fielding's women are likened to literature's great men": *Fictions of Authority: Women Writers and Narrative Voice* (Ithaca: Cornell University Press, 1992), 50. Conversely, Marianne Novy suggests that "three images of Shakespeare have particular resonance for women's history: the outsider, the artist of wide-ranging identification—later sympathy—and the actor": *Engaging with Shakespeare: Responses of George Eliot and other Women Novelists* (Athens, GA: University of Georgia Press, 1994), 8.

9. Michael Dobson and Stanley Wells, eds., *The Oxford Companion to Shakespeare* (Oxford: Oxford University Press, 2001), 137.

10. *OED*, "propriety, n.," definition 7a.

11. Samuel Johnson, *Dictionary of the English Language on CD-Rom*, ed. Anne McDermott (Cambridge: Cambridge University Press, 1996).

12. It is also connected to linguistic precision in definition 5a: "Correctness or purity of diction or language."

13. Adam Smith, *The Theory of Moral Sentiments*, ed. D. D. Raphael and A. L. Macfie (Oxford: Oxford University Press, 1976), 18. Further references will be given parenthetically.

14. For further discussion of this process in Smith's *Theory*, see Nigel Wood's essay in this volume.

15. John Mullan, *Sentiment and Sociability: The Language of Feeling in the Eighteenth Century* (Oxford: Clarendon Press, 1988), 44; Terry Eagleton, *Trouble with Strangers: A Study of Ethics* (Chichester: Wiley-Blackwell, 2009), 71.

16. Smith says that a "mediocrity" of passions—neither too high nor too low—best elicits sympathy from the observer (27).

17. Gerard A. Barker, "*David Simple*: The Novel of Sensibility in Embryo," *Modern Language Studies* 12, no. 2 (Spring 1982): 69–80; Sara Gadeken, "Sarah Fielding and the Salic Law of Wit," *Studies in English Literature* 42 (2002): 547, 550.

18. Sarah Fielding, *The Governess; or, The Little Female Academy*, ed. Candace Ward (Peterborough, Ont.: Broadview, 2005), 87. She later says, "For if you read Plays, and consider them as you ought, you will neglect and despise what is light and useless, whilst you will imprint on your Minds every useful Lesson that is to be drawn from them" (150).

19. Fielding and Collier, *The Cry*, 3:84, 69, 174, 279.

20. Henry Fielding, *The History of Tom Jones, A Foundling*, ed. Fredson Bowers, 2 vols. (Oxford: Clarendon Press, 1974), 1:204; Samuel Richardson, *The History of Sir Charles Grandison*, ed. Jocelyn Harris, 3 vols. (London: Oxford University Press, 1972), 3:153.

21. Frances Burney, *Evelina*, ed. Edward A. Bloom (Oxford: Oxford University Press, 2002), 43.

22. See the entries for Margaret Cavendish and Elizabeth Montagu in *Women Reading Shakespeare, 1660–1900: An Anthology of Criticism*, ed. Ann Thompson and Sasha Roberts (Manchester: Manchester University Press, 1997), 13, 26.

23. Richardson, *Clarissa; or, The History of a Young Lady*, 7 vols. (London: S. Richardson, 1748), 3:503; *Clarissa*, 3rd ed., 8 vols. (London: S. Richardson, 1750–1751), 3:24.

24. Dobson, *Making of the National Poet*, chap. 4.

25. Margreta de Grazia, "Shakespeare in Quotation Marks," in *The Appropriation of Shakespeare: Post-Renaissance Reconstructions of the Works and the Myth*, ed. Jean I. Marsden (New York: Harvester Wheatsheaf, 1991), 64.

26. Smith, *Lectures on Rhetoric and Belles Lettres*, ed. John M. Lothian (Edinburgh: Thomas Nelson and Sons, 1963), 74.

27. William Dodd's *The Beauties of Shakespear* (London: T. Waller, 1752) was the first collection dedicated solely to the playwright.

28. Dodd, *The Sisters; or, The History of Lucy and Caroline Sanson, Entrusted to a False Friend*, 2 vols. (London: T. Waller, 1754), 2:171.

29. See Liz Bellamy, *Commerce, Morality and the Eighteenth-Century Novel* (Cambridge: Cambridge University Press, 1992).

30. Eagleton, *Trouble with Strangers*, 75.

31. "Shakespeare, William: confusion of metaphors, 27; Hamlet's soliloquies parodied, 42; indirect description in King Lear, 60; descriptions more animated than Spenser's, 63; often uses contradictory epithets, 73; grave-diggers break unity of Hamlet, 117; breaks unity of time, 118; of place, 119; vast variety of characters, 122; breaches of decorum and propriety, 122; *Othello*, 125": Smith, *Rhetoric and Belles Lettres*, 203.

32. Smith, *Rhetoric and Belles Lettres*, 122.

33. Johnson, "Preface to Shakespeare," in *Johnson on Shakespeare*, 7:70.

34. Fielding, *The Adventures of David Simple and Volume the Last*, ed. Peter Sabor (Lexington: University Press of Kentucky, 1998), 346 (Appendix 1).

35. See Betty Schellenberg, *The Professionalization of Women Writers in Eighteenth-Century Britain* (Cambridge: Cambridge University Press, 2005), 94–119; Linda Bree, *Sarah Fielding* (New York: Twayne, 1996); and Peter Sabor, "Richardson, Henry Fielding, and Sarah Fielding," in *The Cambridge Companion to English Literature, 1740–1830*, ed. Thomas Keymer and Jon Mee (Cambridge: Cambridge University Press, 2004), 139–56.

36. Bree, *Sarah Fielding*, 94; Susan Catto, "Modest Ambition: The Influence of Henry Fielding, Samuel Richardson and the Idea of Female Diffidence on Sarah Fielding, Charlotte Lennox and Frances Brooke" (PhD dissertation, University of Oxford, 1998), 104–5. However, Tim Parnell's discussion of Sterne's revisions for his bookseller, Dodsley—including its expansion, and the addition of contemporary quotations, to make the whole "more saleable"—suggests that Sterne might not be exempt from such comments either: "'The whole made more saleable': Young's *Conjectures on Original Composition* and the Reworking of 'The Life & Opinions of Tristram Shandy,'" *Shandean* 20 (2009): 28–36.

37. Schellenberg, *Professionalization of Women Writers*, 95; Catto, "Modest Ambition," 14; Bree, *Sarah Fielding*, vii.

Part VI

CONCLUSION: READING 1759

11

WRITERS, REVIEWERS, AND
THE CULTURE OF READING

SHAUN REGAN

I
N A LETTER TO RICHARD GRAVES of 26 October 1759, the poet, William Shenstone, recorded that "I have purchased 'Gerard upon Taste,' the author of which is a Professor at Edinburgh, and the book commended in the Review—you will say that the Reviewers are partial to Scotch-people—I know nothing of that, but the book is learned, and on a pleasing subject—I may perhaps add a very *important* one—for surely it is altogether unquestionable that taste *naturally* leads to virtue. I am however in some doubt whether it will give you that amusement which Burke's has done."[1] The letter offers a useful entry point for a consideration of the practice, protocols, and conditions of reading within the literary culture of 1759. As Shenstone noted, Alexander Gerard's *Essay on Taste* had been favorably evaluated by the *Critical Review*—the review journal noted for its Scottish personnel—in May 1759. The work was also praised by William Rose in the *Monthly Review* for June, the reviewer observing that "the word *taste*, though in almost every body's mouth, is used in a very loose and indeterminate sense."[2] The journals' commendation of Gerard's treatise could have come as no great surprise, given the centrality of the concept of taste to the reviewers' own enterprise and to the wider discourse of aesthetic appreciation. As Gerard noted in the *Essay*, taste—which, in his definition, chiefly consisted in "the improvement of those principles, which are commonly called *the powers of imagination*"—not only gave "the last finishing to genius in the *author* or performer" but also constituted the "fundamental ingredient in the character of the *critic*."[3] For the reviewers, as for Shenstone, taste was thus both a "pleasing" subject and an "*important*" one; the very barometer, indeed, of a civilized sensibility. As Shenstone's letter of 26 October attests, moreover, readers of the latest publications in 1759 were only too

aware of the review journals' recent establishment as arbiters of taste in the literary world—notwithstanding the perceived Scottish bias of Archibald Hamilton and Tobias Smollett's *Critical Review*.

Shenstone was far from unique among literary letter-writers this year in reflecting upon taste, or indeed in noting the reviewers' judgments, recommending recent publications to friends, or evaluating comparatively between texts (as here between Gerard's "learned" work and Edmund Burke's more enjoyable one).[4] This essay examines two privileged groups of readers within the literary culture of 1759—the reviewers and the 'literati'—whose public pronouncements and personal correspondence provide substantial evidence of what was being read during the year, of how particular works were being judged, and of the relationship between public and private (or, more often, between public and semi-personal, or 'public-private') tastes in reading. Following on from essays earlier in this volume that have considered the reception of particular works and writers (such as James Watt and Moyra Haslett's coverage of the reviewers' mixed responses to *Rasselas* and *Tristram Shandy*), the present essay addresses the state, and the status, of literary reviewing in 1759. As Richard Taylor suggests, "the idea of competing review journals," as emerged in the middle decades of the century, was "utterly novel"; while, as Frank Donoghue has argued, the founding of the *Critical Review* in 1756 had already caused a change in the reviewing practices of the *Monthly*, from mere description of works (to enable readers to make their own choices) to more prescriptive reviews, grounded in assumptions about polite reading standards and the ill social effects of bad writing.[5] The year 1759 marked the tenth anniversary of the commencement of the *Monthly*, but it also witnessed a series of challenges to the authority of the reviewers—not least those at the upstart *Critical Review*, whose sometimes high-handed manner was a cause of particular resentment this year.

Following on also from Rebecca Ford's examination of the letters of the French Encyclopedists, this essay draws substantially on discussions of reading in writers' letters from this year, with a focus in this instance on the British context of reception (which itself includes responses to publications by French authors such as Voltaire, Rousseau, and Helvétius). As Stephen Colclough has cautioned, "no source simply offers an unmediated insight into reading," and writers' letters from this period need to be approached with an awareness of certain limitations to their status as evidence.[6] For a start, the coverage of letters available to modern scholars is necessarily partial. As Harry Solomon notes, the relatively large number of letters that survive from the publisher-poet, Robert Dodsley, to William Shenstone can give a misleading impression of Dodsley's letter-writing overall; for

1759 specifically, only nine Dodsley letters survive, all of which were written to Shenstone.[7] For a number of writers, it is necessary also to bear in mind the partly 'public' aspect of the familiar letter—not least in the case of the Bluestockings, whose letters, as Betty Schellenberg observes, were "read aloud in domestic circles as a regular practice" and "no doubt . . . written with an awareness of potential audiences other than the individual recipient."[8] Such caveats notwithstanding, the sizeable body of writers' letters available for this year can tell us much about what some of the major figures within the literary culture were reading, about how they discussed and debated the value of particular works, and about the terms on which these well-informed individuals wished the cultural conversation about literature to proceed.

By no means all of the texts either publicly reviewed or (semi-)privately read this year were published or indeed written during 1759. It was during this year, for instance, that James Beattie engaged in a detailed reading of Samuel Richardson's *Clarissa*, first published just over a decade previously (in 1747–1748) and judged by Beattie, in the current terms of the day, to be a work of "original sentiment" (if also "tedious to a fault").[9] In the journals, similarly, coverage was occasionally belated, and reviews of foreign publications in particular lagged behind their actual dates of production due to the difficulty of procuring copies—an effect that was exacerbated by the war, as the *Monthly* noted in March 1759.[10] The majority of works reviewed during the year, though, came fresh from the printing presses—and writers' letters from this period provide ample testimony to familiarity with significant recent publications, a marked desire to keep up-to-date with the developing literary scene. In a letter to Thomas Percy of 23 November, William Shenstone again both displays and seeks to engender interest in a selection of the year's works, as he asks: "Have you seen Gerard on Taste? D[r] Smith on Moral Sentiments? Hurd's Dialogues Moral & Political? All of which I've bought, but not quite read—."[11] Shenstone's concluding comment here necessarily suggests a further caveat to any consideration of writing *about* reading at this time: neither the purchase of the most recently published works, nor even discussion of them, necessarily constitutes evidence of actual reading (Shenstone's "not quite read" is nicely imprecise). If purchasing books and reading them were not quite the same things, though, what Shenstone's letters usefully demonstrate is the extent to which contemporary literary circles also functioned as miniature reading communities, within which writers discussed, evaluated, and recommended texts and—in certain cases—circulated them among their authorial acquaintances. These texts were often manuscripts or other pre-publication copies, read not simply for enjoyment but also with an eye to correction and revision. More frequently, they were what were deemed to be the most significant published works of the day—the works that any self-respecting member of the literary community needed to get to grips with (even if not necessarily to praise). One of the benefits of addressing the reading culture of the single year of 1759 is that it enables consideration of a number of these circles simultaneously. As such an analysis will suggest, behind the established public institutions of reading, the major review journals, lay clusters of reading networks—sometimes overlapping, occasionally antagonistic, and often sustained by letter-writing—that participated in and helped to direct the cultural discourse about literature, and literary value, at this time.

Engaging the full extent of 'literature' in its expansive, contemporary meaning, the critical reviewers of the mid-eighteenth century endeavored to encompass all areas of writing and knowledge, whether historical, biographical, mathematical, military, agricultural, horticultural, oratorical, legal, philosophical, theological, eschatological, architectural, musical, botanical, physiological, medical, surgical, navigational, commercial, political, polemical, or poetical ("most of 'em ending," as Sterne's *Tristram Shandy* put it this year, "in *ical*").[12] In comprehending this diverse and increasingly specialized realm of literature, the review journals aimed to refer it to common standards that might offer control and order. These standards were the standards of literary taste and correct style. As the *Critical* noted in October (in a review that has been attributed to Smollett), the reviewers had assumed to themselves "the delicate task of directing the public taste with respect to literature and science."[13] For authors themselves, the golden rule was the Horatian dictum, *utile dulce*—"A precept no less important in philosophy than in poetry and the arts," as the *Critical* observed in March—while the exemplary author was one who wrote like "a Gentleman, a Scholar, and a Christian," as the *Monthly* put it of one commentator on Warburton in September.[14] Conversely, 'low' subject matter, particularly of a sexual kind, was invariably chastised—as with the "few smutty tales" included in *Venus Unmasked*, or the "Miserable, lying, obscene trash" of *The Juvenile Adventures of Miss Kitty F----r* (to cite the *Monthly*'s assessments of these publications).[15]

Yet even as debates continued over whether it was possible to establish one true standard of taste, adaptation to current tastes was encouraged in certain respects. Although translations of classical works were often granted pride of place in leading articles within the journals' monthly issues, modern imitations of ancient works were not always so well-favored. As William Kenrick noted in the *Monthly* for June, William Mason's *Caractacus*, modeled as it was on ancient tragedy, was not necessarily conformable to the present taste. In a more personal exchange, Thomas Percy wrote to Shenstone of William Wilkie's *Epigoniad* (the second edition of which was published this year) that while "the Writer seems animated with a true poetical flame," the epic cast of the work was to be lamented, as the "ancient Homerican Heroes are now worn threadbare."[16] Such animation, and imitation of the ancient authors' creativity (as opposed to imitation of their texts), lay at the heart of the theory of originality that was outlined this year in Edward Young's *Conjectures on Original Composition*, which constituted an important modification of, indeed challenge to, prevailing notions of 'polite' taste. Young's treatise itself received a largely favorable reception as a spirited work that belied the author's advanced years—though Kenrick in the *Monthly* observed that it might have been more accurately titled a "*rhapsody*" on original composition, and William Warburton wryly noted the work's lack of practical help for aspiring authors: "the wisest and kindest part of his work, is advising writers to be original, and not imitators; that is, to be geniuses rather than blockheads."[17] During the latter half of 1759, the terms of Young's treatise were sufficiently familiar to be invoked in reviews of other works—as in the *Critical*'s response to one of the many texts to appear this year from the perennial scribbler, John Hill, which saw the reviewer (possibly Smollett) distinguishing between the "forced productions of necessity" and the "spontaneous growth of genius."[18] Authorial individuality was not, though, always to be fully commended. Broadly speaking, 'originality' was only just filtering in to reviews as a decisive marker of value at this point, and it was adherence to the standards of correct style and taste that continued to direct readers—and reviewers especially—in their critical responses.

To encourage and enforce these standards, the reviewers counseled extensively against the manifold possible deviations from the correct and polite: against verbal imprecision, obscurity of meaning, labored expression, failures of concision, unnecessary coinages, excessive displays of learning, provincialisms, Scotticisms, and—with particular patriotic edge at this time—Gallicisms. During the first half of 1759, the pages of the *Monthly* incorporated criticism of the "*provincial expressions*" of Edward Lisle; the "rambles" of Rousseau; the "diffusive, moralizing strain" of Jonas Hanway; the Scotticisms of Robert Maxwell's *The Practical Husbandman*, which "offend our eye"; and the style of Walter Harte, which was maligned unequivocally as "turgid, even to burlesque."[19] For particularly egregious failings, the keyword of response was 'disgust' (literally, dis-taste)—as when the *Critical* for December found the "uncouthness of stile" of William Hillary to be "exceedingly disgusting to a reader of taste."[20] Some degree of specialization in the intended audience for a work might be allowed, although the critics might also then bracket out anything that was not suitable for a polite, non-specialized readership: given that much of Sir Geoffrey Gilbert's *Treatise on the Court of Exchequer* was of concern only to "officers of the revenue, and men of the law," Owen Ruffhead indicated in the *Monthly*, he would confine his remarks to "such general heads, as are most proper for the attention of the gentleman and the man of literature."[21] Notably, though, while some problems of style might be overlooked in works designed to "promote useful knowledge," a correct and decorous style was deemed important for every kind of writing, including works of algebra or ophthalmology, and even for texts on military matters. Reviewing Thomas More Molyneux's timely work on *Conjunct Expeditions* (i.e., combined operations involving both the army and the navy, as had been employed in the taking of Louisbourg the previous year), the *Monthly's* reviewer, John Berkenhout, took exception against its often "prolix and tedious" expression, averring regretfully that "we must, in justice to our reputation, declare the language and stile of this performance to be extremely poor, and frequently ungrammatical" and concluding that, in sum, "he is really a bad writer."[22]

Against such blots on the literary landscape, accurate and elegant style could strongly inform positive responses. For the *Critical* in April, the "easy" and "correct" style of Sarah Fielding's *The Countess of Dellwyn* was one of the factors that raised it above the regular run of—usually maligned—prose narratives.[23] Given that "North-British idioms" (aka Scotticisms) were regarded as offensive to critical sensibilities, a striking feature of this year in reviewing and readerly response was the praise that was accorded to the literary style of Scottish authors.[24] The weight given to aesthetic considerations at this time would be nowhere more marked than in Burke's evaluation of Adam Smith's *The Theory of Moral Sentiments* (in the *Annual Register* for 1759) as "one of the most beautiful fabrics of moral theory, that has perhaps ever appeared."[25] Both in the reviews and in writers' letters, though, the work of 1759 most lauded for its stylistic decorum was William Robertson's *History of Scotland*. In an article that has been attributed to Hume, February's issue of the *Critical* described Robertson's style as "such as becomes the dignity of history; nervous, regular, chaste, and uniformly supported."[26] In March, meanwhile, Walpole informed Robertson himself that his work was "what all the world now allows the best modern history," written "in the purest English, and with as much seeming knowledge of men and courts as if he had passed all his life in important embassies."[27]

Praise of Robertson's *History*, and of its stylistic elegance, was often accompanied by criticism of works that, for one reason or another, were deemed to have fallen short of the mark. Writing to Richard Hurd on 30 January, William Warburton judged that "Robertson's History is, I think, extremely well written"—as against Smollett's successful *History of England*, haughtily dismissed by Warburton as the work of a "vagabond Scot" who writes "nonsense." Writing four days later to Sir Edward Littleton, Hurd parroted the words of his mentor ("It is extremely well-written . . .") while comparing the *History* to John Jortin's *Life of Erasmus*, the first volume of which had been published the previous year.[28] Perhaps most strikingly, on 16 April the Earl of Chesterfield wrote to his illegitimate son, Philip Stanhope, of Robertson's "clearness, purity, and dignity of style," contrasting this to Walter Harte's *History of the Life of Gustavus Adolphus*, the style of which was "execrable," and original only in an unfortunate way: "it is a bad style, of a new and singular kind; it is full of Latinisms, Gallicisms, Germanisms, and all *isms* but Anglicisms; in some places pompous, in others vulgar and low."[29] Chesterfield's critique cast Harte's work as a compendium of 'disgusting' writing, comprising a litany of modern infelicities. Indeed, where Robertson's *History*, as Walpole put it, met with "but one opinion . . . universal approbation," the style of Harte's met with universal disfavor, even from well-disposed readers such as Chesterfield (a patron to Harte, who was travelling tutor to Stanhope). As Adam Ferguson summarized in a letter to William Cullen, while Harte's work might have appeared "as like Hume & Robertson on the outside as can be conceived," within its pages was to be found an appalling literary spectacle, "the most amazing Stuff that ever was seen."[30]

Stylistically, then, the ideal manner in 1759 was clear, precise, decorous, and bold (or "manly") writing.[31] The favor of mid-eighteenth-century readers did not, though, depend exclusively on matters of aesthetics. For works of science and learning, utility was also essential. As extensive extracts from the papers of the Royal Society suggest, an important aspect of the review journals was their engagement with Enlightenment science, and their encouragement of projects that might lead to practical improvements in areas such as navigation, computation, and ventilation. A final, crucial but potentially more controversial criterion of value concerned religious belief. In its review of Smith's *Theory of Moral Sentiments*, the *Critical* adjudged that the two main merits of the work were its "lively, perspicuous, manly, unaffected stile" and its "strict regard" to "the principles of religion."[32] The former, certainly, could not succeed without the latter: works that failed the test of Christian faith would not be spared for their aesthetic elegancies. In 1759, it was French authors, and Voltaire particularly, who most offended Anglophone readers on the score of irreligion. For the *Critical* (in another review attributed to Smollett), *Candide* was a "satire upon the Creator of the Universe" that was written to "disgrace human nature" (though deserving of some merit for its "keen satire upon the vices and follies of mankind"); while in the *Monthly*, Kenrick lambasted the work as misanthropic and impious, relating the "detestable story of the *Yahoos*" in Swift's *Gulliver's Travels* (1726) to "the abominable one of *Candide*."[33] Readers of various stamps sought to pin down the precise object of Voltaire's satiric attack. Writing to Smith in April, Hume described the work as "full of Sprightliness & Impiety" and "a Satyre upon Providence, under Pretext of criticizing the Leibnitian System"; while for Warburton, writing to Hurd, if its "professed design" was "to ridicule the *Optimisme*," the "real design" of *Candide* was "to recommend *Naturalism*" (that is, natural religion, or deism).[34] Outside of the reviews, probably the most decisive expressions of offense at the work this year appear in correspondence between the Bluestockings, Elizabeth Montagu and Elizabeth Carter. Writing to Carter about Young's *Conjectures*, Montagu observed that "it abounds with the violets and primroses of a vernal imagination," and contrasted the florid textscape of Young's work to the "rank weeds of Voltaire's." Based on this comparative account, Carter replied on 4 June that she found herself "much more tempted to look out for Dr. Young's harmless bouquet, than the infernal composition of deadly weeds, made up by Voltaire," and asked "Is there no law in force in any Christian country against moral poisoning?" By 20 June, Carter had acquired the work for herself, "and begun it, and read enough to find it so horrid in all respects, that I threw it aside, and nothing, I believe, will tempt me ever to look into it again"; while by late July, Montagu was writing to Carter of her own "detestation" of *Candide*.[35] For the Bluestockings, as for Richard Hurd, Voltaire was evidently "the most infamous writer of his age," and there was little appreciation here for *Candide*'s wide-ranging critique of moral, social, and religious injustices, as surveyed by Simon Davies in this volume.[36] Indeed, between the reviewers, the Warburton circle, and the Bluestockings, Voltaire's satire proved itself inimical to professional, pious, and proper readers within the literary culture of mid-eighteenth-century Britain.

As these letter-writers' comments about Voltaire and *Candide* might suggest, epistolary correspondence concerning reading formed an important part of the practice of literary circles at this time. Within various circles, discussions about books helped both to forge and to reinforce group identities and aesthetic values. The texts read and discussed within such contexts were not necessarily in printed form: Betty Schellenberg has written recently about Shenstone's practice of exchanging texts in manuscript (that were not necessarily intended for print publication) with "overlapping circles" of readers, who included Richard Graves, Lady Luxborough, George Lyttleton, Robert Dodsley, Joseph Spence, and Thomas Percy.[37] Nor did all writers have the luxury of such contacts. The beginning of the year saw Laurence Sterne, as yet unknown to the wider world, awaiting publication of the ill-fated *A Political Romance*, which had been read and commented on by a local acquaintance, John Blake. During the course of 1759, Sterne would respond to readers of his developing novel, "the Life & Opinions of Tristram Shandy," and attempt to cultivate the kinds of alliances that might secure him both readers and sales—not least through the commercial patronage of Robert Dodsley. (He would also read, or perhaps merely handle, Johnson's *Rasselas*, the "Sise [sic] . . . paper and Type" of which he proposed as a model for his own work).[38] Only in 1760 would Sterne become fully part of the recognized literati of the period, and even then as something of an eccentric oddity, whose primary connections arguably lay away from the metropolitan scene, with John Hall-Stevenson and his fellow 'Demoniacs' back in provincial Yorkshire. Other writers were more fortunate in their connections, and texts destined for publication could receive close attention from experienced and successful authors prior to printing. Notably this year, Samuel Richardson, a friend and the work's addressee, corresponded with Edward Young about his *Conjectures on Original Composition* during the period leading up to its publication. Once a text had been published, literary allies might also write with news of other readers' responses—as did Warburton to Hurd in July 1759, concerning various reactions to Hurd's *Moral and Political Dialogues*.[39] Writers within any given circle did not, of course, always agree about the merits and qualities of particular publications, even of each other's writings. Yet they frequently did so, and, in a broad view, such circles of literary acquaintance performed a range of mutually reinforcing functions: as reading forums, support networks, interpretive communities, and literary interest-groups.

The buttressing of group identity through reading, and the influence of group perspectives on literary evaluation, can be seen at work in the letters of the Bluestockings. As Carter and Montagu's correspondence about *Candide* shows, letters within literary circles facilitated hermeneutic reading circles, as an initial, personal response to a text was confirmed and perhaps modified through subsequent correspondence, and a broader group response formed—a process that issued, in this instance, in a confirmation and perhaps hardening of Montagu's original view of Voltaire's 'detestable' satire. This process could be especially important where controversial texts were concerned, and a correct (validated) judgment required. In the case of *Candide*, Montagu and Carter were perhaps always likely to come to a shared view; where they differed was not in their detestation but in how to deal with such works. As Jacqueline Pearson has argued, Montagu and Carter's discussions of *Candide* incorporated a debate over "how a female reader should deal with questionable texts"—over whether it was better to retain purity of mind by avoiding them (as Carter held—hence her throwing aside of the "horrid" object) or to trust to one's self not to be corrupted by them (as did Montagu).[40] More broadly, the Bluestockings actively endeavored to forge a common outlook through the sharing both of books and of responses to books. As Elizabeth Eger notes, Montagu and Carter in particular were "voracious readers," who often planned to read books at the same time.[41] These works were not simply recommended but also circulated—physically shared—among the members of the group. Letters from 1759 show Montagu passing books to Carter, while a letter to Carter from Catherine Talbot reinforces these connections between physical circulation, sharing of readerly opinion, and group outlook: "I have read through all your books, and am undone for more, but will have them of nobody's chusing but your's."[42] In such ways did reading and textual discussion—often facilitated by the distribution of books, and conducted through letters—underpin the activities and values of literary circles at this time.

The interests of a particular literary community could also be served by promoting books produced from within that community, both to attract more readers and to encourage a positive reception in the wider public sphere. Preeminent among the publicists of other authors this year was Hume, who was actively engaged in advancing the works of fellow Scots. Having seen Gerard's *Essay* through the press, corrected the galleys of Robertson's *History*, and possibly written a favorable review of the latter, Hume also sent to the *Critical* an unsigned letter that contested the journal's appraisal of Wilkie's *Epigoniad*, noting that the second edition of the work had been corrected following the reviewer's strictures in 1757 (the journal allowed the justice of Hume's retort).[43] As well as easing texts into print and publishing favorable reports of them, Hume was well aware of the power of getting copies of books into the right hands—the hands, that is, of important individuals, and potentially influential readers. As he noted to Adam Smith while regaling him with the early success of his *Theory*, it was important to send copies to "good judges, and proper to spread the reputation of the book." Such encouragements to good publicity were not made at the expense of critical assessment; Hume was himself one of the closest of early readers of the *Theory*, as his letter to Smith of 28 July, recommending alterations to the second edition (concerning the issue of whether "all kinds of Sympathy are necessarily Agreeable"), attests.[44] Intellectual engagement, though, need not be at odds with cultural and commercial promotion, and in June Robertson was able to relay news received from London (via John Home) that Smith's *Theory* was "in the hands of all persons of the best fashion; that it meets with great approbation both on account of the matter and stile; and that it is impossible for any book on so serious a subject to be received in a more gracious manner."⁴⁵ The importance of promotional activities and positive reviews in gaining both readers for and favorable readings of books would be borne out by the responses of Burke, who was (as Hume reported to Smith in July) "much taken" with the *Theory of Moral Sentiments*, and whose own elaboration on this in September ("I am not only pleased with the ingenuity of your Theory; I am convinced of its solidity and Truth") echoed the review of the work in the *Critical*—a review that may possibly have been written by Hume himself, who had also arranged for a copy of Smith's text to be sent to Burke.⁴⁶

If Hume helped facilitate the successful reception of key works of the Scottish Enlightenment by Robertson and Smith this year, his own publication of 1759, the second installment of his *History of England*, did not fare quite so well. In the reviews, the volumes received a positive response, which included coverage over the April and May issues of the *Monthly* and a generally favorable review in the *Critical*, which noted the "elegance, variety, and force of his elocution" (though also some words of "doubtful authority").⁴⁷ Elsewhere, responses were more mixed—to the extent that, in "My Own Life" (his memoir of 1776), Hume would recall ruefully that "In 1759 I published my History of the House of Tudor. The Clamour against this Performance was almost equal to that against the History of the two first Stuarts."⁴⁸ The reception of Hume's volumes is instructive in revealing the potential for friction between different groups of writers; the way in which one literary reading-community might work against the texts, values, and interests of another. Negative responses to Hume partly reflected what—*contra* the *Critical*'s review—was perceived to be its slapdash manner. To Horace Walpole, for instance, the installment appeared a "hasty" work, "inaccurate and careless."⁴⁹ As with the reaction against Voltaire, though, it was in relation to religion that opposition to Hume was strongest. In particular, Hume's volumes antagonized Warburton and his circle. Writing to Hurd in early March, Warburton opined that "Hume has out-done himself in this new History, in shewing his contempt of Religion," contrasting this to the "*decency*" of Robertson's *History*. Warburton was reading a pre-publication copy obtained from the work's publisher, Andrew Millar, in consequence of which he asked Hurd to "say nothing of it till it be published, for I engaged my word to Millar to be silent about it till that time." This early reading did though allow Warburton and his allies extra time to consider a public response, which arrived in the form of a postscript to Hurd's *Dialogues* that Hurd, on Warburton's advice, added to his delayed work in place of a "*Dissertation on Chivalry*" (an early version of his *Letters on Chivalry and Romance* [1762]).[50] The focus of the *Dialogues'* attack on Hume's *History* was "his apology for the unhappy Scotish [sic] line" (that is, the Catholic Stuarts), rather than his "contempt of Religion" *per se*.[51] Hume, who had had dealings previously with Hurd (who had written against his *Natural History of Religion* [1757]), was in no doubt about the provenance of the attack; as he wrote to Smith in July, "You have probably seen Hurd's Abuse of me. He is of the Warburtonian School; and consequently very insolent and very scurrilous."[52] The later bishops of Gloucester and Worcester were always unlikely, of course, to find common cause with the 'atheist' philosopher. In the event, Hurd's own text was not well received either, not on account of its attack on Hume but due to another perceived antagonism contained in its preface: an imaginary dialogue (or verbal confrontation) between the "editor" and a "bookseller" which, as Shenstone noted, "sneers Dodsley, very causelessly."[53]

As its mixture of concerns about taste and authorial antagonisms suggests, the literary culture of the late 1750s was a locus of competition and contestation as well as of textual elegance and refinement. If writers, and writers' circles, sometimes engaged in ungenteel literary combat, the same was true of writers and their public readers, the reviewers. Relationships between authors and the new professional critics were by no means always fraught: many works met with praise, and the roles of author and reviewer often overlapped. Negative reviews there were, though, and the summary catalogues that appeared towards the end of each number of the review journals provided the critics with an opportunity to exercise their wit against the worst of books, in a monthly ritual of barbed high-handedness. In curtly dismissive reviews, the *Monthly* maligned *Hymen* as "Old rubbish," Charles Martin's *A Treatise on the Gout* as "Quackery," and *An Essay, to Prove the Superiority of the Present Age and Nation over that of any Former* as "A Rhapsody of nonsense"; while the *Critical* declared of Martin's work that "What we chiefly applaud in this production, is the broad margin with the large print."[54] Authors' responses to negative reviews could take various forms. While Johnson, according to Smollett, sent a "very petulant Card" to the printer of the *Critical Review* following the journal's review of *Rasselas*, Robert Dodsley sought to make more productive use of the critics' responses to *Cleone* (his play of the previous year), writing to Shenstone of his revisions for a third edition that "I will consider . . . every thing that has been said against it in the Reviews & Magazines, & endeavour by this means to make my Enemies to do me the Office of Friends."[55] Nor were the two journals identical in their attitudes towards authors. In 1759, the newer *Critical Review* was still straining to assert its difference from its more established rival. Against the *Monthly*, the *Critical* appealed to higher principles of critical disinterest and sought to distance itself from the grubby milieu of the hack and the mercenary bookseller—as in its review of Goldsmith's *Enquiry into the Present State of Polite Learning*, which observed that, in making his argument that the critics were to blame for the decay of polite literature, the *Enquiry*'s author had "indiscriminately censured the two Reviews, confounding a work undertaken from public spirit, with one supported for the sordid purposes of a bookseller."[56] As Antonia Forster observes, for all these high-minded (or, high-sounding) claims, "in practice the differences [between the two journals] are difficult to see." As Forster also continues, though, "the operation of prejudice, interest, faction, envy and malevolence is rather more striking in the *Critical Review* than the *Monthly Review*."[57] During 1759, certainly, the *Critical* was both more minute and more acute in its criticisms than was the *Monthly*, and more prone to pick up on hits at the critics in the publications under its scrutiny. In seeking to differentiate itself from the *Monthly*, moreover, Smollett and Hamilton's journal also embroiled itself in undignified disputes with the very writers who found themselves at the receiving end of its proud Parnassian sneer.

Attacks upon the reviewers were by no means unique to 1759. The immediately preceding years had seen John Shebbeare's attack on the "*Scotch* Tribunal" of the *Critical*, along with John Brown's lambasting of the "two notorious Gangs of *monthly* and *critical* Book-Thieves"; while in 1760, a major sally in the ongoing campaign would appear in the form of the satirical *Battle of the Reviews*.[58] 1759, though, had its share of skirmishes, along with some key sallies that raised questions about the very legitimacy of the reviewers' (and particularly the *Critical*'s) enterprise. Early in the year, for instance, William Kenrick entered into the fray with *A Scrutiny; or, The Criticks Criticis'd*, responding to the mixed review of his *Epistles Philosophical and Moral* in the *Critical* for December 1758, which had pointed out both some stylistic problems and some more serious departures from religious orthodoxy.[59] Kenrick's pamphlet response confronted the "censorial undertaking" of the "hypercritical *criticks*," arguing that the *Critical*'s reviewers were rather "*judicial*" than "*judicious*."[60] Thickening the plot, in another article that has been attributed to Smollett the *Critical* for February also reviewed Kenrick's pamphlet attack (the *Scrutiny*), noting the journal's ability to endure the slings and arrows of outrageous authors ("We have already sustained the resentment of

Dr. Sh—re, and other formidable antagonists. The Critical Review has weathered many a storm . . .") and declaring that the "efforts of revenge" of angry writers such as Kenrick "serve no other purposes, but those of propagating their own want of talent and temper, and of increasing the demand for the Critical Review." In a further twist, Kenrick then reviewed his own pamphlet in the *Monthly* for March; declining, with mock coyness, to name the *Critical's* reviewers as the critics "here complained of."[61]

Further reviewer-directed sorties this year included Joseph Reed's *A Sop in the Pan for a Physical Critick*: a somewhat tardy response, from this authorial halter-maker, to the negative review of his burlesque play, *Madrigal and Trulletta*, in the *Critical Review* for August 1758. The main event of the year, though, was the running battle between the *Critical* and James Grainger, a former reviewer for the *Monthly* whose *Poetical Translation of the Elegies of Tibullus* had received a negative and perhaps unfair review (attributed to Smollett) in the *Critical* for December 1758.[62] In *A Letter to Tobias Smollet, M.D.*, Grainger offered repeated demonstrations of the journal's failure to live up to the principles outlined in its original 'Plan', and concluded by advising Smollett—"if you have any Shame left"—to "drop the Rod of *Aristarchus*."[63] Epistolary discussions of the controversy convey the sometimes personalized and pugilistic atmosphere of the writer-reviewer relationship at this time. Responding to the *Critical's* review of his *Poetical Translation* in a letter of 10 January, Grainger told Percy that Smollett "has a personal pique to me, which upon this occasion has betrayed him into many false criticisms, delivered in very illiberal expressions," and pondered whether to give Smollett a literary "drubbing." Writing to Shenstone on 4 February, Percy expressed his concern at Grainger's entering into the fray via his retaliatory *Letter* to Smollett: "I know Smollett has laid himself open enough to rebuke: but who would fight with a Scavenger in the Street!"[64] As Percy's depiction of Smollett as a "Scavenger" implies, such public disputes with critics could be regarded as indecorous affrays with merely second-order literary agents, cast here as the lower orders within the literary hierarchy of the mid-eighteenth century.

Exacerbating matters, Grainger's *Letter to Tobias Smollet* itself received a long review, or rather corrective response, in the *Critical* for February 1759. This review elaborates further the tensions between authors and reviewers, the literary self-fashioning of the *Critical*, and the distinction that the latter sought to uphold between itself and its main rival. Defending the *Critical* against Grainger's charges in the *Letter*, the review (which has been attributed to Smollett) compared Smollett to Pope (both of whom are abused by the "dunces of the age"); aligned

Grainger with Shebbeare; denied that Smollett was a writer for bread; hinted (perhaps mendaciously) that Smollett might not have written the original review; and noted that the ungrateful Grainger had been "hospitably treated" at Smollett's table. The *Critical* also took the opportunity presented by Grainger's *Letter* to contrast the two journals: "The Critical Review is not written by a parcel of obscure hirelings, under the restraint of a bookseller and his wife, who presume to revise, alter, and amend the articles occasionally. The principal writers in the Critical Review are unconnected with booksellers, unawed by old women, and independent of each other."[65] With its references to geniuses and dunces, Pope and his enemies, independent authors versus commercial publishers, this oft-cited review fully displays the *Critical*'s post-Scriblerian self-image.[66] Such high-cultural hauteur did not go unchallenged. Arguing that Grainger in his *Letter* had "(for the most part) fully obviated the censures of his antagonist, who seems to have attacked the Dr.'s translation, under the influence of malice and private pique," and noting also Smollett's "furious" reply in the *Critical*'s review, the *Monthly* took the opportunity to cast the editor of its rival periodical as unsuited to the art of genteel criticism to which both journals purported to adhere.[67] As at other points this year, the *Critical*'s hits at the *Monthly*, in its review of Grainger's *Letter*, contain more than a hint of an attempt to manufacture a literary controversy with the more established publication. If the review journals were indeed the new arbiters of taste in the literary sphere, the process of establishing this position was fissured with tensions and with unseemly squabbles—often encouraged by the *Critical*—between not only the critics and the authors whose works they reviewed but, also, between the review journals themselves.

The reviewers' claims to interpretative authority, then, met with a good deal of resistance during the 1750s and early 1760s, engendering a pamphlet war which, among other things, saw reviewers reviewing pamphlet attacks on the reviewers by writers whose works had been slightingly reviewed, in a kind of mini-industry of reviewer-related controversy. A challenge of a different kind emerged during 1759 in the form of the *Annual Register*, established by Dodsley with Burke as editor. The issue here was not so much the reviewers' critical standards or institutional behavior, but rather their reach. One of the principal rationales for the review journals was their exhaustive coverage of all new publications. An unfortunate by-product of this attempt at inclusivity was that, as well as giving extensive attention to the most significant works of the day, the journals also acted as an unofficial record of all the less exalted aspects of the literary culture of the period, the full force of the contemporary deluge of print. These included works that lay at the outer fringes of responsible publication, such as the more aberrant of religious texts included in the 'Religious and Controversial' section of the monthly catalogues, along with the ceaseless outpourings of scribbling authors. During 1759, the journals thus found themselves covering the numerous contributions to what Walpole termed the "paper wars" over the conduct of Lord George Sackville, and the various new works generated by John Hill.[68] The desideratum of inclusivity had involved the journals in a double bind, and the reviewers for the *Monthly* and the *Critical* often regretted the need to cover all new publications: as the *Monthly* put it in a review of *A Letter to David Garrick* in October, "we are sorry that our plan obliges us to record the titles of such contemptible performances."[69] In a move that might seem to respond to such laments, Burke, in the first number of the *Annual Register* (published in May 1759), emphasized the selectivity of coverage in the *Register*'s own reviews section. The *Annual Register*, he declared, focused on the "best books" only: "We have observed upon none which we could not praise; not that we pretend to have observed on all that are praiseworthy. Those that do not deserve to be well spoken of, do not deserve to be spoken of at all."[70] While other publications at this time also included selective reviews, Burke's comments were clearly directed at the *Monthly* and the *Critical*. As this declaration of intent concisely intimated, the review journals' exhaustiveness of coverage was actually at odds with their role as arbiters of taste, incorporating into their numbers the very books, and kinds of books, that they hoped to discourage. By contrast, the *Annual Register*'s filtered reviewing would serve to cosset readers from even second-hand exposure to such unworthy, distasteful, productions.[71]

If the *Annual Register*'s more selective approach to reviewing showed that this new periodical enterprise had the courage of its own taste, it also hinted that readers should perhaps be precluded from making their own judgments about books. To this extent, the *Register* only reinforced attitudes towards the broader 'public' of readers that were already present in the *Monthly* and the *Critical*. Peppered through the journals are comments that reveal a less than flattering attitude towards the bulk of the contemporary reading audience, and a need for regulation, as well as mere direction, of popular tastes. Revealing here is the *Monthly*'s review of the published *Statutes and Rules* regarding use of the British Museum, a new institutional space for reading that was opened to the public on 15 January. In the reviewer's opinion, such guidelines were necessary, as the Museum was intended as a rational, reflective space for the use of the "learned," not as a vulgar spectacle "to raise the wonder, and occasion a great resort, of the illiterate, by standing in competition with *Punchionello, and all his merry family.*"[72] In December, the failure (or, cessation) of Goldsmith's periodical, *The Bee*, was attributed by the *Critical* to "the want of taste or attention" of the public; while, earlier in the year, the bad taste of the reading public in preferring the arts over the sciences was offered by the journal as a reason "why we constantly have a scanty harvest in science and true knowledge, while the fungous crop of romance, novel, and amusement, is without measure."[73] As this latter comment indicates, it was works of prose fiction, and the errant individuals who chose to read them, that were the worst of literary malefactors in the eyes of the reviewers. Like the puppet-show displays of Punchinello, romances such as *The Life and Real Adventures of Hamilton Murray* were "chiefly calculated for, and read by, the lower class of mankind"; while a novel titled *The Auction* was found to be engaging enough for "our idle and unexperienced [sic] readers." Novels in particular appeared to be proliferating (or breeding) exponentially, to the extent that, as the *Critical* put it in May, "every month, every week produces its monsters."[74] The reviewers' rhetoric against novels and their readers undoubtedly outstripped the actuality of novel-production and reading. James Raven's check-list of prose fiction gives sixty individual titles plus ten miscellanies for this year (fifty-five in total if we remove all multiple editions), included in which are romances, translations, foreign language works, prostitute narratives (of the kind discussed by Mary Peace in this volume), and reprints of earlier works by Behn, Defoe, Richardson, and Fielding. Moreover, as Christopher Flint has recently cautioned, "while novel reading seems to have increased" during this period, "it still accounted for a small portion of overall reading."[75] As the quintessentially modern genre, though, the novel appeared to epitomize everything that was wrong with literary culture, and even the occasional departure from anti-novel feeling could be taken to prove the general point. Granting *The History of Wilhelmina Susannah Dormer* a review in a main article, for instance, the *Critical* presented this success as an exception to the more general problem of prose fiction, and cast the readers of such fictions as more passionate than rational. (Over at the *Monthly*, the work was more characteristically dismissed, as "unintelligible and romantic").[76]

Less acerbic, but similarly equivocal attitudes to the public at large can be observed in writers' letters. One of the more conflicted authors in this regard was Richard Hurd, whose *Dialogues* were not entirely well-received this year. In late June, Hurd revealed to Mason his trepidation about the work's reception: "I have much to apprehend. For even You are a little squeamish about the Notes, and Millar [the publisher] makes no scruple to condemn the Preface."[77] Attempting to cope with the negative response the work did receive, Hurd was uncertain whether to defer to the general view or to criticize the public for failing to construe the work in the way the author had intended. Despite Warburton's more pugnacious opinion (expressed in a letter in early July) that "the publick is a malicious monster," Hurd remained uncertain in late August: arguing defensively that he could "not see one paragraph, no nor one sentence" in the widely criticized parts of the work "that should give any reasonable disgust," while also reiterating his "deference" to the public, if "this opinion" should turn out to be "so general." In a letter to Warburton, he now seemed resigned to the negative reaction to the work's notes and preface ("this playful part of my book"); proceeding, in proto-Shandean manner, to accept that "there is no disputing about tastes."[78] Responding to concerns about the possible reaction to *Tristram Shandy*, Sterne himself this year observed that "I depend much upon the candour of the publick"—though in carefully overseeing the printing of the work, he did everything he could to ensure its success.[79] It was, though, Hurd's antagonist, Hume, who offered the most intriguing reflection this year on the public and the context of reception. Writing on 12 April concerning the favorable response to *The Theory of Moral Sentiments*, Hume informed Smith that "your book has been very unfortunate; for the public seem disposed to applaud it extremely. It was looked for by the foolish people with some impatience; and the mob of literati are beginning already to be very loud in its praises. Three bishops called yesterday at Millar's shop in order to buy copies."[80] In playing with the terms of, and complicating, the distinction between the high literati and the general mob of readers, Hume's report urbanely exposed both the uncertain relationship between privileged readers and the reading public at large, and the variegated nature of the contemporary reading audience, with its—perhaps unstable—hierarchies and distinctions of status, taste, and interest.

As Hume's report also indicates, the perceived success of a book might depend on what one took to be the true barometer of such success: whether popular acclaim, commercial sales, or literary-critical approval. The tyranny of 'taste' might well have caused writers of literary letters to be circumspect both in their judgments and in the kinds of texts that they chose to write about: the evidence of such letters from this year is that the "mob of literati" only rarely perused—at least, rarely discussed—the "Trash" works that fell within the purview of the review journals' monthly catalogues.[81] To what extent authors and others were now being led in their choices by the reviewers' recommendations is not absolutely clear—particularly in cases where the journals themselves disagreed in their assessments.

What is more clear is that the reviewers and their judgments were themselves subjects of discussion among literary circles, and that the establishment of the reviews marked a significant shift in literary power-relations (and thus in the contours of taste) during the third quarter of the century. Taking a broad view, James Basker has argued that "All the evidence points to a rapid realignment of power and influence in the literary world, with authors conceding authority to the review critics and looking to them, rather than to an amorphous and unpredictable public, to articulate critical standards."[82] As we have seen, the broad categories of polite taste and correct style were standards shared by writers and reviewers alike (both which groups could be mistrustful of the tastes of the anonymous reading public), and the journals, certainly, were not slow to highlight instances of authors revising their works in the light of the reviewers' strictures. At the same time, the relationship between authors and reviewers was more mixed than is suggested by any blanket notion of writers deferring to critics: during the period of the Seven Years' War, there was considerable resistance to the reviewers' assumption of authority, even if this resistance itself demonstrated the impact that the journals had made on the literary scene.

Moreover, as the evidence of literary letters from this year abundantly demonstrates, the two roles were not mutually exclusive: writers were also readers, and readers—at least, readers of *taste*—were also critics. As David Allan states, "familiarity with informed opinion" was "an important foundation of modern taste," yet simply "knowing about the critics' opinions was insufficient. Ultimately, it was necessary to *share* them—to take on the persona of the critic."[83] Yet even shared protocols of reading did not necessarily entail identical evaluations of specific works; judgments that merely reflected prevailing opinion could themselves be regarded as lacking the interest of particular insight or novelty. At the very beginning of the year, Thomas Gray sprang something of a surprise by recording a favorable response to the most recent laureate odes of William Whitehead, on the king's birthday and the new year; as Gray remarked, "I like both Whithed's Odes in great measure, but no body else does."[84] As this unfashionable response attests, even in the midst of various attempts to steer and to regulate literary reception, individual readers might still develop tastes peculiar to themselves. For all the emphasis at this time on the standard (and the virtue) of taste, Gray's singular view thus represented an entirely appropriate opening to the year 1759 in reading. It also provides an apt note on which to conclude a volume on a singular year in eighteenth-century literary culture.

Notes

1. William Shenstone to Richard Graves, 26 October 1759, in *The Letters of William Shenstone*, ed. Marjorie Williams (Oxford: Basil Blackwell, 1939), 529.

2. *Monthly Review* 20 (June 1759), 534. Endnote references to the *Monthly Review* and the *Critical Review* will be abbreviated to *MR* and *CR* respectively. Unless otherwise indicated, all references to reviews are to numbers published in 1759.

3. Alexander Gerard, *An Essay on Taste* (London: A. Millar, A. Kincaid, and J. Bell, 1759), 1, 181.

4. Shenstone had strongly recommended the second edition of Burke's *Enquiry* to Graves in a letter of 3 October, stating "Of all books whatever, read Burke (second edit.) 'Of the Sublime and Beautiful'": *Letters of William Shenstone*, 525.

5. Richard C. Taylor, *Goldsmith as Journalist* (Rutherford, Madison, Teaneck: Fairleigh Dickinson University Press; London: Associated University Presses, 1993), 105; Frank Donoghue, "Colonizing Readers: Review Criticism and the Formation of a Reading Public," in *The Consumption of Culture, 1600–1800: Image, Object, Text*, ed. Ann Bermingham and John Brewer (London: Routledge, 1995), 59–62.

6. Stephen Colclough, *Consuming Texts: Readers and Reading Communities, 1695–1870* (Basingstoke: Palgrave Macmillan, 2007), ix.

7. Harry M. Solomon, *The Rise of Robert Dodsley: Creating the New Age of Print* (Carbondale and Edwardsville: Southern Illinois University Press, 1996), 305–6n75.

8. Betty A. Schellenberg, "Bluestocking Women and the Negotiation of Oral, Manuscript, and Print Cultures," in *The History of British Women's Writing, 1750–1830*, ed. Jacqueline M. Labbe (Basingstoke: Palgrave Macmillan, 2010), 69.

9. James Beattie to Dr John Ogilvie, 20 August 1759, in *An Account of the Life and Writings of James Beattie, LL.D.*, ed. Sir William Forbes (New York: Isaac Riley and Co.; Philadelphia: William F. McLaughlin, 1806), 27, 28.

10. *MR* 20 (March), 257.

11. Shenstone to Thomas Percy, 23 November 1759, in *Letters of William Shenstone*, 532.

12. Laurence Sterne, *The Life and Opinions of Tristram Shandy, Gentleman: The Text*, ed. Melvyn New and Joan New, vols. 1–2 of *The Florida Edition of the Works of Laurence Sterne* (Gainesville: University Presses of Florida, 1978), 1.21.72.

13. *CR* 8 (October), 271. For a summary of reviews attributed to Smollett (including those attributed by Basker), see James G. Basker, *Tobias Smollett: Critic and Journalist* (Newark: University of Delaware Press; London: Associated University Presses, 1988), 220–78.

14. *CR* 7 (March), 206; *MR* 21 (September), 225.

15. *MR* 20 (May), 468; *MR* 20 (March), 276.

16. *MR* 20 (June), 507; Percy to Shenstone, 9 August 1759, in *The Correspondence of Thomas Percy and William Shenstone*, ed. Cleanth Brooks (New Haven: Yale University Press, 1977), 33.

17. *MR* 20 (June), 502; William Warburton to Richard Hurd, 17 May 1759, in *Letters from a Late Eminent Prelate to One of his Friends*, 2nd ed. (London: T. Cadell and W. Davies, 1809), 285.

18. *CR* 8 (October), 271–72.

19. *MR* 20 for May (438), February (115), April (303), June (582), and May (445).

20. *CR* 8 (December), 432.

21. *MR* 20 (February), 98.

22. *MR* 21 (November), 373; *MR* 21 (September), 192.

23. *CR* 7 (April), 378.

24. *MR* 20 (January), 26.

25. *The Annual Register; or, A View of the History, Politicks, and Literature, of the Year 1759* (London: R. and J. Dodsley, 1760), 485.

26. *CR* 7 (February), 91. Unusually, this was a leading article that had been sent in to the journal. For the attribution see David R. Raynor, "Hume and Robertson's *History of Scotland*," *British Journal for Eighteenth-Century Studies* 10 (1987): 59–63.

27. Horace Walpole to William Robertson, 4 March 1759, in *The Letters of Horace Walpole, Fourth Earl of Orford*, ed. Paget Toynbee, vol. 4 (Oxford: Clarendon Press, 1903), 245.

28. Warburton to Hurd, 30 January 1759, in *Letters from a Late Eminent Prelate*, 278; Hurd to Sir Edward Littleton, 3 February 1759, in *The Early Letters of Bishop Richard Hurd, 1739–1762*, ed. Sarah Brewer (Woodbridge: Boydell Press, 1995), 332.

29. Lord Chesterfield to his son, 16 April 1759, in *Letters*, ed. David Roberts (Oxford: Oxford University Press, 1992), 331.

30. Walpole to Sir David Dalrymple, 25 February 1759, in *Letters of Horace Walpole*, 4:243–44; Adam Ferguson to [William Cullen], 17 April 1759, in *The Correspondence of Adam Ferguson*, ed. Vincenzo Merolle, 2 vols. (London: Pickering and Chatto, 1995), 1:32.

31. In late January, prior to its publication, Garrick called Robertson's *History* "a most noble manly performance": James E. Tierney, "Unpublished Garrick Letters to Robertson and Millar," *Yearbook of English Studies* 5 (1975): 133.

32. *CR* 7 (May), 398–99.

33. *CR* 7 (June), 550, 551, 554; *MR* 21 (July), 84.

34. David Hume to Adam Smith, 12 April 1759, in *New Letters of David Hume*, ed. Raymond Klibansky and Ernest C. Mossner (Oxford: Clarendon Press, 1954), 53; Warburton to Hurd, 8 July 1759 (postscript), in *Letters from a Late Eminent Prelate*, 289.

35. Elizabeth Montagu to Elizabeth Carter, n.d., in *The Letters of Mrs. Elizabeth Montagu, with some of the Letters of her Correspondents*, 4 vols. (London: T. Cadell and W. Davies, 1809–1813), 4:184–85; Carter to Montagu, 4 June 1759, in *Letters from Mrs. Elizabeth Carter, to Mrs. Montagu, between the Years 1755 and 1800*, ed. Montagu Pennington, 3 vols. (London: F. C. and J. Rivington, 1817), 1:44; Carter to Montagu, 20 June 1759, in *Letters from Mrs. Elizabeth Carter*, 1:49; Montagu to Carter, 25 July 1759, in *Elizabeth Montagu, The Queen of the Blue-Stockings: Her Correspondence from 1720 to 1761*, ed. Emily J. Climenson, 2 vols. (London: John Murray, 1906), 2:163.

36. Hurd to William Mason, 25 June 1759, in *Early Letters*, 339.

37. Schellenberg, "'The Society of Agreeable and Worthy Companions': Bookishness and Manuscript Culture after 1750," in *Bookish Histories: Books, Literature, and Commercial Modernity, 1700–1900*, ed. Ina Ferris and Paul Keen (Basingstoke: Palgrave Macmillan, 2009), 216.

38. Sterne to Robert Dodsley, [5 October 1759], in *The Letters, Part 1: 1739–1764*, ed. Melvyn New and Peter de Voogd, vol. 7 of *Works* (Gainesville: University Press of Florida, 2009), 96–97.

39. Warburton to Hurd, 8 July 1759, in *Letters from a Late Eminent Prelate*, 286, 288.

40. Jacqueline Pearson, *Women's Reading in Britain, 1750–1835: A Dangerous Recreation* (Cambridge: Cambridge University Press, 1999), 139.

41. Elizabeth Eger, *Bluestockings: Women of Reason from Enlightenment to Romanticism* (Basingstoke: Palgrave Macmillan, 2010), 87.

42. Carter to Montagu, 31 January 1759, in *Letters from Mrs. Elizabeth Carter*, 1:25; Catherine Talbot to Carter, 23 September 1759, in *A Series of Letters between Mrs. Elizabeth Carter and Miss Catherine Talbot, from the Year 1741 to 1770*, ed. Montagu Pennington, 4 vols. (London: F. C. and J. Rivington, 1809), 2:297.

43. Hume to William Robertson, 29 May 1759, in *The Letters of David Hume*, ed. J. Y. T. Greig, 2 vols. (Oxford: Clarendon Press, 1932), 1:308; *CR* 7 (April), 323–34.

44. Hume to Smith, 12 April and 28 July 1759, in *Letters of David Hume*, 1:303, 313.

45. Robertson to Smith, 14 June 1759, in *The Correspondence of Adam Smith*, ed. Ernest Campbell Mossner and Ian Simpson Ross, 2nd ed. (Oxford: Oxford University Press, 1987), 40.

46. Hume to Smith, 28 July 1759, in *Letters of David Hume*, 1:312; Edmund Burke to Smith, 10 September 1759, in *The Correspondence of Edmund Burke*, vol. 1, ed. Thomas W. Copeland (London: Cambridge University Press; Chicago: University of Chicago Press, 1958), 129; *CR* 7 (May), 384. For the attribution of this review to Hume see David R. Raynor, "Hume's Abstract of Adam Smith's *Theory of Moral Sentiments*," *Journal of the History of Philosophy* 22 (1984): 51–79.

47. *CR* 7 (April), 291, 290. Attributed to Smollett.

48. *Letters of David Hume*, 1:5.

49. Walpole to Henry Zouch, 15 March 1759, in *Letters of Horace Walpole*, 4:252.

50. Warburton, *Letters from a Late Eminent Prelate*, 282; Hurd to Mason, 4 May 1759, in *Early Letters*, 335.

51. Hurd, *Moral and Political Dialogues* (London: A. Millar, W. Thurlborne, and J. Woodyer, 1759), 284 (a mis-numbered page).

52. Hume to Smith, 28 July 1759, in *Letters of David Hume*, 1:313–14.

53. Shenstone to Percy, 23 November 1759, in *Letters of William Shenstone*, 532.

54. *MR* 21 (November), 449; *MR* 20 (May), 477; *MR* 20 (January), 83; *CR* 7 (March), 281.

55. Tobias Smollett to John Wilkes, 1 April 1759, in *The Letters of Tobias Smollett*, ed. Lewis M. Knapp (Oxford: Clarendon Press, 1970), 77; Robert Dodsley to Shenstone, 20 February 1759, in *The Correspondence of Robert Dodsley, 1733–1764*, ed. James E. Tierney (Cambridge: Cambridge University Press, 1988), 398.

56. *CR* 7 (April), 372.

57. Antonia Forster, "Book Reviewing," in *The Cambridge History of the Book in Britain: Volume 5, 1695–1830*, ed. Michael F. Suarez SJ and Michael L. Turner (Cambridge: Cambridge University Press, 2009), 638.

58. John Shebbeare, *The Occasional Critic; or, The Decrees of the Scotch Tribunal in the Critical Review Rejudged* (London: M. Cooper, 1757), 7; John Brown, *An Estimate of the Manners and Principles of the Times*, vol. 2 (London: L. Davis and C. Reymers, 1758), 75. Jeremy Lewis conjectures that the *Battle of the Reviews* may have been authored by John Hill: *Tobias Smollett* (London: Jonathan Cape, 2003), 181.

59. *CR* 6 (December 1758), 439–53. Attributed to Smollett.

60. William Kenrick, *A Scrutiny; or, The Criticks Criticis'd* (London: T. Wilcox, 1759), 25, 9, 12.

61. *CR* 7 (February), 160–61, 167; *MR* 20 (March), 220.

62. *CR* 6 (December 1758), 475–82. Praising Grainger's versification as "scarce inferior to any in the language," the *Gentleman's Magazine* noted that the *Critical's* review had ignored the errata to the volume, which corrected some of the typographical issues criticised by the journal: *Gentleman's Magazine* 29 (February 1759), 83–84.

63. James Grainger, *A Letter to Tobias Smollet, M.D. Occasioned by his Criticism upon a late Translation of Tibullus* (London: Sold by T. Kinnersly, 1759), 25.

64. Grainger to Percy, 10 January 1759, in John Bowyer Nichols, *Illustrations of the Literary History of the Eighteenth Century*, 8 vols. (London: J. B. Nichols and Son, 1848), 7:268; Percy to Shenstone, 4 February 1759, in *Correspondence of Thomas Percy and William Shenstone*, 23.

65. *CR* 7 (February), 143, 148, 151.

66. On this identity see Donoghue, *The Fame Machine: Book Reviewing and Eighteenth-Century Literary Careers* (Stanford: Stanford University Press, 1996), 37.

67. *MR* 20 (March), 273.

68. Walpole to the Hon. Henry Seymour Conway, 14 October 1759, in *Letters of Horace Walpole*, 4:307. Though claiming distaste of such "paper wars," Walpole here records himself buying "nine or ten" pamphlets on Sackville.

69. *MR* 21 (October), 368.

70. *The Annual Register; or, A View of the History, Politicks, and Literature, of the Year 1758* (London: R. and J. Dodsley, 1759), v–vi.

71. Whether consciously or not, Burke was arguing here for a return to the original aim of the *Monthly Review*, which had been to review only "those productions of the press, as they come out, that are worth notice," as the journal put it in an advertisement that was added to its first volume: see Antonia Forster, "Review Journals and the Reading Public," in *Books and their Readers in Eighteenth-Century England: New Essays*, ed. Isabel Rivers (London: Continuum, 2001), 172–73.

72. *MR* 20 (February), 187.

73. *CR* 8 (December), 499; *CR* 7 (January), 60.

74. *CR* 7 (March), 282; *CR* 8 (December), 458; *CR* 7 (May), 460.

75. James Raven, *British Fiction, 1750–1770: A Chronological Check-List of Prose Fiction Printed in Britain and Ireland* (Newark: University of Delaware Press; London: Associated University Presses, 1987), 147–61; Christopher Flint, "The Eighteenth-Century Novel and Print Culture: A Proposed Modesty," in *A Companion to the Eighteenth-Century English Novel and Culture*, ed. Paula R. Backscheider and Catherine Ingrassia (Oxford: Blackwell, 2005), 352.

76. *CR* 7 (January), 67–68; *MR* 20 (January), 80.

77. Hurd to Mason, 25 June 1759, in *Early Letters*, 339.

78. Warburton to Hurd, 8 July 1759, in *Letters from a Late Eminent Prelate*, 287; Hurd to Mason, 26 August 1759, in *Early Letters*, 343; Hurd to Warburton, 26 August 1759, in *Letters from a Late Eminent Prelate*, 293.

79. Sterne, *Letters*, 105.

80. Hume to Smith, 12 April 1759, in *Letters of David Hume*, 1:305.

81. For the monthly catalogues as repositories of "Trash" publications see *Letters of Tobias Smollett*, 57.

82. James Basker, "Criticism and the Rise of Periodical Literature," in *The Cambridge History of Literary Criticism*, vol. 4, ed. H. B. Nisbet and Claude Rawson (Cambridge: Cambridge University Press, 1997), 328.

83. David Allan, *Commonplace Books and Reading in Georgian England* (Cambridge: Cambridge University Press, 2010), 104–5.

84. Thomas Gray to Mason, 18 January [1759], in *Correspondence of Thomas Gray*, ed. Paget Toynbee and Leonard Whibley, 3 vols. (Oxford: Clarendon Press, 1935), 2:604.

Primary Works

Amory, Thomas. *The Life of John Buncle, Esq*, edited by Moyra Haslett. Dublin: Four Courts Press, 2011.

The Annual Register; or, A View of the History, Politicks, and Literature, of the Year 1758. London: R. and J. Dodsley, 1759.

The Annual Register; or, A View of the History, Politicks, and Literature, of the Year 1759. London: R. and J. Dodsley, 1760.

Archenholz, Johann Wilhelm von. *A Picture of England: Containing a Description of the Laws, Customs, and Manners of England*. 2 vols. London: Edward Jeffery, 1789.

Augustine. *Confessions*, edited and translated by Henry Chadwick. Oxford: Oxford University Press, 2001.

———. *On Christian Teaching*, edited and translated by R. P. H. Green. Oxford: Oxford University Press, 1997.

Barbauld, Anna Laetitia. *The British Novelists: With an Essay and Prefaces, Biographical and Critical*. 50 vols. London: F. C. and J. Rivington, 1820.

Beattie, James. *Dissertations Moral and Critical*. London and Edinburgh: W. Strahan, T. Cadell, and W. Creech, 1783.

Boswell, James. *Boswell's Life of Johnson*, edited by George Birkbeck Hill, revised by L. F. Powell. 6 vols. Oxford: Clarendon Press, 1934–1950.

Brown, John. *An Estimate of the Manners and Principles of the Times*. 2 vols. London: L. Davis and C. Reymers, 1757–1758.

Burke, Edmund. *The Correspondence of Edmund Burke*. Vol. 1, edited by Thomas W. Copeland. London: Cambridge University Press; Chicago: University of Chicago Press, 1958.

———. *A Philosophical Enquiry into the Origin of our Ideas of the Sublime and Beautiful*, edited by J. T. Boulton. London: Routledge, 1958.

Burney, Frances. *Evelina*, edited by Edward A. Bloom. Oxford: Oxford University Press, 2002.

Burns, Robert. *The Poems and Songs of Robert Burns*, edited by James Kinsley. London: Oxford University Press, 1969.

Carter, Elizabeth. *Letters from Mrs. Elizabeth Carter, to Mrs. Montagu, between the Years 1755 and 1800*, edited by Montagu Pennington. 3 vols. London: F. C. and J. Rivington, 1817.

———, and Catherine Talbot. *A Series of Letters between Mrs. Elizabeth Carter and Miss Catherine Talbot, from the Year 1741 to 1770*, edited by Montagu Pennington. 4 vols. London: F. C. and J. Rivington, 1809.

Casanova, G., Chevalier de Seingalt. *History of My Life*, translated by W. R. Trask. New York: Harcourt, 1970.

Charke, Charlotte. *A Narrative of the Life of Mrs Charlotte Charke*, edited by Robert Rehder. London: Pickering and Chatto, 1999.

Chaumeix, Abraham. *Préjugés légitimes contre l'Encyclopédie*. 8 vols. Paris: Herissant, 1758–1759.

Chesterfield, Lord. *Letters*, edited by David Roberts. Oxford: Oxford University Press, 1992.

Cicero. *De Finibus Bonorum et Malorum*, edited by H. Rackham. London: Loeb Library, 1914.

The Clockmakers Outcry against the Author of the Life and Opinions of Tristram Shandy. London: J. Burd, 1760.

Defoe, Daniel. *A Tour thro' the Whole Island of Great Britain*. 6th ed. 4 vols. London: D. Browne, T. Osborne, C. Hitch, and others, 1761–1762.

A Dialogue Betwixt General Wolfe, and the Marquis Montcalm, in the Elysian Fields. [Coventry?]: Sold by E. Jopson, Rivington and Fletcher, and others, 1759.

Diderot, Denis. *Correspondance*, edited by Georges Roth and Jean Varloot. 16 vols. Paris: Editions de Minuit, 1955–1970.

———. *Lettre sur les aveugles*, edited by Marian Hobson and Simon Harvey. Paris: Flammarion, 2000.

———, and Jean Le Rond d'Alembert, eds. *Encyclopédie; ou, dictionnaire raisonné des sciences, des arts, et des métiers*. 28 vols. Paris: Briasson, David, Le Breton, and Durand, 1751–1772.

Dodd, William. *A Sermon on St. Matthew, Chap. IX. Ver. 12, 13*. London: L. Davis and C. Reymers, [1759?].

———. *The Sisters; or, The History of Lucy and Caroline Sanson, Entrusted to a False Friend*. 2 vols. London: T. Waller, 1754.

Dodsley, Robert. *The Correspondence of Robert Dodsley, 1733–1764*, edited by James E. Tierney. Cambridge: Cambridge University Press, 1988.

Dryden, John. *"De Arte Graphica" and Shorter Works*, edited by Alan Roper, vol. 20 of *The California Edition of the Works of John Dryden*, edited by Vinton A. Dearing. Berkeley and Los Angeles: University of California Press, 1989.

Epictetus. *Epictetus his Morals, with Simplicius his Comment, made English from the Greek*, edited and translated by George Stanhope. London: Richard Sare and William Hindmarsh, 1694.

Ferguson, Adam. *The Correspondence of Adam Ferguson*, edited by Vincenzo Merolle. 2 vols. London: Pickering and Chatto, 1995.

Fielding, Henry. *The History of Tom Jones, A Foundling*, edited by Fredson Bowers. 2 vols. Oxford: Clarendon Press, 1974.

Fielding, Sarah. *The Adventures of David Simple and Volume the Last*, edited by Peter Sabor. Lexington: University Press of Kentucky, 1998.

———. *The Governess; or, The Little Female Academy*, edited by Candace Ward. Peterborough, Ont.: Broadview, 2005.

———. *The History of the Countess of Dellwyn*. 2 vols. London: A. Millar, 1759.

———, and Jane Collier. *The Cry: A New Dramatic Fable*. 3 vols. London: R. and J. Dodsley, 1754.

Forbes, Sir William, ed. *An Account of the Life and Writings of James Beattie, LL.D.* New York: Isaac Riley and Co.; Philadelphia: William F. McLaughlin, 1806.

Forster, John. *The Life and Times of Oliver Goldsmith.* 3rd ed. London: Ward, Lock and Co., 1890.

Garrick, David. *The Letters of David Garrick*, edited by David M. Little and George M. Kahrl. 3 vols. London: Oxford University Press, 1963.

Gerard, Alexander. *An Essay on Taste.* London: A. Millar, A. Kincaid, and J. Bell, 1759.

Goldsmith, Oliver. *The Collected Works of Oliver Goldsmith*, edited by Arthur Friedman. 5 vols. Oxford: Clarendon Press, 1966.

Grainger, James. *A Letter to Tobias Smollet, M.D. Occasioned by his Criticism upon a late Translation of Tibullus.* London: Sold by T. Kinnersly, 1759.

Gray, Thomas. *Correspondence of Thomas Gray*, edited by Paget Toynbee and Leonard Whibley. 3 vols. Oxford: Clarendon Press, 1935.

Helvétius, Claude Adrien. *De l'esprit.* Paris: Durand, 1758.

The Histories of Some of the Penitents in the Magdalen-House, As supposed to be Related by Themselves, edited by Jennie Batchelor and Megan Hiatt. London: Pickering and Chatto, 2007.

Hobbes, Thomas. *Leviathan*, edited by Richard Tuck. Cambridge: Cambridge University Press, 1991.

Home, Henry, Lord Kames. *Essays on the Principles of Morality and Natural Religion.* 2nd ed. London: C. Hitch, L. Hawes, R. and J. Dodsley, and others, 1758.

Hume, David. *Enquiries concerning Human Understanding and concerning the Principles of Morals*, edited by L. A. Selby-Bigge. 3rd ed., revised and edited by P. H. Nidditch. Oxford: Clarendon Press, 1996.

———. *Essays Moral, Political and Literary*, edited by Eugene F. Miller. Indianapolis: Liberty Classics, 1987.

———. *The Letters of David Hume*, edited by J. Y. T. Greig. 2 vols. Oxford: Clarendon Press, 1932.

———. *New Letters of David Hume*, edited by Raymond Klibansky and Ernest C. Mossner. Oxford: Clarendon Press, 1954.

———. *A Treatise of Human Nature: A Critical Edition*, edited by David Fate Norton and Mary J. Norton. 2 vols. Oxford: Clarendon Press, 2007.

Hurd, Richard. *The Early Letters of Bishop Richard Hurd, 1739–1762*, edited by Sarah Brewer. Woodbridge: Boydell Press, 1995.

———. *Moral and Political Dialogues.* London: A. Millar, W. Thurlborne, and J. Woodyer, 1759.

Hutcheson, Francis. *An Essay on the Nature and Conduct of the Passions and Affections*, edited by Andrew Ward. Manchester: Clinamen Press, 1999.

———. *An Inquiry into the Original of our Ideas of Beauty and Virtue in Two Treatises*, edited by Wolfgang Leidhold. Indianapolis: Liberty Fund, 2008.

Johnson, Samuel. *A Dictionary of the English Language.* 4th ed. 2 vols. Dublin: Thomas Ewing, 1775.

———. *Dictionary of the English Language on CD-Rom*, edited by Anne McDermott. Cambridge: Cambridge University Press, 1996.

———. *The History of Rasselas, Prince of Abissinia*, edited by Thomas Keymer. Oxford: Oxford University Press, 2009.

———. *The Idler and The Adventurer*, edited by W. J. Bate, John M. Bullitt, and L. F. Powell, vol. 2 of *The Yale Edition of the Works of Samuel Johnson.* New Haven: Yale University Press, 1963.

BIBLIOGRAPHY

——. *Johnson on Shakespeare*, edited by Arthur Sherbo, vols. 7–8 of *The Yale Edition of the Works of Samuel Johnson*. New Haven: Yale University Press, 1968.

——. *The Plan of a Dictionary of the English Language*. London: J. and P. Knapton and others, 1747.

——. *Poems*, edited by E. L. McAdam, Jr., with George Milne, vol. 6 of *The Yale Edition of the Works of Samuel Johnson*. New Haven: Yale University Press, 1964.

——. *Political Writings*, edited by Donald J. Greene, vol. 10 of *The Yale Edition of the Works of Samuel Johnson*. New Haven: Yale University Press, 1977.

——. *The Rambler*, edited by W. J. Bate and Albrecht B. Strauss, vols. 3–5 of *The Yale Edition of the Works of Samuel Johnson*. New Haven: Yale University Press, 1969.

——. *Rasselas and Other Tales*, edited by Gwin J. Kolb, vol. 16 of *The Yale Edition of the Works of Samuel Johnson*. New Haven: Yale University Press, 1990.

——. *Samuel Johnson: The Major Works*, edited by Donald Greene. Oxford: Oxford University Press, 1984; revised ed., 2000.

——. *A Voyage to Abyssinia*, edited by Joel J. Gold, vol. 15 of *The Yale Edition of the Works of Samuel Johnson*. New Haven: Yale University Press, 1985.

——, and Ellis Cornelia Knight. *"The History of Rasselas, Prince of Abissinia" and "Dinarbas: A Tale,"* edited by Lynne Meloccaro. London: J. M. Dent, 1994.

Kenrick, William. *A Scrutiny; or, The Criticks Criticis'd*. London: T. Wilcox, 1759.

Leland, John. *A View of the Principal Deistical Writers of the Last and Present Century*. London: B. Dod, 1755.

Lowth, Robert. *Lectures on the Sacred Poetry of the Hebrews*, translated by G. Gregory. 2 vols. London: Johnson, 1787.

Macaulay, Thomas Babington. *Selected Writings*, edited by John Clive. Chicago: University of Chicago Press, 1972.

The Memoirs of the Celebrated Miss Fanny Murray, Interspersed with the Intrigues and Amours of Several Eminent Personages, Founded on Real Facts. 2 vols. Dublin: S. Smith, 1759.

Montagu, Elizabeth. *Elizabeth Montagu, The Queen of the Blue-Stockings: Her Correspondence from 1720 to 1761*, edited by Emily J. Climenson. 2 vols. London: John Murray, 1906.

——. *The Letters of Mrs. Elizabeth Montagu, with some of the Letters of her Correspondents*. 4 vols. London: T. Cadell and W. Davies, 1809–1813.

Montagu, E. W., junior, Esq. *Reflections on the Rise and Fall of the Antient Republicks. Adapted to the Present State of Great Britain*. London: A. Millar, 1759.

More, Henry. *Conjectura Cabbalistica; or, A Conjectural Essay of Interpreting the Mind of Moses according to a Threefold Cabbala*. London: Fletcher, 1653.

Nichols, John Bowyer. *Illustrations of the Literary History of the Eighteenth Century*. 8 vols. London: J. B. Nichols and Son, 1848.

Percy, Thomas, and William Shenstone. *The Correspondence of Thomas Percy and William Shenstone*, edited by Cleanth Brooks. New Haven: Yale University Press, 1977.

Plato. *The Republic of Plato*, translated by Francis Macdonald Cornford. Oxford: Clarendon Press, 1941.

Ralph, James. *The Case of Authors by Profession or Trade, Stated*. London: R. Griffiths, 1758.

Richardson, Samuel. *Clarissa; or, The History of a Young Lady*. 7 vols. London: S. Richardson, 1748.

[236]

———. *Clarissa; or, The History of a Young Lady.* 3rd ed. 8 vols. London: S. Richardson, 1750–1751.

———. *The History of Sir Charles Grandison*, edited by Jocelyn Harris. 3 vols. London: Oxford University Press, 1972.

Rider, William. *A New Universal English Dictionary.* London: W. Griffin, 1759.

Rousseau, Jean-Jacques. *Julie ou la Nouvelle Héloïse*, edited by René Pomeau. Paris: Garnier, 1960.

———. *Oeuvres complètes*, edited by Bernard Gagnebin and Marcel Raymond. 5 vols. Paris: Gallimard, 1959–1995.

Scott, Sir Walter. *Lives of the Novelists.* London: Oxford University Press, 1934.

Shebbeare, John. *The Occasional Critic; or, The Decrees of the Scotch Tribunal in the Critical Review Rejudged.* London: M. Cooper, 1757.

Shenstone, William. *The Letters of William Shenstone*, edited by Marjorie Williams. Oxford: Basil Blackwell, 1939.

Smart, Christopher. *The Poetical Works of Christopher Smart*, edited by Karina Williamson and Marcus Walsh. 6 vols. Oxford: Oxford University Press, 1980–1996.

Smith, Adam. *The Correspondence of Adam Smith*, edited by Ernest Campbell Mossner and Ian Simpson Ross. 2nd ed. Oxford: Oxford University Press, 1987.

———. *An Inquiry into the Nature and Causes of the Wealth of Nations*, edited by R. H. Campbell, A. S. Skinner, and W. B. Todd. 2 vols. Oxford: Oxford University Press, 1976.

———. *Lectures on Rhetoric and Belles Lettres*, edited by John M. Lothian. Edinburgh: Thomas Nelson and Sons, 1963.

———. *The Theory of Moral Sentiments*, edited by D. D. Raphael and A. L. Macfie. Oxford: Oxford University Press, 1976.

———. *The Theory of Moral Sentiments.* 6th ed. London: W. Strahan and T. Cadell, 1790.

Smollett, Tobias. *The Letters of Tobias Smollett*, edited by Lewis M. Knapp. Oxford: Clarendon Press, 1970.

The Spectator, edited by Donald F. Bond. 5 vols. Oxford: Clarendon Press, 1965.

Sterne, Laurence. *The Letters, Part 1: 1739–1764*, edited by Melvyn New and Peter de Voogd, vol. 7 of *The Florida Edition of the Works of Laurence Sterne.* Gainesville: University Press of Florida, 2009.

———. *The Life and Opinions of Tristram Shandy, Gentleman: The Notes*, by Melvyn New, with Richard A. Davies and W. G. Day, vol. 3 of *The Florida Edition of the Works of Laurence Sterne.* Gainesville: University Presses of Florida, 1984.

———. *The Life and Opinions of Tristram Shandy, Gentleman: The Text*, edited by Melvyn New and Joan New, vols. 1–2 of *The Florida Edition of the Works of Laurence Sterne.* Gainesville: University Presses of Florida, 1978.

The Tryal of Lady Allurea Luxury, Before the Lord Chief-Justice Upright, on an Information for a Conspiracy. London: F. Noble, 1757.

*The Uncommon Adventures of Miss Kitty F****r.* 2 vols. London: Thomas Bailey, 1759.

Voltaire. *Au Roi en son conseil*, edited by Robert Granderoute, in vol. 72 of *The Complete Works of Voltaire*, 264–303. Oxford: Voltaire Foundation, 2011.

———. *Candide*, edited by René Pomeau, vol. 48 of *The Complete Works of Voltaire.* Oxford: Voltaire Foundation, 1980.

———. *Candide and Other Stories*, translated by Roger Pearson. Oxford: Oxford University Press, 1998.

———. *Contes en Vers et en Prose*, edited by Sylvain Menant. 2 vols. Paris: Garnier, 1992.

———. *Correspondence and Related Documents*, edited by Theodore Besterman, vols. 85–135 of *The Complete Works of Voltaire*. Oxford: Voltaire Foundation, 1968–1977.

———. *Essai sur les moeurs*, edited by René Pomeau. 2 vols. Paris: Garnier, 1963.

———. *Oeuvres complètes de Voltaire*, edited by Louis Moland. 52 vols. Paris: Garnier, 1877–1885.

Walpole, Horace. *The Letters of Horace Walpole, Fourth Earl of Orford*, edited by Paget Toynbee. Vol. 4. Oxford: Clarendon Press, 1903.

Warburton, William. *Letters from a Late Eminent Prelate to One of his Friends*. 2nd ed. London: T. Cadell and W. Davies, 1809.

Watts, Isaac. *The Works of the Late Reverend and Learned Isaac Watts*. 6 vols. London: Longman, 1753.

Wilkins, John. *Of the Principles and Duties of Natural Religion*. 8th ed. London: R. Bonwicke, W. Freeman, J. Walthoe, and others, 1722.

The World Displayed. 20 vols. London: J. Newbery, 1759–1761.

Yorick's Meditations upon Various Interesting and Important Subjects. Dublin: James Hunter, 1760.

Young, Edward. *Conjectures on Original Composition: In a Letter to the Author of "Sir Charles Grandison."* London: A. Millar and R. and J. Dodsley, 1759.

Secondary Works

Adams, David. "Slavery in the *Encyclopédie*." In *The Enterprise of Enlightenment*, edited by Terry Pratt and David McCallum, 127–40. Oxford: Peter Lang, 2004.

Alkon, Paul K. "The Intention and Reception of Johnson's *Life of Savage*." *Modern Philology* 72 (1974): 139–50.

Allan, David. *Commonplace Books and Reading in Georgian England*. Cambridge: Cambridge University Press, 2010.

Barker, Gerard A. "*David Simple*: The Novel of Sensibility in Embryo." *Modern Language Studies* 12, no. 2 (Spring 1982): 69–80.

Barker, Nicholas. "The Library Catalogue of Laurence Sterne." *Shandean* 1 (1989): 8–24.

Bar-On Santor, Gefen. "Looking for 'Newtonian' Laws in Shakespeare: The Mystifying Case of the Character of Hamlet." In *Shakespeare and the Eighteenth Century*, edited by Peter Sabor and Paul Yachnin, 151–64. Aldershot: Ashgate, 2008.

Barrell, John. *English Literature in History, 1730–1780: An Equal, Wide Survey*. London: Hutchinson and Co., 1983.

Basker, James. "Criticism and the Rise of Periodical Literature." In *The Cambridge History of Literary Criticism*. Vol. 4, edited by H. B. Nisbet and Claude Rawson, 316–32. Cambridge: Cambridge University Press, 1997.

———. "Scotticisms and the Problem of Cultural Identity in Eighteenth-Century Britain." *Eighteenth-Century Life* 15 (February and May 1991): 81–95.

———. *Tobias Smollett: Critic and Journalist*. Newark: University of Delaware Press; London: Associated University Presses, 1988.

Beebee, Helen. *Hume on Causation*. London: Routledge, 2006.

Bellamy, Liz. *Commerce, Morality and the Eighteenth-Century Novel*. Cambridge: Cambridge University Press, 1992.

Berry, Christopher. *The Idea of Luxury: A Conceptual and Historical Investigation*. Cambridge: Cambridge University Press, 1994.

Blom, Philip. *Encyclopédie: The Triumph of Reason in an Unreasonable Age*. London: Fourth Estate, 2004.

Bree, Linda. *Sarah Fielding*. New York: Twayne, 1996.

Broadie, Alexander. *The Scottish Enlightenment: The Historical Age of the Historical Nation*. Edinburgh: Birlinn, 2001.

———. "Sympathy and the Impartial Spectator." In *The Cambridge Companion to Adam Smith*, edited by Knud Haakonssen, 158–88. Cambridge: Cambridge University Press, 2006.

Brown, Stewart J. "William Robertson (1721-1793) and the Scottish Enlightenment." In *William Robertson and the Expansion of Empire*, edited by Stewart J. Brown, 7–35. Cambridge: Cambridge University Press, 1997.

Brown, Vivienne. "Dialogism, the Gaze, and the Emergence of Economic Discourse." *New Literary History* 28 (1997): 697–710.

Campbell, T. D. *Adam Smith's Science of Morals*. London: George Allen and Unwin, 1971.

Cardwell, M. John. *Arts and Arms: Literature, Politics and Patriotism during the Seven Years War*. Manchester: Manchester University Press, 2004.

Catto, Susan. "Modest Ambition: The Influence of Henry Fielding, Samuel Richardson and the Idea of Female Diffidence on Sarah Fielding, Charlotte Lennox and Frances Brooke." PhD dissertation, University of Oxford, 1998.

Chandler, James. *England in 1819: The Politics of Literary Culture and the Case of Romantic Historicism*. Chicago: University of Chicago Press, 1998.

Chibka, Robert L. "The Stranger within Young's *Conjectures*." *ELH* 53 (1986): 541–65.

Clery, Emma. *The Feminization Debate in Eighteenth-Century England: Literature, Commerce and Luxury*. London: Palgrave, 2004.

Clifford, James L. *Dictionary Johnson: The Middle Years of Samuel Johnson*. London: Heinemann, 1979.

Cohen, Murray. *Sensible Words: Linguistic Practice in England, 1640–1785*. Baltimore: Johns Hopkins University Press, 1977.

Colclough, Stephen. *Consuming Texts: Readers and Reading Communities, 1695–1870*. Basingstoke: Palgrave Macmillan, 2007.

Compson, H. F. B. *The Story of a Great Charity*. London: Society for Promoting Christian Knowledge, 1917.

Cronk, Nicholas. "The Voltairean Genre of the *conte philosophique*: Does it Exist?" *Nottingham French Studies* 48, no. 3 (2009): 61–73.

Curley, Thomas M. *Samuel Johnson and the Age of Travel*. Athens, GA: University of Georgia Press, 1976.

Damrosch, Leo. *Fictions of Reality in the Age of Hume and Johnson*. Madison, WI: University of Wisconsin Press, 1989.

Darnton, Robert. *The Business of Enlightenment: A Publishing History of the "Encyclopédie," 1775–1800*. Cambridge, MA: The Belknap Press, 1979.

David, Alun Morris. "Christopher Smart and the Hebrew Bible." PhD dissertation, University of Cambridge, 1994.

Davie, Donald. *A Travelling Man: Eighteenth-Century Bearings*. Manchester: Carcanet, 2003.

Davies, Simon. "Reflections on Voltaire and his Idea of Colonies." *SVEC* 332 (1995): 61–69.

———. "Voltaire et *Le Voltaire*." *Revue d'histoire littéraire de la France* 4 (1991): 756–61.

———. "Whither/Wither France: Voltaire's View from Ferney." In *Peripheries of the Enlightenment*, edited by Richard Butterwick, Simon Davies, and Gabriel Sánchez Espinosa, 17–27. Oxford: Voltaire Foundation, 2008.

Davis, Cicely. "Ut Pictura Poesis." *Modern Language Review* 30 (1935): 159–69.

De Grazia, Margreta. "Shakespeare in Quotation Marks." In *The Appropriation of Shakespeare: Post-Renaissance Reconstructions of the Works and the Myth*, edited by Jean I. Marsden, 57–91. New York: Harvester Wheatsheaf, 1991.

Deloffre, Frédéric. "Genèse de *Candide*: étude de la création des personnages et de l'élaboration du roman." In *Bestiaires de Voltaire, Genese de Candide, et Autres Etudes sur Voltaire*, edited by Christiane Mervaud and Frédéric Deloffre, 201–302. Oxford: Voltaire Foundation, 2006.

De Voogd, Peter. "Henry William Bunbury, Illustrator of *Tristram Shandy*." *Shandean* 3 (1991): 138–44.

Dobie, Madeleine. *Colonization and Slavery in Eighteenth-Century French Culture*. Ithaca: Cornell University Press, 2010.

Dobson, Michael. *The Making of the National Poet: Shakespeare, Adaptation, and Authorship, 1660–1769*. Oxford: Clarendon Press, 1992.

———, and Stanley Wells, eds. *The Oxford Companion to Shakespeare*. Oxford: Oxford University Press, 2001.

Donoghue, Frank. "Colonizing Readers: Review Criticism and the Formation of a Reading Public." In *The Consumption of Culture, 1600–1800: Image, Object, Text*, edited by Ann Bermingham and John Brewer, 54–74. London: Routledge, 1995.

———. *The Fame Machine: Book Reviewing and Eighteenth-Century Literary Careers*. Stanford: Stanford University Press, 1996.

Eagleton, Terry. *Trouble with Strangers: A Study of Ethics*. Chichester: Wiley-Blackwell, 2009.

Eger, Elizabeth. *Bluestockings: Women of Reason from Enlightenment to Romanticism*. Basingstoke: Palgrave Macmillan, 2010.

Ehrard, Jean. *Lumières et esclavage: l'esclavage colonial et l'opinion publique en France au xviiie siècle*. Brussels: André Versaille, 2008.

Evensky, Jerry. *Adam Smith's Moral Philosophy: A Historical and Contemporary Perspective on Markets, Law, Ethics, and Culture*. Cambridge: Cambridge University Press, 2005.

Flint, Christopher. "The Eighteenth-Century Novel and Print Culture: A Proposed Modesty." In *A Companion to the Eighteenth-Century English Novel and Culture*, edited by Paula R. Backscheider and Catherine Ingrassia, 343–64. Oxford: Blackwell, 2005.

Folkenflik, Robert. *Samuel Johnson, Biographer*. Ithaca: Cornell University Press, 1978.

———. "*Tristram Shandy* and Eighteenth-Century Narrative." In *The Cambridge Companion to Laurence Sterne*, edited by Thomas Keymer, 49–63. Cambridge: Cambridge University Press, 2009.

Forster, Antonia. "Book Reviewing." In *The Cambridge History of the Book in Britain: Volume 5, 1695–1830*, edited by Michael F. Suarez SJ and Michael L. Turner, 631–48. Cambridge: Cambridge University Press, 2009.

———. "Review Journals and the Reading Public." In *Books and their Readers in Eighteenth-Century England: New Essays*, edited by Isabel Rivers, 171–90. London: Continuum, 2001.

Freeman, Edward. "Le combat naval de Minorque: l'exécution de l'Amiral Byng et l'intervention de Voltaire." In *La Méditerranée au XVIIIe Siècle*, edited by F. Paknadel, 41–59. Aix-en-Provence: Université de Provence, 1987.

Gadeken, Sara. "Sarah Fielding and the Salic Law of Wit." *Studies in English Literature* 42 (2002): 541–57.

Geertz, Clifford. *The Interpretation of Cultures*. New York: Basic Books, 1973.

Goring, Paul. *The Rhetoric of Sensibility in Eighteenth-Century Culture*. Cambridge: Cambridge University Press, 2005.

Griffin, Dustin. *Literary Patronage in England, 1650–1800*. Cambridge: Cambridge University Press, 1996.

Griswold, Charles L. "Imagination: Morals, Sciences, and Arts." In *The Cambridge Companion to Adam Smith*, edited by Knud Haakonssen, 22–56. Cambridge: Cambridge University Press, 2006.

Hammond, Brean S. *Professional Imaginative Writing in England, 1670–1740: "Hackney for Bread."* Oxford: Clarendon Press, 1997.

Harkin, Maureen. "Mackenzie's *Man of Feeling*: Embalming Sensibility." *ELH* 61 (1994): 317–40.

Hartman, Geoffrey H. "Christopher Smart's 'Magnificat': Toward a Theory of Representation." *ELH* 41 (1974): 429–54.

Hawes, Clement. "Johnson and Imperialism." In *The Cambridge Companion to Samuel Johnson*, edited by Greg Clingham, 114–26. Cambridge: Cambridge University Press, 1997.

———. *Mania and Literary Style: The Rhetoric of Enthusiasm from the Ranters to Christopher Smart*. Cambridge: Cambridge University Press, 1996.

Hudson, Nicholas. *Samuel Johnson and Eighteenth-Century Thought*. Oxford: Clarendon Press, 1988.

———. *Samuel Johnson and the Making of Modern England*. Cambridge: Cambridge University Press, 2003.

Kallich, Martin. "Samuel Johnson's Principles of Criticism and Imlac's 'Dissertation upon Poetry.'" *Journal of Aesthetics and Art Criticism* 25 (1966): 71–82.

Kaul, Suvir. *Eighteenth-Century British Literature and Postcolonial Studies*. Edinburgh: Edinburgh University Press, 2009.

Kenny, Robert W. "Ralph's *Case of Authors*: Its Influence on Goldsmith and Isaac D'Israeli." *PMLA* 52 (1937): 104–13.

Kernan, Alvin. *Printing Technology, Letters and Samuel Johnson*. Princeton: Princeton University Press, 1987.

Keymer, Tom. "Presenting Jeopardy: Language, Authority, and the Voice of Smart in *Jubilate Agno*." In *Presenting Poetry: Composition, Publication, Reception*, edited by Howard Erskine-Hill and Richard A. McCabe, 97–116. Cambridge: Cambridge University Press, 1995.

———. *Sterne, the Moderns, and the Novel*. Oxford: Oxford University Press, 2002.

Kidd, Colin. "The Ideological Significance of Robertson's *History of Scotland.*" In *William Robertson and the Expansion of Empire*, edited by Stewart J. Brown, 122–44. Cambridge: Cambridge University Press, 1997.

Kirk, Robert. *Zombies and Consciousness*. Oxford: Clarendon Press, 2005.

Lamb, Jonathan. *Sterne's Fiction and the Double Principle*. Cambridge: Cambridge University Press, 1989.

———. "Sterne's System of Imitation." *Modern Language Review* 76 (1981): 794–810.

Lammenranta, Markus. "The Pyrrhonian Problematic." In *The Oxford Handbook of Skepticism*, edited by John Greco, 9–33. Oxford: Oxford University Press, 2008.

Langford, Paul. *Englishness Identified: Manners and Character, 1650–1850*. Oxford: Oxford University Press, 2000.

Lanser, Susan Sniader. *Fictions of Authority: Women Writers and Narrative Voice*. Ithaca: Cornell University Press, 1992.

Latour, Bruno. *We Have Never Been Modern*, translated by Catherine Porter. London: Prentice Hall, 1993.

Lavigne, Claudine. "Les Stratégies de Voltaire face à la censure." In *Censure, autocensure et art d'écrire: de l'antiquité à nos jours*, edited by Jacques Domenech, 165–82. Paris: Editions Complexes, 2005.

Leask, Nigel. *Curiosity and the Aesthetics of Travel-Writing: "From an Antique Land."* Oxford: Oxford University Press, 2002.

Lewis, Jeremy. *Tobias Smollett*. London: Jonathan Cape, 2003.

Lloyd, Sarah. "Pleasure's Golden Bait: Prostitution, Poverty and the Magdalen Hospital." *History Workshop Journal* 41 (1996): 51–72.

Lopez, Jean-François. "Les investissements de Voltaire dans le commerce colonial et la traite négrière: clarifications et malentendus." *Cahiers Voltaire* 7 (2008): 124–39.

Loptson, Peter. "Hellenism, Freedom, and Morality in Hume and Johnson." *Hume Studies* 37 (2001): 161–72.

Lough, John. *The "Encyclopédie."* London: Longman, 1971.

Lynch, Deidre. "Overloaded Portraits: The Excesses of Character and Countenance." In *Body and Text in the Eighteenth Century*, edited by Veronica Kelly and Dorothea E. von Mücke, 112–43. Stanford: Stanford University Press, 1994.

Lynn, Steven. *Samuel Johnson after Deconstruction: Rhetoric and "The Rambler."* Carbondale, IL: Southern Illinois University Press, 1992.

Maire, Catherine. "L'Entrée des Lumières à l'Index: le tournant de la double censure de l'*Encyclopédie* en 1759." *Recherches sur Diderot et sur l'Encyclopédie* 42 (2007): http://rde.revues.org/index 2363.html.

Mann, Elizabeth L. "The Problem of Originality in English Literary Criticism, 1750–1800." *Philological Quarterly* 18 (1939): 97–118.

Marshall, David. *The Figure of Theater: Shaftesbury, Defoe, Adam Smith, and George Eliot*. New York: Columbia University Press, 1986.

Matt, Daniel C. *The Essential Kabbalah: The Heart of Jewish Mysticism*. New York: HarperSanFrancisco, 1996.

McKillop, Alan D. "Richardson, Young, and the *Conjectures*." *Modern Philology* 22 (1925): 391–404.

McLynn, Frank. *1759: The Year Britain Became Master of the World*. London: Jonathan Cape, 2004.

Mervaud, Christiane. "Du carnaval au carnavalesque: l'épisode vénitien de *Candide*." In *Le Siècle de Voltaire: Hommage à René Pomeau*, edited by C. Mervaud and S. Menant, 2:651–62. Oxford: Voltaire Foundation, 1986.

———. *Voltaire à table*. Paris: Desjonquères, 1998.

Milbank, John. "Beauty and the Soul." In *Theological Perspectives on God and Beauty*, edited by J. Milbank, Graham Ward, and Edith Wyschogrod, 1–24. Harrisburg: Trinity Press International, 2003.

Miller, Christopher L. *The French Atlantic Triangle: Literature and Culture of the Slave Trade*. Durham: Duke University Press, 2008.

Monkman, Kenneth. "*Tristram* in Dublin." *Transactions of the Cambridge Bibliographical Society* 7 (1979): 343–68.

Mullan, John. *Sentiment and Sociability: The Language of Feeling in the Eighteenth Century*. Oxford: Clarendon Press, 1988.

Neill, Anna. *British Discovery Literature and the Rise of Global Commerce*. Basingstoke: Palgrave, 2002.

Norton, David Fate, ed. *The Cambridge Companion to Hume*. Cambridge: Cambridge University Press, 1993.

Novak, M. E. "Satirical Form and Realistic Fiction in *Tristram Shandy*." In *Approaches to Teaching Sterne's "Tristram Shandy*,*"* edited by Melvyn New, 137–45. New York: MLA, 1989.

Novy, Marianne. *Engaging with Shakespeare: Responses of George Eliot and other Women Novelists*. Athens, GA: University of Georgia Press, 1994.

O'Brien, Karen. "Empire, History and Emigration from Enlightenment to Liberalism." In *Race, Nation and Empire: Making Histories, 1750 to the Present*, edited by Catherine Hall and Keith McClelland, 15–35. Manchester: Manchester University Press, 2010.

Odell, D. W. "The Argument of Young's *Conjectures on Original Composition*." *Studies in Philology* 78 (1981): 87–106.

Parke, Catherine N. *Samuel Johnson and Biographical Thinking*. Columbia, MI: University of Missouri Press, 1991.

Parker, Fred. *Scepticism and Literature: An Essay on Pope, Hume, Sterne, and Johnson*. Oxford: Oxford University Press, 2003.

———. "The Skepticism of *Rasselas*." In *The Cambridge Companion to Samuel Johnson*, edited by Greg Clingham, 127–42. Cambridge: Cambridge University Press, 1997.

Parnell, Tim. "'The whole made more saleable': Young's *Conjectures on Original Composition* and the Reworking of 'The Life & Opinions of Tristram Shandy.'" *Shandean* 20 (2009): 28–36.

Peace, Mary V. "The Magdalen Hospital and the Fortunes of Whiggish Sentimentality in Mid-Eighteenth-Century Britain: 'Well-Grounded' Exemplarity vs. 'Romantic' Exceptionality." *Eighteenth Century* 48 (2007): 125–48.

Pearson, Jacqueline. *Women's Reading in Britain, 1750–1835: A Dangerous Recreation*. Cambridge: Cambridge University Press, 1999.

Pearson, Roger. *The Fables of Reason: A Study of Voltaire's "contes philosophiques."* Oxford: Clarendon Press, 1993.

Phillipson, Nicholas. *Adam Smith: An Enlightened Life*. London: Allen Lane, 2010.

Pierse, Síofra. *Voltaire Historiographer: Narrative Paradigms*. Oxford: Voltaire Foundation, 2008.

Pocock, J. G. A. *The Machiavellian Moment: Florentine Political Thought and the Atlantic Republican Tradition*. Princeton: Princeton University Press, 1975.

Pointon, Marcia. "The Lives of Kitty Fisher." *British Journal for Eighteenth-Century Studies* 27 (2004): 77–97.

Popkin, Richard. *The High Road to Pyrrhonism*, edited by Richard A. Watson and James E. Force. San Diego: Austin Hill, 1980.

Porter, Roy. *Enlightenment: Britain and the Creation of the Modern World*. Harmondsworth: Penguin, 2000.

Potkay, Adam. *The Passion for Happiness: Samuel Johnson and David Hume*. Ithaca: Cornell University Press, 2000.

———. "The Spirit of Ending in Johnson and Hume." *Eighteenth-Century Life* 16 (1992): 153–66.

Raphael, D. D. *The Impartial Spectator: Adam Smith's Moral Philosophy*. Oxford: Clarendon Press, 2007.

Raven, James. *British Fiction, 1750–1770: A Chronological Check-List of Prose Fiction Printed in Britain and Ireland*. Newark: University of Delaware Press; London: Associated University Presses, 1987.

Raynor, David R. "Hume and Robertson's *History of Scotland*." *British Journal for Eighteenth-Century Studies* 10 (1987): 59–63.

———. "Hume's Abstract of Adam Smith's *Theory of Moral Sentiments*." *Journal of the History of Philosophy* 22 (1984): 51–79.

Read, Rupert, and Kenneth A. Richman, eds. *The New Hume Debate*. London: Routledge, 2000.

Richardson, John. "Imagining Military Conflict during the Seven Years' War." *Studies in English Literature* 48 (2008): 585–611.

———. "Sterne's Patriotic Shandeism." *Essays in Criticism* 58 (2008): 20–42.

Rogers, Pat. *Grub Street: Studies in a Subculture*. London: Methuen, 1972.

Rose, Mark. *Authors and Owners: The Invention of Copyright*. Cambridge, MA: Harvard University Press, 1993.

Rosenberg, Alexander. "Hume and the Philosophy of Science." In *The Cambridge Companion to Hume*, edited by David Fate Norton, 64–89. Cambridge: Cambridge University Press, 1993.

———, and Tom L. Beauchamp. *Hume and the Problem of Causation*. Oxford: Oxford University Press, 1981.

Rosenthal, Laura J. *Infamous Commerce: Prostitution in Eighteenth-Century British Literature and Culture*. Ithaca: Cornell University Press, 2006.

Ross, Ian Simpson. *The Life of Adam Smith*. 2nd ed. Oxford: Oxford University Press, 2010.

Routley, Erik. *Church Music and the Christian Faith*. London: Collins, 1980.

Sabor, Peter. "Richardson, Henry Fielding, and Sarah Fielding." In *The Cambridge Companion to English Literature, 1740–1830*, edited by Thomas Keymer and Jon Mee, 139–56. Cambridge: Cambridge University Press, 2004.

Saintsbury, George. *The English Novel*. London: Dent, 1913.

———. *The Peace of the Augustans: A Survey of Eighteenth-Century Literature as a Place of Rest and Refreshment.* London: G. Bell and Sons, 1916.

Schellenberg, Betty A. "Bluestocking Women and the Negotiation of Oral, Manuscript, and Print Cultures." In *The History of British Women's Writing, 1750–1830*, edited by Jacqueline M. Labbe, 63–83. Basingstoke: Palgrave Macmillan, 2010.

———. "'The Measured Lines of the Copyist': Sequels, Reviews, and the Discourse of Authorship in England, 1749–1800." In *On Second Thought: Updating the Eighteenth-Century Text*, edited by Debra Taylor Bourdeau and Elizabeth Kraft, 25–42. Cranbury, NJ: Associated University Presses, 2007.

———. *The Professionalization of Women Writers in Eighteenth-Century Britain.* Cambridge: Cambridge University Press, 2005.

———. "'The Society of Agreeable and Worthy Companions': Bookishness and Manuscript Culture after 1750." In *Bookish Histories: Books, Literature, and Commercial Modernity, 1700–1900*, edited by Ina Ferris and Paul Keen, 213–31. Basingstoke: Palgrave Macmillan, 2009.

Scherwatzky, Steven. "Johnson, *Rasselas*, and the Politics of Empire." *Eighteenth-Century Life* 16 (1992): 103–13.

Shaw, Philip. *The Sublime.* London: Routledge, 2006.

Solomon, Harry M. *The Rise of Robert Dodsley: Creating the New Age of Print.* Carbondale and Edwardsville: Southern Illinois University Press, 1996.

Spacks, Patricia Meyer. *Novel Beginnings: Experiments in Eighteenth-Century Fiction.* New Haven: Yale University Press, 2006.

Stenger, Gerhard. *L'Affaire des cacouacs: trois pamphlets contre les philosophes des Lumieres.* Saint-Etienne: Publications de l'Université de Saint-Etienne, 2004.

Strawson, Galen. *The Secret Connexion: Causation, Realism, and David Hume.* Oxford: Clarendon Press, 1989.

Taylor, Richard C. *Goldsmith as Journalist.* Rutherford, Madison, Teaneck: Fairleigh Dickinson University Press; London: Associated University Presses, 1993.

Terry, Richard. *The Plagiarism Allegation in English Literature from Butler to Sterne.* Basingstoke: Palgrave Macmillan, 2010.

Thompson, Ann, and Sasha Roberts, eds. *Women Reading Shakespeare, 1660–1900: An Anthology of Criticism.* Manchester: Manchester University Press, 1997.

Tierney, James E. "Unpublished Garrick Letters to Robertson and Millar." *Yearbook of English Studies* 5 (1975): 130–35.

Trumpener, Katie. *Bardic Nationalism: The Romantic Novel and the British Empire.* Princeton, NJ: Princeton University Press, 1997.

Viladesau, Richard. *Theology and the Arts: Encountering God through Music, Art and Rhetoric.* New York: Paulist Press, 2000.

Volpilhac-Auger, Catherine. "Voltaire and History." In *The Cambridge Companion to Voltaire*, edited by Nicholas Cronk, 139–52. Cambridge: Cambridge University Press, 2009.

Walker, Jeanne Murray. "*Jubilate Agno* as Psalm." *Studies in English Literature* 20 (1980): 449–59.

Walvin, James. *Making the Black Atlantic: Britain and the African Diaspora.* London: Cassell, 2000.

Watts, Carol. *The Cultural Work of Empire: The Seven Years' War and the Imagining of the Shandean State.* Toronto: University of Toronto Press, 2007.

Weinsheimer, Joel. "Conjectures on Unoriginal Composition." *Eighteenth Century* 22 (1981): 58–73.

Westermeyer, Paul. *Te Deum: The Church and Music; A Textbook, A Reference, An Essay.* Minneapolis: Fortress Press, 1998.

West, Shearer. "The Darly Macaroni Prints and the Politics of 'Private Man.'" *Eighteenth-Century Life* 25 (2001): 170–82.

Wildermuth, Mark E. *Print, Chaos, and Complexity: Samuel Johnson and Eighteenth-Century Media Culture.* Newark: University of Delaware Press, 2008.

Williams, Michael. "Hume's Skepticism." In *The Oxford Handbook of Skepticism*, edited by John Greco, 80–107. Oxford: Oxford University Press, 2008.

Williams, Raymond. *Marxism and Literature.* Oxford: Oxford University Press, 1977.

———. *Modern Tragedy.* London: Hogarth, 1992.

Wilson, Kathleen. *The Sense of the People: Politics, Culture, and Imperialism in England, 1715–1785.* Cambridge: Cambridge University Press, 1995.

Wolper, Roy. "Candide: Gull in the Garden." *Eighteenth-Century Studies* 111 (1969–1970): 265–77.

Woodmansee, Martha. *The Author, Art, and the Market: Rereading the History of Aesthetics.* New York: Columbia University Press, 1994.

Wright, John P. "Hume's Causal Realism: Recovering a Traditional Interpretation." In *The New Hume Debate*, edited by Rupert Read and Kenneth A. Richman, 88–99. London: Routledge, 2000.

Zionkowski, Linda. "Aesthetics, Copyright, and 'The Goods of the Mind.'" *British Journal for Eighteenth-Century Studies* 15 (1992): 163–74.

———. "Territorial Disputes in the Republic of Letters: Canon Formation and the Literary Profession." *Eighteenth Century* 31 (1990): 3–22.

Simon Davies is Honorary Professor of Enlightenment Studies at Queen's University Belfast, and was the founding Director of its Centre for Eighteenth-Century Studies. He is a past Secretary-General of the International Society for Eighteenth-Century Studies, and a current Research Fellow of the Voltaire Foundation (Oxford). In recent years, he has specialized in scholarly editing, producing modern texts of works by Chamfort, Crébillon fils, and particularly Voltaire. He is on the editorial boards of the *Complete Works* of Voltaire and of the correspondence and the *Complete Works* of Bernardin de Saint-Pierre.

Rebecca Ford is a Lecturer in French at the University of Nottingham. Her research interests include eighteenth-century science and thought, correspondence, and social and intellectual networks. She is currently working on projects relating to the *Encyclopédie* and to the French writer Bernardin de Saint-Pierre.

Moyra Haslett is a Senior Lecturer in English at Queen's University Belfast. She is the author of *Byron's Don Juan and the Don Juan Legend* (Clarendon, 1997), *Marxist Literary and Cultural Theories* (Macmillan, 2000), and *Pope to Burney, Scriblerians to Bluestockings* (Palgrave, 2003), and editor of Thomas Amory's *The Life of John Buncle, Esq* (Four Courts, 2011).

Mary Peace is a Senior Lecturer in English at Sheffield Hallam University. Her research interests include the figure of the prostitute in eighteenth-century sentimental literature and Romantic-era writing by women. She has published essays and articles on Sarah Scott, the Magdalen Hospital, and mid-eighteenth-century medicine, and has edited Charles Lucas's *The Infernal Quixote* (Pickering and Chatto, 2005).

Rosalind Powell holds degrees from the University of Cambridge and from the University of St Andrews, where she completed her doctorate on Christopher Smart and translation in 2012. She currently teaches at St Andrews and is a research assistant for the Digital Miscellanies Index project at the University of Oxford.

Shaun Regan is a Lecturer in Eighteenth-Century and Romantic literature at Queen's University Belfast. With Professor Brean Hammond (University of Nottingham), he is the author of *Making the Novel: Fiction and Society in Britain, 1660–1789* (Palgrave Macmillan, 2006). He has published articles on Sterne, satire, print culture, and the novel, and on narrative and testimony in Olaudah Equiano's *The Interesting Narrative*. With Professor Frans De Bruyn (University of Ottawa), he is currently editing a volume of essays on the culture of the Seven Years' War.

Adam Rounce is a Senior Lecturer at Manchester Metropolitan University. He has written on Dryden, Johnson, Churchill, Cowper, Akenside, Warburton, Joseph Warton, and Godwin. His main ongoing research is with the Cambridge edition of the *Complete Works of Jonathan Swift*, for which he is co-editing two volumes and contributing a Chronology.

Kate Rumbold is a Lecturer in English Literature at the University of Birmingham. Her primary research interest is the reception of Shakespeare during the eighteenth century. She has published on Shakespearean anthologies, quotation and cultural authority, and the heritage industry, and she is currently completing a book on Shakespeare in the eighteenth-century novel.

James Ward is a Lecturer in the School of English and History at the University of Ulster, Coleraine. He has published on Jonathan Swift and eighteenth-century Ireland, on representations of rubbish in literature and film, and on appropriations of the 'long' eighteenth century in modern fiction and film. He is currently writing a book on this last topic.

James Watt is a Senior Lecturer in the Department of English and Related Literature at the University of York, where he convenes the Global Eighteenth Century pathway of the MA in Eighteenth-Century Studies. He is the author of *Contesting* *the Gothic: Fiction, Genre, and Cultural Conflict 1764–1832* (Cambridge, 1999), and is currently completing a book on British Orientalist representation from the Seven Years' War to the 1830s.

Nigel Wood is Professor of Literature at Loughborough University. He is the author of *Swift* (Harvester, 1986) and editor of the World's Classics volume of *She Stoops to Conquer and other Comedies* (Oxford, 2007) and of a *Selection of the Journals and Diaries of Fanny Burney* (Oxford Text Archive and Bristol Classical Press, 1993). He is currently editing Evelyn Waugh's *Put Out More Flags* for Oxford University Press.

www.ingramcontent.com/pod-product-compliance
Lightning Source LLC
Chambersburg PA
CBHW071510110726
47908CB00003B/785